"Dzogchen Ponlop Rinpoche is an amazing person. For seven lifetimes he has been a recognized master of Mahamudra and Dzogchen meditation. In this lifetime, he was first in his class at the Nalanda Institute of Buddhist Philosophy. He has studied modern psychology and has an intimate understanding of the Western mind, having lived and taught in Europe and North America for many years. This book he has written is like a shining lamp that illuminates the path to realizing your own basic nature. Read it and let it open you up to the wish-fulfilling jewel of your own true nature of mind."

—KHENPO TSÜLTRIM GYAMTSO, author of *The Sun of Wisdom*

"A fascinating and daring description of the tantric journey by one of the very finest contemporary Tibetan teachers. Deeply informed by impeccable scholarship, this book is a profound and subtle evocation of the experience of Mahamudra and Dzogchen that modern people will find clear, inspiring, and compelling."

—REGINALD A. RAY, author of *Indestructible Truth* and *Secret of the Vajra World*

Wild
Awakening

The Heart of
Mahamudra & Dzogchen

DZOGCHEN PONLOP

SHAMBHALA · *Boston & London* · 2003

SHAMBHALA PUBLICATIONS, INC.
Horticultural Hall
300 Massachusetts Avenue
Boston, Massachusetts 02115
www.shambhala.com

9 8 7 6 5 4 3 2 1

FIRST EDITION
Printed in the United States of America

♾ This edition is printed on acid-free paper that meets
the American National Standards Institute z39.48 Standard.

Distributed in the United States by Random House, Inc.,
and in Canada by Random House of Canada Ltd

LIBRARY OF CONGRESS CATALOGING-IN-PUBLICATION DATA
Dzogchen Ponlop, Rinpoche.
Wild awakening: The heart of Mahamudra and Dzogchen/
Dzogchen Ponlop Rinponche.
p.   cm.
Includes index.
ISBN 1-59030-096-3 (paperback)
1. Mahāmudrā (tantric rite) 2. Rdzogs-chen (Rāniçn-ma-pa)
I. Title.
BQ8921.M35 D96 2003
294.3'443—dc21
2003003550

To my guru, Khenpo Tsültrim Gyamtso Rinpoche,
who pointed out the heart of Mahamudra and Dzogchen

Contents

THESE DAYS THERE IS growing interest in Buddhist teachings and practices, particularly among people who, faced with the rapid and far-reaching changes that science and technology are making in the external world, are seeking ways to achieve a corresponding inner development. Like other spiritual traditions, Buddhism presents many ways to generate, enhance, and strengthen fundamental positive human values such as love and compassion, and it does so by cultivating positive states of mind.

Mahamudra and Dzogchen are among the most exalted teachings of the Tibetan Buddhist tradition. The focus of these profound and advanced practices is the very nature of the mind itself and as such they go straight to the point. However, it would be a mistake to think that they therefore offer some kind of shortcut. Without understanding the context of compassion, the awakening mind, and the emptiness of intrinsic existence within which they function, the methods of Mahamudra and Dzogchen would not only be ineffective, but could also be easily misunderstood. On the other hand, cultivating these qualities will lend their practice resolution and vigor. Moreover, as several acquaintances of mine, great practitioners of Dzogchen or Mahamudra, have told me that when their meditation was invigorated by intense feelings of respect toward their lama, they were able to realize the ultimate nature of their minds and were able to gain wonderful qualities, hence a personal relationship with a qualified teacher is a prerequisite, too.

This book by Dzogchen Ponlop Rinpoche, a teacher and practitioner with close acquaintance with both Mahamudra and Dzogchen, is timely. His thorough account of these marvelous traditions will be a valuable source of inspiration and clarity to many readers. As it is said, if you can purify the open sky of the mind of the clouds of conceptual thoughts, the constellations of omniscience will shine forth.

THE DALAI LAMA
APRIL 16, 2003

Now that we have taken a human birth endowed with intelligence and discrimination, it is essential that we make the best use of it through exerting ourselves in accomplishing genuine happiness and benefiting others. However, we will be ignorant of how to proceed with respect to these concerns if we do not rely upon an effective spiritual path. Therefore, study of the Buddhadharma, which is rich in paths of skillful means and knowledge, is a most meaningful endeavor.

Though in general the doctrines of Buddhadharma are limitless, the path of Secret Mantra is especially swift and profound, and all of its practices are included within the two stages of creation and completion. In recent times, The Dzogchen Ponlop Rinpoche, Karma Sungrab Ngedön Tenpay Gyaltsen, a master endowed with great wisdom and intelligence with respect to the Buddhadharma, has taught on Mahamudra and Dzogchen, the heart practices of the completion stage path of simplicity. These discourses have been compiled and published here by his students. I rejoice in this publication and pray that the enlightened activity connected with these teachings will vastly increase.

THE KARMAPA, OGYEN TRINLEY DORJE
MARCH 23, 2003

Editors' Preface

IN *Wild Awakening,* The Dzogchen Ponlop Rinpoche presents the heart essence of the two great practice traditions of Mahamudra and Dzogchen. *Mahamudra* refers to the unfabricated and unconditioned wisdom nature of mind; it is the luminous, empty, and unceasing nature of all reality. *Dzogchen* refers to the primordially awake mind—perfect in its own state and completely full of the qualities of enlightenment. These two streams of wisdom are regarded as possessing great blessings and transformative power. It is helpful to examine them together, not only to appreciate the richness of the wisdom they share, but also to discover in their uniqueness the directions our individual path of practice could potentially take. They offer the practitioner a variety of approaches to meditation practice and a vast array of methods through which to recognize one's confusion and transform it into wisdom. However, if not for the instructions that demonstrate how to properly approach these paths, their power might remain out of our reach. For those interested in following these paths, The Dzogchen Ponlop Rinpoche's clear and detailed introduction to the landscape of the journey is itself something of a revelation.

   Wild Awakening begins with a discussion of the nature of the spiritual journey all together, reflecting on issues of blind faith, religion, and culture in relation to our path. Buddhism is presented as a science of mind, in contrast to a religion, and as a body of wisdom that is fundamentally free of any cultural forms and that is accessible to all. However, The Dzogchen Ponlop Rinpoche reminds us that if we intend to practice these instructions, then it is imperative to prepare ourselves thoroughly for what lies ahead. If we have prepared ourselves through reflection, study, and proper training in meditation, and have developed a heart of devotion, then we possess "a complete and perfect path." From the point of view of these traditions, devotion and realization are inseparably linked. The open heart of devotion is directed toward one's guru and the lineage, but ultimately it is also directed toward one's own enlightened heart.

As practitioners, we soon learn that we need not only the perfect path, but also the perfect guide, since there are many pitfalls and opportunities for misunderstanding along the way. The great literature of all cultures abounds with stories of the comic-poignant struggles of those who set out on the path of transcendence—a journey that leads us to a state that is powerfully awake, immaculately present, and full of the qualities of selfless love and compassion. The great teachers of the lineage have always embodied the realization of this journey's fruition and have kindly communicated to students the way to travel this path successfully.

There is great benefit in studying how the path works from the ground up, how it unfolds as we gradually penetrate our confusion with an increasingly sharp and precise faculty of mind. Here, The Dzogchen Ponlop Rinpoche uses the classic Buddhist logic of the three stages of ground, path, and fruition to describe a progressive path. The ground stage introduces us to the view of Buddhist philosophy on an intellectual level and to the basics of mind training through the practices of study, contemplation, and meditation. The path stage consists of the instructions of the guru, particularly the "pointing-out" instructions, which convey an immediate experience of awakening, and the specific meditation practices of shamatha and vipashyana. The fruition stage is arrived at as a result of our journey through the first two stages. At the same time, The Dzogchen Ponlop Rinpoche offers a view of this journey from the perspective of its fruition—a view in which the state of enlightenment is present all along, where each moment offers equal opportunities for sinking into confusion or leaping into wakefulness. From the conventional point of view, such a leap is madness. From the point of view of the wisdom of Mahamudra and Dzogchen, not even confusion can mask our utterly pure and awake nature. What *is* this "wild awakening"? The Dzogchen Ponlop Rinpoche points to the experience of sudden awakening—the state of exhilaration, joy, and fearlessness—that comes when we are finally free of the elaborations and restrictions of clinging to ego.

Throughout the text, references to this utterly pure and awake nature appear in various forms. Here, we would like to point out how the term *buddha* is often used, not as a reference to the historical Buddha known as Shakyamuni, but as a synonym for the enlightened state itself or for the ineffable qualities of enlightenment. For example, when The Dzogchen Ponlop Rinpoche refers to buddha mind or the heart of buddha, he is pointing to the most fundamental reality of mind that is its unobscured, fully awake essence of wisdom and compassion. Furthermore, mind and heart in this sense are not polarities, as we sometimes view them in the West; they are indistinguishable. The seat of mind is in the heart.

While detailed descriptions of the Buddhist path can become very technical, these presentations of Mahamudra and Dzogchen are straightforward in offering the main points—working with ego and emotions. Many of these teachings are conveyed in metaphors or stories. Overall, the path described here is one of great humanity and practicality—an inward journey that enables us to make a connection with the actual experiences of awakened heart and vast awareness here and now.

May all who encounter these teachings develop wisdom and compassion equal to that of all the buddhas, and may all beings without exception follow a complete and perfect path to buddhahood.

THE NALANDABODHI EDITORIAL COMMITTEE
Cindy Shelton, Anna-Brown Griswold,
Marg Cooke, and Tim Lyons

PART ONE

Surveying
the Path

The Nature of the Path

BUDDHISM IS A PERSONAL JOURNEY into the depths of one's heart and mind—an exploration of who we are and what we are. The teachings of the Buddha show us how to rediscover that essence and come to a full realization of that reality. Among all Buddhist paths, the lineages of Mahamudra and Dzogchen represent the heart essence of the Buddha's teachings. Undertaking the practices of either of these two paths opens the way to a profound journey. These are the lineages that provide us with the most skillful means to experience the fully awakened state and directly taste the reality of our mind and environment.

Yet the spiritual journey can be very tricky. It can start with great power, energy, intellect, skepticism, and inquisitiveness. Nonetheless, it can ultimately result in nothing more than a kind of religion based completely on blind faith. That is the principal danger for Buddhist practitioners. It is easy to fall into this trap without really noticing it. We think we are being very skeptical and inquisitive. Then suddenly we find ourselves in a totally blind tradition of religious dogma. We find ourselves in the midst of a great darkness—still walking, but not knowing where we are going.

There is a tremendous need to reflect again and again on the nature of our spiritual path. What is our purpose in being here? What is the basic motivation that brought us to this path? Is it a genuine interest in awakening, in enlightenment, in freedom? Or do we have other reasons? Every now and then we have to remind ourselves of our purpose and motivation. We have to go back to the most basic questions: Do I really want to attain enlightenment? Am I really willing to achieve that? It is not a question of how difficult it is or how long it takes to become enlightened. The question is, Do I really want to wake up from this dream?

From the perspective of the Mahamudra and Dzogchen teachings, we can wake up right now. When we wake up from our confused state of mind, that is enlightenment. There is no difference between this moment and enlightenment. The nature of our mind is fully awakened right from the beginning, and this awakened state is nothing other than our ordinary experience of emotions, thoughts, and perceptions. If we can genuinely see our emotions, senses, and thoughts just as they are, without trying to change them or improve our way of seeing them, then we can see the basic state of wakefulness. The state of fruition is simply the recognition of this nature of mind. That is what we call "nirvana," or "freedom from samsara." There is nothing more.

At the same time, there is a sense of making a journey, undergoing a gradual process of evolving our consciousness. This journey is the mutual effort of teacher and student. It is a process of developing the qualities of faith, trust, and confidence in an atmosphere of total openness. Such a relationship can develop only when the student has thoroughly examined and processed the teachings and has developed a clear, precise foundation of knowledge. At some point, as practitioners of these lineages, we must go beyond the level of conceptual experience in order to open fully to our guru and the lineage. This is the experience of devotion, which is the intense and powerful experience of the naked reality of mind. The experience of devotion is not blind faith. Rather, it is deeply rooted in wisdom and knowledge. Genuine devotion arises when we develop a firm ground of trust and confidence in our own enlightened heart. Ultimately, our commitment is to the nature of our own mind.

BUDDHISM: THE SCIENCE OF MIND

Accordingly, the path of Buddhist spirituality is not a religion per se. Rather, it is a genuine science of mind that uncovers the very nature of the mind and the phenomena that we experience. It is also a genuine philosophy of life—an approach to life that deals with its meaning and helps us understand how we can overcome the suffering of the world. To say that Buddhism is a science does not mean the dry science of analyzing material things. It is something much deeper. It means going into the depths of the reality of our inner world, which is the most powerful world. The teachings of this tradition show us the pure reality of both our own mind and our environment.

There are parallels between the inner science of mind and the outer sciences. For example, in the outer sciences, we bring our concepts and ideas into the laboratory for testing. Those tests produce certain results, which are the fruition of our ideas. In a similar way, we might hear or read about a concept taught by Buddha. From a Buddhist perspective, we then examine this concept using the inner science of mind. We analyze it thoroughly in the lab of the mind. The result of our analysis is an experience of meditation that reveals to us whether the concept was accurate or not. We can say, "Yes, this is accurate" or "No, it is not true." Thus, as a science of mind, the path utilizes the skillful means with which we explore the intrinsic, true nature of our mind or consciousness. Then, our ensuing understanding of mind itself brings us greater clarity about how to lead our lives effectively and meaningfully.

Although Buddhism is relatively new to the West, it is finding its place in the modern global cultures of the twenty-first century. However, when something becomes a part of popular culture, its form changes. To genuinely understand the teachings of Buddha, we have to go beyond any trappings of culture and language. This truth that Buddha taught, known as the Dharma, can be likened to pure water, which we are trying to pour into various cultural containers. We can pour this water into an elegant, beautifully crafted Indian pot, a decorative silver and gold Tibetan cup, a beautiful European crystal glass, or a North American paper cup. The water will adopt the shape and reflect the colors of its container, whether it is made of ceramic, gold, crystal, or paper. The reflections of colors in the water are similar to the languages and social forms of each culture. Although the water might come to taste and even smell a little bit like its new country, the pure essence of the water does not change.

When we reflect on this variety of containers, it is crucial for us to contemplate the nature of the pure essence of the water and not merely the container in which we find it. This essence is beyond all language and form. Moreover, the process of bringing this pure water from one culture and language into a new culture and language requires tremendous precision, mindfulness, compassion, and patience. There is a tendency for the new culture to become obsessed with the old container—to become fascinated by its beauty, novelty, and freshness. However, if we become trapped in an obsession with the cultural container, then our attachment to that form can become so strong that it blocks us from achieving any realization.

Therefore, we should approach the path of spirituality with discrimination. Buddha said that people should examine his teachings like a merchant who wants to purchase genuine gold. When you purchase gold, you do not want to buy something that merely resembles gold. You want the real thing. In ancient India merchants had a process to determine whether or not a piece of gold was genuine. First, they would burn the gold, then cut it, and finally rub it. In a similar way, we should examine the Buddha's teachings thoroughly. Buddha said that, after this process, we should either accept the teachings, practicing them until we achieve full accomplishment, or leave them alone. He said that we should not accept these teachings solely because they were taught by a personage of high rank or wide acclaim, such as a prince or a buddha. We must analyze and examine them ourselves to find out if they are beneficial. It is up to us.

Buddhism teaches that there is no creator outside our mind. There is no external source of our suffering, our pain, our pleasure, and our happiness. The good, the bad, and the ugly that we experience in our world are purely the creation of our minds. There is no outer force, energy, or supernatural entity that has power over us or controls us. Not even buddhas have the power to control our world. It is entirely the creation of our individual and group karma. Therefore, there is a sense of total, individual responsibility and complete freedom and power on this path. This becomes the basis of our personal journey— our path of working with our mind and actions.

Because we are making this journey to discover who and what we are, we have to start where we are. On the Buddhist path, starting where we are involves a certain degree of courage and fearlessness. It takes fearlessness to look in the mirror and see one's own face. We might have to look in the mirror in the early morning when we first get up, before we have taken a shower; or we might have to look at ourselves after an accident. Nevertheless, we have to cut through any fear of looking at that reality. Whatever is reflected in the mirror, whatever is reflected in our experience, we can be courageous enough to explore that reality further, accept it, and start the journey from that very spot. In Buddhism, that is the beginning. We cut through all our conceptualizations, expectations, projections, and fantasies, such as, "Oh, if I were that person, I could do much better on the path." This is not a healthy way to begin the journey. The main requirement is to be who we are and start where we are. That is the simplest way to begin our journey, and it is the most direct way to discover our mind and its nature.

PREPARING FOR THE JOURNEY

Mahamudra and Dzogchen are similar to all other Buddhist journeys in that there is a beginning, a middle, and an end, which correspond to the ground, path, and fruition stages of the path. The journey starts at the beginning, which is called "ground," and not at the end, which is called "fruition." However, the fruition aspect cannot be isolated from the ground aspect; they both are aspects of a whole path. Nevertheless, it is necessary to go through these progressive stages because of the vast accumulations of karmic garbage that we carry with us and bring to the path. These stages are not necessary from the point of view of enlightenment. They are necessary only from the point of view of our own neurosis. Thus, it is the extent of our neurosis that determines the complexity of the path and our need to be led through a gradual process of working with ego-clinging and emotions.

From a Buddhist perspective, *neurosis* refers to our experience of ordinary, conventional reality, in which we undergo various forms of suffering based on a mistaken perception that the "I" or "self" is a truly existing, permanent entity. Based on this fundamental misperception, we grasp onto the imagined self, and this clinging—often referred to as *ego-clinging*—then serves as a basis for the arising of disturbing emotions and karmic actions.

Seen from the perspective of enlightenment, the whole journey is unnecessary: There are no paths or stages to achieve. However, each individual practitioner taking this journey needs to go through the progressive levels and follow the detailed instructions and methods of the path in order to attain realization. It is not possible to jump straight to the fruition stage, saying, "I just want to be there." It is not that easy or that simple. To jump straight in would be to set out on this journey in haste, without taking the time to prepare carefully. Imagine taking a journey to some unknown place, such as the Sahara Desert. If you do not prepare for your journey properly, if you do not take sufficient time to think about the place you are trying to reach and the amount of time required to get there, then, in your great hurry, you will forget to pack something very important, such as your Tylenol, your water, or your first aid kit.

Preparing for this particular journey might seem to require too much effort or too much intellectual exertion, or it might simply seem inordinately detailed and mundane. You might not want to think about the difficulties. Because the preparation is both difficult and painful, you might decide to skip some of the details and set off in haste, saying, "I just want to be there, at the level of enlightenment. I do not want to think about the preparation or the process. I do not want to practice this progressive stuff. It is too painful."

However, without proper preparation, you could get a severe headache in the middle of the journey and not know what to do. There is no drugstore in this wild Sahara Desert, no grocery store where you can buy Evian water. There is no stream of water here, and anyway, you forgot to pack your water bottle. You begin to ask yourself whether you want to continue struggling and pushing through this headache and thirst in order to reach your destination. You are not sure whether you can make it or not. You might decide to go back home and get your Tylenol.

This happens to many of us. After beginning our journey, we go through a period of struggle only to find out that we are missing certain things that are absolutely necessary for our journey. Then we find ourselves in a very difficult position. We have to decide whether to go back to where we were, make proper preparations, and begin the journey again, from scratch, or whether to force ourselves to continue our journey with a severe headache, dehydration, or any other unknown or unexpected experiences for which we are unprepared. In the end, it may take us longer to reach our destination if we start in haste and try to zoom through our journey than if we take time at the beginning to prepare fully.

Generally, the paths of Mahamudra and Dzogchen are introduced in progressive stages. By going through these basic stages of the path, we become fully prepared. We examine every possible aspect of our journey, every potential problem that might cause us to end up in a miserable state. Then we explore every possible means of protecting ourselves and of solving the problems that we might face. We learn what can be prevented and how to work with the situations that we will inevitably face.

THE STAGES OF MAHAMUDRA AND DZOGCHEN
One Dharma, Many Yanas

Yana is a Sanskrit term that means "vehicle." Literally, it means "the vehicle that brings us to our destination." Our destination here is enlightenment, liberation from samsara; that is where the vehicle will bring us. According to Shakyamuni Buddha, we can understand *yana* in two different ways. We can understand the term to mean "the yana that brings us to our destination" or "the yana that brought us here"—in other words, to where we are right now.

The first meaning of *yana,* "the yana that brings us to our destination," orients us toward the future. The yana, or vehicle, is the cause that brings us to our result: we are brought to the fruition stage, which is our destination. When we define yana in this way, it is known as the causal yana.

The second meaning of *yana,* "the yana that brought us here," refers to the result or fruition. It is called the resultant yana, or fruition yana, because we have already been conveyed to our destination. We are already there.

Although we speak of the Buddhist path as being divided into various stages, such as the three or nine yanas, fundamentally, Shakyamuni Buddha taught only one Dharma. That Dharma is the true reality of absolute and relative phenomena. That is all that Buddha taught. However, that one Dharma was heard in various ways by many listeners, who had diverse, individual capacities. Some heard this Dharma in a way that relates to the fundamental details of relative truth. Others heard it in a way that relates to the most profound level of absolute reality. Still, all in all, Buddha taught only one Dharma and one truth, and that truth is the reality of all phenomena. However, Buddha also taught that there can be as many yanas as there are thoughts, concepts, or modes of ego-clinging.

The general Buddhist path is divided into three yanas, or vehicles. The most familiar understanding of the three yanas in the West consists of the Hinayana, the Mahayana, and the Vajrayana. The Mahamudra journey is based on this three-yana classification. However, in the Dzogchen approach, the journey is divided into nine yanas, which include the previous three. Thus, although the views of Mahamudra and Dzogchen are inseparable, the Mahamudra and Dzogchen paths are laid out in slightly different ways. In both systems of classification, the path is a gradual process of the evolution of mind. The practices of Mahamudra and Dzogchen are the final stages of their respective paths.

First, we will briefly review the essential characteristics of three-yana system, which comes to fruition in the Mahamudra path. Later, we will outline the nine-yana journey, which is the heart of the Dzogchen path.

The Three-Yana Journey

In the general three-yana process, we look first at ourselves, then at others, and finally at the whole environment. In the first yana, the Hinayana, we learn to relate more closely to our individual experiences. Before we can extend ourselves to others, as we do in the Mahayana, we need to experience our own emotions and work with our own suffering. Having gone through that process, we undertake the Mahayana journey, the second yana, the essence of which is using profound insight to interact with others. Finally, on the Vajrayana journey, any and all of our experiences are viewed as opportunities for awakening. From this perspective, we are continually relating to the whole environment without making dualistic distinctions between, for example, "good" and "bad" or "awake" and "asleep."

THE HINAYANA

The Hinayana, which is associated with the first cycle of the Buddha's teaching, is translated as the "lower vehicle." However, this does not mean that the Hinayana is lower in quality. "Lower" refers to that which occurs at the beginning, the most fundamental part of our journey. The Hinayana is said to be lower than the other two vehicles in the same way that the foundation of a house or building is lower than the upper floors. In order to build a house, we have to start by building a foundation. Ultimately, how many floors we will be able to build depends on how well we lay the foundation.

Many of the other factors that affect our journey are determined by how well we lay the foundation of the Hinayana path. If we attempt to leap right into Mahamudra or Dzogchen, then we are forgetting about Hinayana, which means that we are forgetting about our foundation. On the three-yana journey, when we forget about our groundwork, we end up merely dreaming. We dream about the ninth floor. We dream about how beautiful it is and all the lovely things we have heard about it. In fact, however, we have not made any serious effort to build the foundation necessary to get there.

The foundation that we are trying to develop consists of the Hinayana view of selflessness, the understanding of interdependent origination, and the path of revulsion and renunciation. In order to properly understand selflessness, which is the view of the nonexistence of an individual self or ego, we need to understand that all phenomena of the relative world of samsaric existence arise only in dependence upon causes and conditions. There are no phenomena that arise independently. Upon examination, we can see that all phenomena constituting individual existence are impermanent, momentary, and composite. We can also see that such conditioned existence is full of suffering and pain. Samsaric existence is, in fact, a repetitive cycle of suffering, arising through the causes and conditions of ignorance, disturbing emotions, and their resulting negative karmic actions.

When we understand that suffering is the real truth of samsaric existence, we develop a genuine feeling of revulsion, which leads to renunciation. Seeing this reality becomes the primary motivation for us to connect with the pure Dharma, the genuine path. Revulsion and renunciation are similar. Revulsion is the state of feeling disgust with the suffering of samsara. Renunciation is simply seeing samsaric suffering clearly and wanting to be free from such suffering, wanting to achieve ultimate happiness and peace.

Such an understanding of samsara leads us onto the path of liberation. We could say that developing renunciation helps us to start the engine of our vehicle so that we can navigate on the road and find a suitable exit from suffering. We do not want to take just any exit. We do not want to get off at an exit that leads to the local bar, or at one that leads to a Himalayan cave. Simply being physically present in a Himalayan cave will not help, because we inevitably bring our whole samsaric mind with us. Instead, when we develop true revulsion, we can renounce our habitual tendencies, the deeply ingrained, subtle habits of mind that are ignorant, disturbing, and harmful to our mental well-being.

When we develop a genuine understanding of suffering, renunciation, and the selfless nature of ego, we can properly enter the path of Mahayana.

THE MAHAYANA

The Mahayana, which is known as the "greater vehicle," is associated with the second and third cycles of the Buddha's teachings. These cycles contain the Prajnaparamita sutras, or the sutras on transcendental knowledge, and the teachings on buddha nature. At this point, we are saying that we are working not only for our own benefit but for the benefit of all living beings. However, if we cannot work with our own ego-clinging, how can we work with genuine compassion for the benefit of others? We will be pretending. It will be as if we are making ourselves a great T-shirt that says "Bodhisattva" or "Mahayanist," but it will not mean anything. We will simply be wearing a T-shirt displaying a label that says "Bodhisattva" or "I Am Compassionate. I Work for You Guys."

It is only when we have properly understood the Hinayana notion of suffering and the view of selflessness that it becomes possible to generate genuine loving-kindness and compassion. When we have directly recognized our own suffering and its causes, we can easily understand that other beings are also suffering in samsara, just like us. With this understanding, compassion is not very difficult to develop. It requires only a slight shift in our motivation, a slight shift in our point of reference, from a self-centered view to the view of caring for all sentient beings. We shift from being concerned solely with our own welfare to having concern for the welfare of all living beings around us. Therefore, when we truly enter the Mahayana path, we become genuine practitioners of compassion, practicing our whole path for the benefit of others. Our concern for the happiness and welfare of all beings surpasses our concern for our own happiness.

This kind of motivation is called *bodhichitta,* which is translated as "the heart of enlightenment." The heart of enlightenment has two aspects: relative and ultimate. Relative bodhichitta is the desire to achieve enlightenment in order to benefit all living beings. We want to bring all sentient beings into the state of buddhahood. Ultimate bodhi-chitta is the realization of emptiness combined with compassion. Emptiness, or *shunyata* in Sanskrit, refers to the true nature of all phenomena. That nature is devoid of true, inherent, and independent existence and is beyond all levels of conceptual elaboration. This genuine understanding of shunyata is not limited to knowing the emptiness of self, but also includes knowing the selfless nature of the whole universe. Thus, the Mahayana path leads us one step further than the Hinayana path. It leads us to the development of genuine compassion and love and to a deeper understanding of emptiness. Once we have established the fundamental groundwork of the Hinayana and Mahayana paths, we can enter the path of Vajrayana.

THE VAJRAYANA

The goal of Vajrayana practice, which is the realization of complete freedom, is not different from the goal of any other Buddhist path. However, the approach of this yana is quite distinct. In Vajrayana practice, we are not aiming toward attaining enlightenment. Rather, enlightenment is seen as existing in every state of being. There is a basic sense of the continuity of enlightened mind that is like the thread that runs through a string of prayer beads. This thread runs through beads of all different sizes and forms. In a similar way, the continuity of the enlightened heart is present in every state of mind and in every situation of samsara. In the Vajrayana, we do not see enlightenment as our final goal because it is here already. It is present in every state of mind: in every state of confusion as well as in every state of clarity and wisdom.

From the Vajrayana point of view, whenever we are fully experiencing the chaos of samsara and of our emotions, we are experiencing complete enlightenment, or full awakening. It does not matter how we label these experiences. There is a basic sharpness in our emotions that awakens us by itself. No outer method or remedy is required to wake us up. The basic sharpness and basic space of experience awaken us to the reality of enlightenment.

From a conventional point of view, the Vajrayana view is a little bit insane. For example, it does not see any difference between being awake and being asleep. The very experience of sleep is awake. Sleep is nothing but dense clarity. The very experience of emotions is the very experience of enlightenment. Essentially, the Vajrayana approach toward our whole environment and our emotions is to see them as our guru. What is the function of a guru? A guru wakes us up from the sleep of samsara. What is the function of emotions? They wake us up as well. Therefore, Vajrayana practitioners see opportunities for awakening in the nature of all experiences, all emotions, and all environments. There is no awakening outside these very experiences. What we variously call buddhahood, enlightenment, or buddha mind is present in this very moment.

The Nine-Yana Journey

From the Dzogchen perspective, the journey is broken down into nine stages, which are grouped into three sets of yanas. These stages are described very briefly here. A full presentation of the nine-yana journey is presented in part 3 of this book.

The first set of three yanas—the Shravakayana, the Pratyeka-buddhayana, and the Bodhisattvayana—is called the Vehicle of Directing the Cause of Suffering. It is known as the causal vehicle because it brings us gradually to the final result by taking the causes of awakening as the path. Within the three-yana system, the Shravakayana and the Pratyeka-buddhayana are included in the Hinayana, while the Bodhisattvayana accords with the general Mahayana.

In contrast to the gradual path of the causal vehicle, the next two sets of yanas are known as fruition yanas. They bring one more rapidly to the accomplishment of the final result by taking the state of fruition itself as the path.

The second set of yanas is called the Vehicle of Austerity and Awareness, which consists of the three lower or outer tantras: Kriya tantra, Upa tantra, and Yoga tantra. With these three yanas, we begin the Vajrayana journey. In Dzogchen, we go through not only the causal yanas of the basic Buddhist path, but also the progression of the lower tantras, which are not commonly practiced on the Mahamudra path. This set of yanas provides us with the skillful means to relate more directly with the fundamental nature of mind.

The last set of three yanas is called the Vehicle of Overpowering Means, which consists of the three inner tantras of Maha yoga, Anu yoga, and Ati yoga. Also known as the resultant yana, this vehicle comprises the final stages of the path, where we come to the innermost essence of the whole journey. The last of these three yanas, Ati yoga, is what is usually referred to in Tibetan as Dzogchen. This is the point where the journey ends and where we have exhausted all our karmic garbage. It is like a giant *full stop*—the period at the end of a sentence. There is a sense of fullness and completeness. At the same time, everything stops here: samsara has been exhausted. It does not go beyond this. That is Dzogchen.

ENTERING THE PATH

The Buddha taught that there is no enlightenment and no wisdom outside our own minds. From this perspective, what we gain from teachers, from scriptures, or from following the spiritual path through all its stages is not something new or external to us. When we follow the path, we simply gain more skillful methods to uncover our own wisdom and our own enlightenment. The teachings of the Mahamudra and Dzogchen paths show us that wisdom and enlightenment are found right within our emotions and right within our ordinary world. From the Buddhist point of view, the most profound way to relate to the realm of our emotions and the entire universe is to simply experience each moment as it is, each phenomenon as it arises, without concepts and labels. If we are looking for a better way, we are wasting our time.

The paths of Mahamudra and Dzogchen are the most immediate routes to this realization. These two paths are not essentially different, even though they use different terminologies and slightly different methods. Many great masters have taught that Mahamudra and Dzogchen are of an inseparable nature. Their instructions and methods function like extremely precise and powerful energy-recycling machines that can instantly process all our karmic hangovers, residues, and refuse. If we have reflected on our motivation and know why we are here, if we are certain about our goal and if we can apply all the power, energy, and sharpness of our inquisitive mind to our journey, then—and only then—are we prepared to enter the most profound paths of Mahamudra and Dzogchen.

The great Indian mahasiddha, Maitripa, with his disciple, the renowned Marpa the translator.

PART TWO

The
Mahamudra
Journey

MAHAMUDRA: THE GREAT SEAL

The unfabricated and unconditioned
wisdom nature of mind;
The luminous, empty, and unceasing
nature of all reality.

Mahamudra

The Great Seal

T HE ESSENTIAL NATURE of Mahamudra is like all-encompassing space; it rests nowhere and is free from all conceptions. The Mahamudra teachings come from the direct teachings of Lord Buddha Shakyamuni, the historical Buddha. The lineage of these Mahamudra teachings has continued from the time of the historical Buddha until now in an unbroken lineage. There is an oral transmission or "ear-whispered" lineage and a textual transmission lineage.

The Sanskrit term *mahamudra* is *chak gya chenpo* (*phyag rgya chen po*) in Tibetan. The meaning of *chak gya chenpo* is explained in many different ways in our tradition, one of the principal sources for these explanations being the *Mahamudratilaka Tantra*.[1] Overall, *chak gya chenpo* traditionally comprises three aspects, found in the meaning of the syllables *chak, gya,* and *chenpo*.

The first syllable, *chak,* refers to emptiness or shunyata, and the experience of emptiness, which in the Mahamudra tradition must become personal and genuine. *Chak* thus stands for the innermost awareness or insight of shunyata, the realization of the inseparability of samsara and nirvana in their nature of emptiness.

The second syllable, *gya,* literally means "seal" or "symbol." In its deeper sense, *gya* refers to the unaltered, unfabricated, or unconditioned nature of wisdom: the experience of going beyond samsaric existence, of freedom from the subtle fetters of complexities. *Gya* signifies the intrinsic quality or abiding reality of all things, which transcends duality. It is the primordial purity that encompasses everything.

The third syllable, *chenpo,* means "great" or "pervading." The fundamental nature of mind is all-pervasive and the nature of everything. It is the union of emptiness and wisdom. *Chenpo* signifies this union and the realization that freedom is innate in the true nature of reality.

Therefore, literally speaking, Mahamudra means "great symbol" or "great seal." It also means "great gesture." The term *great seal* is used in the sense of an emperor's seal. When an emperor signs a constitutional decree, at the end there is a seal that carries the full weight of this authority. Until it is sealed, the law means nothing, but once it has been sealed, there is nothing that is beyond that law. In this case, the seal is the nature of all reality. In other words, there is no other nature or reality that exists beyond this nature of luminosity and emptiness, this nature of appearance and emptiness. The nature of ego is great emptiness. The nature of self is selflessness. The nature of the phenomenal world is nonexistence. It is empty yet appearing. That is why it is said that emptiness is inseparable from appearance, from luminosity itself.

The term *great symbol* is also used, but "symbol" is not meant in the conventional sense of something that stands for or suggests something else; instead, it is the thing itself—the real thing, the actual stuff. For example, we could say that spaghetti is the symbol of Italian food. However, when we eat spaghetti we are not eating a symbol. We are eating actual Italian food. In a similar way, the "great symbol" is not like a picture that represents a real place somewhere else. The great symbol is the great nature of true reality. It is the actual taste of the true nature of inseparable emptiness-luminosity.

Maitripa, a great Indian *mahasiddha* and one of the forefathers of the Kagyu lineage, explains the definition of Mahamudra in this way:

Mahamudra is nondual awareness that transcends intellect; it is nonconceptual and lucid, like all-pervading space. Though manifesting boundless compassion, it is devoid of self-nature. It is like the reflection of the moon on the lake's surface. It is lucid and undefinable, without center or circumference, unstained, undefiled, and free from fear and desire. Like the dream of a mute, it is inexpressible.[2]

The Mahamudra teachings are the essence teachings of the New Translation school of Tibetan Buddhism. This school refers to those traditions that developed in Tibet during the second spreading of the Buddhist doctrine, beginning in the eleventh century. In particular, the New Translation school includes the Kagyu, Sakya, and Gelugpa schools. The Old Translation school refers to the Nyingma lineage. The fundamental elements of Mahamudra are presented in the Mahayana journey in the teachings on transcendental wisdom or knowledge called *prajnaparamita*. The teachings on Mahamudra are also taught in the different tantras and *shastras*. The tantras refer to the scriptures or teachings of the Buddha that form the basis of the Mantrayana. Shastras are commentaries or philosophical treatises that elucidate the Buddha's teachings.

THE GLACIER MOUNTAIN

The Sun of Devotion

In order to follow the path of Mahamudra, we need the genuine transmission from the lineage and the lineage masters. From the Mahamudra point of view, the guru plays a very important role because no matter how well, how directly, and how perfectly Shakyamuni Buddha transmitted the Mahamudra teachings, we are not able to be in his presence now. However, we are able to be in the presence of our gurus, and it is only through their blessings that we are able to directly receive, connect with, and realize this heart of Mahamudra. In the Mahamudra tradition it is said that the compassion of the guru and buddhas is equal—there is no difference in their compassion. However, in terms of kindness, our guru is more kind to us than all the buddhas of the three times, because he or she directly points out our true nature. Thus, the key to Mahamudra experience or realization is our devotion to the guru and the lineage. Without devotion, there is no *adhishthana,* or blessing transmission. Without adhishthana, there is no way for us to realize the true nature of mind.

In one of the songs of realization, it is said that devotion is like the sun shining on a snow mountain. This mountain is like the guru. If the sun of devotion does not shine on the glacier mountain of the four *kayas* of the guru, then the river flow of blessings will not descend. This metaphor shows us whether or not we will be able to receive the transmission of Mahamudra. The more intensely the sun of devotion shines, the more strongly the stream of blessings will flow. If it is too cold, or too cloudy, or if no sun is shining, then the glacier mountain remains frozen. It is always beautiful, it is always pure, but the stream does not come down from that mountain. Therefore, generating devotion is very important if we are to receive these blessings. It is important to pay close attention to our mind of devotion. Because devotion to the guru, to the lineage, and to the teachings of Mahamudra is so strongly emphasized, the path of Mahamudra is frequently known as the path of devotion.

Devotion is the path, and devotion is realization. Devotion is experience and devotion is fruition. Whenever we experience genuine devotion, we experience Mahamudra mind; and whenever we realize the depth of devotion, we realize the true state of Mahamudra mind.

Devotion is not simply blind faith; rather, the experience or taste of devotion is an experience of the naked reality of our mind, especially of our emotions. Devotion comes from trust and from surrendering ourselves. Such surrender and trust come from confidence, which comes from knowledge. Therefore, this devotion is deeply rooted in wisdom and knowledge.

Passionate Devotion: Working with Emotions

The experience of devotion is extremely personal in terms of its degree and its way and power of manifestation. Devotion is something that we need to connect with naturally, without preconceptions. For example, we do not need to sit down for an hour in order to try to figure out how or what it should be, or toward which object it should arise. Devotion has to arise naturally with the help of the lineage and with the help of our emotions. The power of a genuine experience of devotion is utterly beyond concept. When we fully experience devotion, it transcends all conceptuality. When we fully experience devotion, it helps us to transcend emotions, even though it arises from or is based on emotions.

As with every aspect of the path, devotion does not arise naturally or easily for everybody, nor is it something that is necessarily constant. It is similar to our experience of meditation practice. Every time we sit and meditate, it is different. Sometimes our practice is deep and calm. We might feel that our practice is a wonderful achievement and that we can work with all of our thoughts and emotions. At other times we might feel as though we have never sat on a cushion before. We might feel that we have lost everything, including all qualities of calmness. The same is true for devotion, except that it fluctuates even more.

Ultimately speaking, devotion is not directed outside our mind. We direct devotion toward "ordinary mind," which is the Mahamudra mind, and to the genuine heart of enlightenment that is within us and within our emotions. We direct devotion to the mind of enlightenment that is right within our fear and hope. There is no Mahamudra mind outside these experiences.

Devotion involves working with our emotions very directly. In fact, the two are closely tied together. Within devotion, we can find elements of all our emotions. There are elements of passion. There are surely elements of jealousy, and there are elements of aggression and pride as well. While there are elements of every emotion within devotion, the strongest is passion, followed closely by jealousy. It is important for us to process these emotions rather than deny them. We need to see them clearly while also trying to remember the kindness, wisdom, *prajna*, and skillful means that we have received from our guru and the lineage. We should continue to try to develop our devotion further, no matter how much or what kind of emotion arises.

Jealousy is frequently involved with devotion because we tend to compare ourselves with others and become competitive. For example, in a class, there are many students but only one teacher. When the teacher acknowledges another student, you might feel, "Oh, my colleague is doing better than I am." Because the teacher acknowledged that person and forgot to acknowledge you or even smile, you might suddenly think, "What's wrong? He smiled at the other guy over there. Did I do something wrong?" There is a lot of fear involved with these thoughts.

We might not be totally crazy with jealousy, but there is sometimes a sense of feeling incompetent or unworthy. This also arises from making comparisons. For example, you might compare yourself with other students and think, "Oh, I'm not worthy. They can do things better than I can." At other times, you might say the opposite: "I can do things better than they can." Either way, it becomes problematic.

Having some sense of openness, willingness, and courage to work with such emotions when they arise becomes a powerful way to realize and experience true devotion. Sometimes it is necessary to recognize the helpful nature of our emotions and to acknowledge their power and potential to be of benefit to us. It is not fair to accuse and blame our emotions all the time.

Original Devotion

Trust in our own enlightened heart can be reinforced through trusting the heart of the guru. We call this "merging our mind with the mind of the guru" or "mixing our heart with the heart of the guru." We have to do this intentionally in the beginning, with trust and with effort. Gradually, however, it does become effortless. Sometimes when we focus totally and one-pointedly on the guru's mind, we have the experience of merging—the experience of being one person. What happens in the next moment? We might feel claustrophobic and run out of the room.

Try to generate devotion—in any amount, in any style, in any way you can. You can cultivate devotion in your own way. Do not worry about how someone else does it. If you simply mimic others because you think that devotion should be uniform, then that will not be genuine. Do not be afraid to express devotion in your own way, whether it is a Tibetan way, an American way, a European way, an Asian way, a Russian way, or any other way. It does not matter. Pure devotion does not have any standardized form or mold to fill. If there were a standard form for devotion, then teachers would have handed it out a long time ago, but there is no checklist or fill-in-the-blanks for devotion. Every individual way of expressing devotion should be as authentic, original, and individual as possible. Then there will be a real sense of connecting with your heart—not in exactly the same way that someone else's heart is connecting, but in a way that you can feel your own heart connection. That is the most important part of our whole journey.

The Mahamudra path is very different from the Hinayana-Mahayana journey in this respect. In the Hinayana-Mahayana journey, there are standard forms. There are checklists. If you are taking monastic ordination or bodhisattva vows, there is a checklist for what you can and cannot do. There is a standard way to conduct yourself on that path. However, on the Mahamudra path, it is very individualized, and that is why your own personal connection with the lineage becomes so powerful and important.

It has been taught that if someone brings to the practice of Mahamudra the tendency to take great pride in not relying on the spiritual guidance of the guru or in not following the guru's meditation instructions, then such a person might fall into the animal realm. In other words, their practice might lead them into a realm of stupidity, a state of completely spaced-out consciousness. This shows us that on the path of Mahamudra, devotion is beyond any question, such as whether or not we should have it or whether we can substitute something else for it. Devotion is not optional. Mahamudra can be realized only through the path of devotion.

MAHAMUDRA LINEAGE HISTORY

Mahamudra emphasizes the continuity of oral instructions, which are passed on from master to student. This emphasis is reflected in the literal meaning of the name "Kagyu." The first syllable, *ka (bka')*, which means "speech," refers to the scriptures of the Buddha and the oral instructions of the guru. *Ka* carries the sense of the enlightened meaning conveyed by the words of the teacher, as well as the force with which such words of insight are conveyed. The second syllable, *gyu (brgyud)*, means "lineage" or "tradition." Together, these syllables mean "the lineage of the oral instructions."

Over twenty-five hundred years ago, Prince Siddhartha attained enlightenment under the bodhi tree in Bodhgaya and then manifested as the Buddha. According to Buddhist cosmology, he was the fourth historic Buddha of this fortunate aeon. Prince Siddhartha's achievement of enlightenment—the realization itself—is called the *dharmakaya,* or the body of truth. When that realization is expressed through subtle symbols, it is called the *sambhogakaya,* or the body of enjoyment. The physical form of Shakyamuni Buddha, which is the historical manifestation of such realization in a form more accessible to sentient beings, is called the *nirmanakaya,* or the body of manifestation.

The Mahamudra lineage traces its origin back to Shakyamuni Buddha through Marpa Chökyi Lodrö, the great translator and realized yogi who brought the unbroken lineage of Buddha's Mahamudra from India to Tibet. At the age of fifteen, Marpa first trained as a translator under Drogmi Shakya Yeshe and later traveled three times to India and four times to Nepal in search of Buddhist teachings. Marpa is said to have studied with 108 masters and yogis, but his principal teachers were Naropa and Maitripa. Marpa then transmitted the lineage to his heart son, the famous yogi Milarepa.

The great master Gampopa, who is also known as Dakpo Lhaje, and Rechungpa were the principal students of Milarepa. Gampopa was prophesied in the sutras by the Buddha and established the framework of the lineage by unifying Milarepa's Mahamudra lineage with the stages-of-the-path tradition of the Kadampa lineage. The resulting unique tradition, known as the Dakpo Kagyu, was critical to the unfolding of the Kagyu lineage.

Gampopa transmitted this lineage to his three heart sons, one of whom was the First Karmapa, Düsum Khyenpa. In the Kagyu lineage supplication, the line "knower of the three times, omniscient Karmapa" is a reference to the First Karmapa. The transmission was passed from the First Karmapa to his disciple, Drogön Rechenpa, and then from him to the Second Karmapa, Karma Pakshi. It has passed continuously in this way to the present incarnation, who is the Seventeenth Karmapa, Ogyen Trinley Dorje, the youngest living Mahamudra lineage holder. The continuity of this lineage transmission is known as the golden rosary.

In general, there are two main lineages of Mahamudra, which are known as the direct and the indirect lineages. The original source of the transmission of the direct lineage is the Buddha Vajradhara, while the original source of the transmission of the indirect lineage is Shakyamuni Buddha.

The Direct Lineage

The original source of the teachings for the special transmission of the direct lineage is Vajradhara, who is the primordial, or dharmakaya, buddha. Vajradhara expresses the quintessence of buddhahood itself, the essence of the historical Buddha's realization of enlightenment. The skylike dharmakaya nature of Vajradhara is depicted in paintings by his dark blue color. Vajradhara is central to the Kagyu lineage because Tilopa received the Vajrayana teachings directly from Vajradhara, who is synonymous with the dharmakaya, the source of all manifestations of enlightenment. Thus, the Kagyu lineage originated from the very nature of buddhahood.

Tilopa acknowledged the origin of this Mahamudra lineage in his songs. He sang, "I, the yogi Tilopa, do not have any human teacher; I do not have any human master to follow. My teacher, my guru, is the great Vajradhara, the dharmakaya nature of Vajradhara." This shows that the lineage came directly from Vajradhara to Tilopa.

The Indirect Lineage

The line of transmission originating with Shakyamuni Buddha, which is known as the indirect lineage, is also referred to as the oral instruction lineage. Tilopa originally inherited four main streams of wisdom that were transmitted by Indian mahasiddhas such as Saraha, Nagarjuna, Aryadeva, Chandrakirti, and Matangi. Tilopa then condensed these four special transmission lineages into one and transmitted it to Naropa. This stream then passed from teacher to disciple: from Naropa to Marpa, Marpa to Milarepa, and then Milarepa to Gampopa.

However, Gampopa received the transmissions of two different Indian lineages. One was the tantric lineage, which came from Tilopa to Naropa to Marpa and then to Milarepa. That tradition conveys a very strong Vajrayana element. Gampopa also received the full transmission of the Indian master Atisha, which is known as the Kadampa lineage.

Atisha was trained at Nalanda University and became a great Buddhist master. He also served as the discipline master at Nalanda University. During the time of Marpa, he came to Tibet and transmitted many Sutrayana teachings. He was responsible for the transmission of both the philosophical and the practice traditions of the Prajnaparamita teachings. Thus, Atisha's lineage was based primarily on the sutras, although he also transmitted some tantric and Mahamudra practices.

Therefore, when the Mahamudra lineage came to Gampopa, it was a rich mixture of the tantra and sutra traditions. Gampopa presented the Mahamudra lineage by teaching three different methods of practicing Mahamudra.

THREE CLASSIFICATIONS OF MAHAMUDRA

According to the teachings and tradition of Lord Gampopa's lineage, the three classifications of Mahamudra are Sutra Mahamudra, Mantra Mahamudra, and Essence Mahamudra. Sutra Mahamudra is primarily based on the sutra teachings, and Mantra Mahamudra is primarily based on the mantra teachings. Essence Mahamudra draws from both sutra and mantra, but is traditionally distinguished as the devotional path based on blessings.

Sutra Mahamudra: The Secret Road in the City

The general teachings of Mahamudra were presented by Lord Buddha and his followers in such sutras as the Prajnaparamita sutras or the discourses on transcendental knowledge. These sutras teach primarily "the great emptiness." The shortest of the Prajnaparamita sutras is the *Heart Sutra,* which teaches the inseparability of form and emptiness. That sutra, along with the whole collection of Prajnaparamita teachings, is one of the bases for Sutra Mahamudra.

The teachings on buddha nature are the other basis for Sutra Mahamudra.[3] The buddha-nature teachings point out that the nature of our mind, emotions, and thoughts is complete wakefulness. That wakefulness is what we call buddhahood, or enlightenment. Furthermore, that enlightenment is the nature of all sentient beings. This essence of enlightenment is what we call buddha nature or *tathagatagarbha* in Sanskrit.

These two streams of teachings form the basis for the sutra aspect of Mahamudra. The practice of Sutra Mahamudra essentially involves the study and contemplation of these sutras, followed by meditation. We contemplate the teachings on emptiness, or shunyata, as well as the teachings on buddha nature, which is our fundamental wakefulness. Through this process, we discover our own heart of enlightenment. We discover that enlightenment is nothing external to us but is found within this very mind—within our emotions, thoughts, and perceptions. It is within these experiences that we see the basic state of enlightenment.

The meditation of Sutra Mahamudra essentially consists of resting one's mind, free of mental activity, in the state of nonconceptual wisdom. This is the fundamental definition of Sutra Mahamudra: mind resting in the state in which it experiences the *dharmadhatu,* which is the expanse or nature of all things. This resting is essentially a noncon-ceptual wisdom beyond all elaboration, or the unity of clarity and emptiness. In this context, one meditates in the following way: The object of one's meditation is luminosity free of any projections; the perceiving subject is the lack of mental engagement; and one meditates without mental engagement. There are many extensive explanations on meditating without mental engagement, found primarily in the teachings of Maitripa and Sahajavajra.

The Sutrayana approach to Mahamudra is seen as a very profound method because it does not require any of the sophisticated and com-plex tantric rituals, deity yoga visualization practices, or *samayas*.[4] It is a simple sutra approach, yet it conveys the direct transmission of the tantric essence of awakening. This particular approach is also known as a secret passage. It can be compared to a secret street within a city—a route that has not been widely discovered. Although it is right in the heart of the city, very few people know about this secret street. What is the difference between this street and the other streets in the city? This street is a shortcut, without traffic or traffic lights, and it is a direct route. This street is right within this very city, and it will take you straight to your destination without any delays. Thus, in order to find this path, you do not have to go far. The direct and profound methods of Sutrayana Mahamudra are found right within the sutra approach, right within the ordinary and simple path of spiritual prac-tice. Through this path, we can attain complete buddhahood by tra-versing the five paths and ten *bhumis*.[5]

Sutra Mahamudra is viewed as being very profound, straight to the point, yet simple. The difference between Sutra Mahamudra and other sutra approaches, such as the general Hinayana and Mahayana paths, is that Sutra Mahamudra has a tradition of skillful means that contains pro-found methods of directly pointing out the selfless and luminous nature of mind. There is a direct method of pointing out, which usually does not exist in other sutra approaches. The skillful methods of pointing out the nature of mind used in Sutra Mahamudra are imported, in a sense, from the Vajrayana tradition. Therefore, the essence of Sutra Mahamudra is usually described as being prajnaparamita, or the transcendental wisdom of emptiness, with a touch of the Vajrayana. Finally, it is called Mahamudra, the great seal, because by using the very words and teachings of the sutras, it brings the realization of Mahamudra.

The Sutra Mahamudra approach is seen as a specialty of the Kagyu tradition and was the central emphasis of Gampopa's teachings. Therefore, although it originated in India and was also taught by Marpa and Milarepa, Gampopa is regarded as the main figure responsible for bringing this teaching to its full development and manifestation.

Mantra Mahamudra: The Path of Great Upaya

The second aspect of the Mahamudra tradition is the approach of the Mantrayana, or the Vajrayana.[6] This approach involves quite profound and sophisticated methods, which include working with creation stage and completion stage deity practices, as well as very detailed instructions on working with *nadi, prana,* and *bindu.*[7] The main presentation of Vajrayana Mahamudra is found in the *Anuttarayoga* tantras and in the instructions of those tantras. These tantras are transmitted through the four principal *abhisheka*s, or empowerments. When Mahamudra is introduced as the naked, natural state through the use of Vajrayana methods, this is called Mantra Mahamudra.

A special feature of the Vajrayana path is the variety and richness of its methods, through which one can realize the nature of mind. This diversity of methods is not emphasized in the Sutra Mahamudra approach, in which there is just one simple pointing-out method for experiencing Mahamudra. In Mantra Mahamudra, there are many means of pointing out mind's nature, such as the process of the four abhishekas. When we go through the initiation process of an abhisheka, we are empowered to practice the mandala of a particular deity, which symbolizes the nature of mind. This is the traditional way in which a student is introduced to the nature of mind. The images of deities represented in paintings and sculptures are actually reflections, mirror images, of the nature of our own mind. By working with such a reflection through the process of visualization, we are working toward the recognition of our own mind. For example, in order to see your own face, you have to rely upon a mirror. When you see your reflection, you can say, "Oh, yes, my face has such and such features," and you can recognize whether your face is clean or dirty. Similarly, the pure and impure aspects of mind are reflected in these symbolic images of a deity. Thus, through deity yoga practice, Mantra Mahamudra reflects to us the nature of mind.

The Mantra Mahamudra deity practice is very profound; at the same time, it is quite easy to misunderstand the images and to misinterpret the deity as an external entity. The practice of the Vajrayana path requires a very strong understanding, and the source of that understanding is the instructions of the lineage and the Vajrayana tantras. When we study the instructions and receive the transmission, our understanding becomes clear. Through this clear understanding, we are able to genuinely relate to Vajrayana deity practice.

Essence Mahamudra: Simultaneous Realization and Liberation

Essence Mahamudra is transmitted through a path more profound and more wondrous than the previous two because it leads to the sudden realization of the true nature of mind, which is called *thamal gyi shepa (tha mal gyi shes pa)*, or ordinary mind.[8]

Essence Mahamudra is practiced when an extremely realized guru bestows a transmission—a particular type of blessing, or adhishthana, that is called "the empowerment of vajra wisdom"—upon an extremely receptive, open, devoted, and qualified student. This empowerment is regarded as the descent of the actual realization of the root and lineage gurus upon or into a student. Through the descent of the blessings of this vajra wisdom, thamal gyi shepa suddenly awakens in that student's heart and is fully recognized on the spot. As a result, the student experiences what is called simultaneous realization and liberation.

On this path, there is no need for either the elaborate methods of Mantra Mahamudra or the gradual training of Sutra Mahamudra. In Sutra Mahamudra, there are still some forms; for example, the practices of *shamatha* and *vipashyana* meditation, as well as the practices of bodhichitta, are retained. There is also a great deal of formal study. In Mantrayana Mahamudra, there is also a certain formality of method that can be seen in the reliance upon ceremony and ritual; for example, there are extensive liturgies, visualizations, and mantra recitations. Thus, in this sense, Vajrayana Mahamudra is also a very formal way of introducing the nature of mind. In contrast, the Essence Mahamudra path is totally formless. The transmission happens instantaneously. Essence Mahamudra is nothing more than one's naked, ordinary mind resting in the unfabricated state.

In the Essence Mahamudra tradition, all conceptual clinging, such as clinging to ideas of sacred and profane or of virtuous and unvirtuous, is cut through, and we work directly with the experience of mind and its nature. The lineage guru points out the nature of mind to us, directly and nakedly. This kind of pointing-out instruction is very genuine. It is not something that we can mimic or repeat. We cannot "try it out" one time and say, "That was just a rehearsal. It did not work out, so okay, let's do the same thing again." That is not how it works. In the tradition of this lineage, we get one direct and naked pointing out, which has an effect. Throughout the history of Essence Mahamudra, pointing out has always happened in a simple, ordinary way. This type of pointing out typifies the Essence Mahamudra approach, where we are working directly with our experiences of ordinary, worldly life, as well as our experience of the nature of mind.

PERSPECTIVES ON THE MAHAMUDRA JOURNEY

We prepare ourselves for the Mahamudra journey first by coming to understand its place within the more general Buddhist journey and, second, by grounding ourselves in its essential meanings, characteristics, and forms. Then we will be ready to look more closely at the details of the three modes of Sutra, Mantra, and Essence Mahamudra.

Ground, Path, and Fruition

The Mahamudra journey is usually viewed from the perspective of ground, path, and fruition. For example, when we begin our Sutra

Mahamudra journey, we enter at the level of ground Mahamudra. At this stage, we are introduced to the fundamental nature of reality, the basic state of our mind and of the phenomenal world. We develop a clear intellectual understanding of the view of emptiness and of the nature of mind through our study, contemplation, and meditation practices. When we are ready to give rise to the actual experience of Mahamudra meditation, we enter the stage of path Mahamudra by first engaging in the preliminary practices and then receiving the pointing-out instructions from our guru, which prepare us to engage in the corresponding meditation practices. Subsequently, we develop our practice more fully through what are known as enhancement practices. The fruition stage is the completion of our journey. It is the point at which we fully discover the nature of our mind, which is the achievement of buddhahood. Thus, whether our Mahamudra journey follows the methods of Sutra, Mantra, or Essence Mahamudra, we relate to the progressive stages of ground, path, and fruition. This is true even though the Mahamudra teachings speak about "sudden awakening."

Sudden Awakening

Even in Sutra Mahamudra, there is some sense of sudden awakening. These teachings are typically distinguished from the Vajrayana Buddhist teachings, yet Gampopa describes the Mahamudra of the Sutrayana tradition as being consistent with the Vajrayana teachings. Therefore, we might well ask what it means to say that Sutra Mahamudra is consistent with the techniques of Vajrayana.

It is important to see that Sutra Mahamudra does not consist only of the teachings on emptiness yoga; it is not simply a philosophical or intellectual approach to understanding emptiness. Sutra Mahamudra introduces a certain method of "clicking," which comes from the Vajrayana tradition. When the "click" occurs, there is a strong sense of force—a sense of something happening suddenly. When the extensive teachings on emptiness are connected to this Vajrayana notion of clicking, they become much more powerful and our journey progresses much more quickly. This clicking is strongly connected to or dependent upon our devotion to the teacher, to the teachings, and to the power of the blessings of the lineage. We suddenly click into a certain state of awakening. We are talking about two states of mind here: asleep and awake. When you are sleeping, you have the potential of being awakened—of being an awake person. You always have that potential, and from the point of view of potential, there is no difference between you lying there asleep and the awake person who is watching you sleep like a log. At the same time, there is a communication taking place between the sleeping mind and the awakened mind. For example, the fully awakened mind of Vajradhara communicated with Tilopa, who was possibly half-awake at a certain point. Then the clicking happened between them, and Tilopa was fully awakened by Vajradhara's teaching.

In one sense, we could see this click as the result of something coming from the outside. Because we experience the world dualistically, we cling to the notion of receiving something from outside ourselves. However, whatever we "receive" is not something foreign to the essence of our minds. It is already there in the same way that the potential for being awake is present in our minds while we are in a state of sleep. In order to wake up, we need only this clicking; it does not matter whether we use an alarm clock to click into the awakened state or another technique, such as a bucket of water, which is much more powerful. However, since we are following a progressive path, if we attempt to use the clicking method to jump into the state of awakening at the beginning of our journey, we might experience some confusion.

In general, our guru, our spiritual friend, guides our journey on the Buddhist path. Because of this, we always have some sense of a reference point and some sense of blessing. However, we should not misconstrue this to mean that our teacher has total power over us. A teacher does not have the power to pull us out of samsara. For example, at the general or basic Sutrayana level of the path, the teacher is simply like an alarm clock. We must make the effort to approach the clock and set the alarm for the right time. Then, when it buzzes in the morning, we have a choice about whether to wake up or go back to sleep. It is our own individual responsibility—we can press the snooze button or we can get up. Thus, there needs to be a sense of balance. Although the teacher or spiritual friend is very important on our journey, he or she is not like God. We have to put in our own effort. This effort begins with ground Mahamudra, which is the fundamental teaching of the Mahamudra path.

3

The Path That Brings Experience

THERE ARE THREE STAGES of path Mahamudra that generate the actual meditation of Mahamudra: the preliminary practices, the pointing-out instructions, and the enhancement
practices.

1. The Preliminary Practices. The purpose of the preliminary practices is to bring about Mahamudra meditation when it has not yet
arisen in the practitioner's mindstream. In other words, at this first
stage, the preliminary practices function so as to bring, generate,
or give rise to Mahamudra mind in our own meditation.

2. The Pointing-Out Instructions. The second stage occurs when
Mahamudra meditation is ready to arise in our mind. Pointing-out
instructions are given at this point in order to make Mahamudra
meditation arise successfully in our mindstream. This is called the
Mahamudra path of pointing out.

3. The Enhancement Practices. When the pointing out has been
done successfully, we develop our practice to its fullest extent in
the third stage of our meditation path through engaging in the
enhancement practices.

Our first introduction to path Mahamudra is through the preliminary practices. They are the means through which one becomes a perfect

candidate for the actual practices of Mahamudra. The great importance of these preliminary practices is expressed succinctly in a traditional aphorism of the lineage: "The preliminary practice is more profound than the actual practice."

The first of the preliminaries, known as the four common preliminaries or the four reminders, is a foundational practice that is common to all Buddhist schools. This essential preliminary is followed by the four uncommon preliminaries, which are common to all Vajrayana and Mahamudra traditions. There is an additional set of four preliminaries, called the four special preliminaries, which precedes the main practice. Following completion of the preliminary practices, students go directly into the path of Mahamudra.

THE FOUR COMMON PRELIMINARIES: THE FOUR REMINDERS

The Mahamudra journey to enlightenment begins with the preliminary practices, which bring the meditation of Mahamudra into one's own being. The four common preliminaries, or four reminders, are the contemplations or reflections on precious human birth, impermanence, karma, and the shortcomings of samsara. Unless we generate a proper experience of the four reminders, it will be very difficult for us to connect with any other experiences on the path.

Precious Human Birth

In the first contemplation, we reflect on what is known as precious human birth. Such a birth is regarded as one that possesses the three essential qualities of confidence, diligence, and wisdom. When we possess these three qualities, our human birth becomes precious.

CONFIDENCE

The first essential quality of a precious human birth is confidence. We develop confidence in our own qualities of buddha nature, in the teachings of the enlightened path, and in the teacher. This first quality is an important aspect of our precious human birth because without these types of confidence we have no sense of protection. When we develop confidence, we develop a form of protection that can be compared to the body of an automobile. The body of an automobile provides us with a certain level of protection, as well as a sense of beauty and comfort. For example, we can enjoy a comfortable seat. We do not have to walk in the rain, in a hailstorm, or under the hot sun because we have the protection of a roof. Developing the quality of confidence is like developing protection all around us. This confidence surrounds and protects our positive qualities and the energy we already possess.

DILIGENCE

The second quality of a precious human birth is diligence. This can be compared to the fuel that is required to run our automobile. Although we have a beautiful car with comfortable seats and a powerful engine, if there is no gasoline, then the car is not going to move. Our enjoyment will be limited to sitting in the car and enjoying its physical qualities. In order to get it moving, we need gasoline. Similarly, in order to move along the path, we need diligence. Without the generation of diligence, we will not get anywhere—we will be stuck with a beautiful concept.

Simply having confidence in our basic buddha nature, in the teachings, and in the teacher does not really move us along the path. Neither faith nor devotion alone is enough to move us. Shantideva said that diligence means being inspired by wholesome or virtuous actions. Diligence does not mean being a workaholic, working hard for twenty-four hours at a time. Both diligence and confidence require a certain degree of understanding and insight. Without such knowledge and wisdom, we cannot have genuine confidence or genuine diligence.

WISDOM

The third quality of precious human birth is wisdom. This quality begins with our fundamental intelligence, our common sense, and our rational mind. When we become involved in matters such as spirituality or religion, we often forget our basic common sense and follow these belief systems without much analysis or examination. In this context, wisdom begins with engaging our basic human wisdom in the form of common sense and rational mind, and it continues all the way to the transcendental wisdom of *prajnaparamita*—the great wisdom of Buddha, of seeing things as they are.

This wisdom is similar to the knowledge of driving. We need to know both how and where to drive. We might have a beautiful car and we might have gasoline, but if we do not know how to drive, then a moving car can become a dangerous weapon. And if we do not know where to drive, then once we have started our car and once we are speeding along the highway, we do not know where we might end up. The wisdom of knowing how to drive comes first; second, we need the wisdom of knowing where we want to go and how to get there.

Possession of these three qualities of confidence, diligence, and wisdom constitutes a precious human birth. Traditionally, this is explained as possessing the eight freedoms and the ten favorable conditions. However, all of these are contained in these three major qualities.

Impermanence

Having reflected on our precious human birth, having seen clearly how difficult it is to obtain and how powerful obtaining this situation is for us, we move on to the second reminder, which is the reflection on impermanence. Once again, we can use the analogy of a car. No matter how safe and beautiful our car might be, no matter how much gasoline we might possess, and no matter how great our knowledge of driving might be, our situation is still impermanent. One day the whole thing will degenerate, either naturally or accidentally. This cannot be prevented, for example, by leaving our car in the garage for a hundred years. It will still degenerate. On the other hand, if we actively drive our car for the next twenty years, it will also degenerate. There is a natural sense of degeneration or falling apart. This is true for the driver as well as for the car. We can see this deterioration very clearly, both in accidents and in natural processes. Reflecting on that, we can appreciate our precious birth and the opportunity we have to use our qualities properly.

Once we have everything we need—the car, the gasoline, the driving skills, along with good eyesight, good memory, and so forth— it is important for us to make use of our situation properly before it falls apart. Contemplating impermanence simply means that we see the nature of impermanence very clearly and we reflect on the natural degeneration of our existence. Reflecting on that is the reminder of impermanence, which is a very powerful contemplation. As Buddha said in the sutras:

> Of all footprints, the elephant's are outstanding; just so, of all subjects of meditation for a follower of the Buddha, the idea of impermanence is unsurpassed.[1]

Nagarjuna in *Sixty Stanzas on Reasoning,* further explained the importance of this contemplation:

> Through understanding arising, one understands cessation.
> Through understanding cessation, one understands
>   impermanence.
> Knowing how to engage impermanence,
> One will realize the genuine Dharma.[2]

This means that if we realize the nature of arising, or birth, then we will realize the nature of cessation, or death. It is through knowing the nature of these two that we realize the truth and depth of impermanence—that we come to truly understand the genuine Dharma and have the wisdom to enter such a path.

This also means that we realize the subtle nature of impermanence—the subtle nature of arising and ceasing or birth and death— which is happening in every moment, every second, in fact. When we contemplate that and see the truth of impermanence, we are not very far from seeing the truth of emptiness. We are getting closer and closer to ultimate truth. Thus, reflecting on the second reminder of impermanence is not only good for the relative aspect of our practice; but it is also a profound contemplation on ultimate truth. This is so because impermanence is the ultimate nature of the relative truth. We can go no

further, as far as relative truth is concerned. Therefore, in order to realize the truth of Mahamudra, it is essential to reflect on impermanence.

Karma

The third reminder is cause and effect or karma. In a literal sense,
karma means "action"; in this particular context, it refers primarily to
mental action. Regardless of the kinds of physical acts in which we might
be engaged, each of these has been preceded by a related mental action.

Generally speaking, we must differentiate between karma and
"fate." The Buddhist view of karma does not propose that the outcome of
an event is 100 percent determined by our karma, our actions from the
past. If we were to say that each person is 100 percent subject to his or her
past karmic actions, then our view of karma would be identical to the
view of fatalism. We would be living in a world in which everything is predetermined. We would all have a blueprint of our lives, and there would
be little point in practicing the path of Buddhism. There would be little
point in Buddha having presented his teachings long ago. If our lives were
completely predetermined by karma, then those who were 100 percent
predetermined by their karma to attain enlightenment would do so regardless of their actions in this life, while those who were 100 percent predetermined not to attain enlightenment because of their karma would be
unable to attain it regardless of any action they took. There would be no
point in presenting the spiritual path of Buddhism and no point in practicing or working hard, unless we had to do it due to a karmic force.

From the Buddhist point of view, when we refer to karma, we are
not talking about fate but about a situation in which our actions from
the past carry a certain weight and power to affect our present lives.
We do have a blueprint, but it is one in which our past karma and our
present karma both carry a certain percentage of the power. For
example, there might be a particular situation in which our past karma
carries 50 percent of the weight. This would mean that there is
space—room for present conditions to arise and affect the current situation—for our present karma also to exert half of the total influence
on that situation. These two together—past and present karma—con-

stitute 100 percent of our karma, or the totality of the causal elements that are present in any given situation.

From this perspective, our previous karma is like the seed of a flower. This seed has the potential to grow and produce a beautiful blossom. However, if we were to leave this flower seed on a table for a hundred years, then it would not produce any result. In order for the seed to produce its potential result, a number of supporting conditions must come together, for example, proper soil, proper temperatures, and sufficient water and sunshine. When these supporting conditions are present at the same time, the seed produces its result, which is a flower.

Each of us faces various challenges in our lives. There are karmic consequences, from the past as well as from the present, taking place in our lives all the time. Even so, these karmic seeds cannot grow without space. We need space in the present moment to grow our results. We have a great opportunity in the present moment to decide how we want to grow this flower and how we want to relate to it. Working with karma means knowing how to balance our previous and present karma, as well as how to work with the energy of the growing seed.

For example, imagine that because of my actions in the past, I have the karmic propensity to kill fish. If that karma from the past is very small—perhaps only 25 percent of the required causal elements—then there will be a natural sense of space so that I can easily avoid repeating the negative actions of killing fish and also the karmic consequences of those actions. Nevertheless, I must make an effort. For example, such a karmically related situation might arise in the form of an invitation for a long weekend or a holiday. A friend might approach me and say, "How about going on a fishing trip? I have a beautiful place in the country on a lake." All of the essential supporting conditions might come together and I might be carried by them toward the fulfillment of this particular past karma. I might follow the 25 percent, thus increasing it to 100 percent. Alternatively, I could work with the situation and make an effort to see how I might transcend that karma.

This is the third reminder: the reflection on cause and effect, which is the natural law of relative truth.

The Shortcomings of Samsara

The fourth reminder is the contemplation of the shortcomings of samsara. This contemplation is very easy to understand if we just think about all of our complaints—our physical and mental sufferings. At this point, we reflect on the fundamental nature of samsara until we see clearly that its basic nature is characterized by suffering and pain. This reminder is simply reflecting on that. Reflecting on the short-comings of samsara is like reflecting on the truth of suffering.

THE FOUR UNCOMMON PRELIMINARIES

The four reminders are followed by the four uncommon prelim-inaries, which are common to all of the Tibetan Buddhist schools. These preliminaries are (1) refuge and bodhichitta, which purify the coarse level of negative karma of the body; (2) Vajrasattva mantra recitation, which purifies karma of speech; (3) mandala practice, which is the basis of acquiring the two accumulations of merit and wis-dom; and (4) guru yoga practice, which invokes the blessings of the lin-eage. More than one hundred thousand repetitions of each of these practices are generally done.

The first of the four uncommon preliminaries is taking refuge and generating bodhichitta. In the Hinayana and Mahayana, there is the threefold refuge of the Buddha, Dharma, and Sangha. In the Vajrayana, there is a sixfold refuge. When we take the sixfold refuge, we are actu-ally entering into the path of the Buddhadharma in general and Vajrayana in particular. We begin by taking refuge in our guru, since the Vajrayana path cannot exist without the guru principle. We also take refuge in the *yidam*s, or deities, and in the protectors.

In order to have a smooth journey and achieve realization, we have to purify our negativities and obscurations, which are obstacles on the path. The second uncommon preliminary is a profound purification practice known as Vajrasattva, one of the supreme methods used in the Vajrayana for overcoming negativities.

The third uncommon preliminary is the mandala offering. In this practice, we work with our attachments, our clinging, and our grasp-ing—our basic sense of ego-mind. Ordinarily, our habitual connection with relative reality tends to enmesh us in conceptual mind and con-ceptual reference points, thus blocking us from achieving the complete state of Mahamudra realization, or buddhahood. The purpose of attain-ing enlightenment is to benefit a limitless number of beings of differ-ent capacities, and it is only through the accumulation of merit that we are able to attain such enlightenment. In order to achieve any glimpse of the nature of mind, we have to let go of our ego-clinging. On the Vajrayana path, we accomplish this through the mandala offering, which is a practice of letting go of our habitual tendencies to grasp and cling to the ego and to the whole universe of phenomena that exists around us.

The most important key to our realization is found through the blessings of our guru, our teachers, our lineage forefathers, and pri-mordial wisdom itself. This transmission is not possible without open-ing ourselves fully to our lineage gurus. Opening to the lineage blessings and transmissions is catalyzed by the practice of guru yoga, which is the fourth uncommon preliminary practice.

These uncommon preliminary practices are taught clearly in a variety of texts such as *The Torch of Certainty* and *The Words of My Perfect Teacher*. We should learn from these texts together with the practical guidance of an instructor. When we engage in the specific practices, we should follow the directions and instructions within the liturgies. For this, it is necessary to work with a practice manual. In addition, it is essential to receive instructions personally from one's teacher.

THE FOUR SPECIAL PRELIMINARIES

There is an additional set of four preliminaries, which are called the four special preliminaries, or the four conditions of Mahamudra practice: (1) the causal condition; (2) the empowering condition; (3) the object condition; and (4) the instantaneous condition.

In order to bring about the actual state of Mahamudra medita-tion, it is necessary to cultivate the four conditions. Developing these four conditions plays a key role in Mahamudra meditation because the actual practice of Mahamudra is one thing, while developing the atmosphere—the right conditions to cultivate that state—is another. If we have not developed these four conditions, it does not matter how hard we try to study and practice what we call "Mahamudra" or how well-versed our teacher may be in giving these instructions—it will not be possible to generate the experience of Mahamudra meditation. For a serious practitioner on this path of simplicity, it is crucial to pay close attention to these four conditions. The alternative is simply to indulge in a fantasy about Mahamudra meditation.

The Causal Condition

The first condition is the causal condition, which is the practice of revulsion. Revulsion is actually the mind that is free from the temporal and immediate concerns of worldly things. That mind becomes the "foot" of meditation, as is taught in the Kagyu lineage supplication. We cannot walk the path of Mahamudra without this "foot."

In this practice, we begin by developing some sense of disgust with our ordinary confusion and acknowledging the garbage that we carry with us all the time. Ordinarily, we think our garbage is very precious. It is as though it is wrapped in beautiful silk, so we do not see it as garbage. Part of developing the first condition is making an effort to acknowledge our karmic garbage for what it is. When we can recognize and accept our own garbage, we can begin to develop genuine revulsion and renunciation.

In addition to developing a certain quality of detachment or revulsion for samsara, we free ourselves from all activities that are not useful or meaningful—activities that bring us into the depths of further confusion and suffering, or activities that cultivate the causes of suffering. In order to develop a clear view of detachment, renunciation, or revulsion, we contemplate the four common preliminaries.

After seeing the precious quality of our human birth, as well as its impermanent nature, we develop a genuine heart of renunciation—wanting and being completely willing to achieve freedom from the pain of samsara. Genuinely and wholeheartedly wanting to be free from samsara becomes very important in the causal condition. A genuine heart of renunciation does not come from someone telling us that samsara is pain and that therefore we must develop renunciation. It is important to carry out our own analysis and analytical meditation and to have our own theoretical and experiential understanding. When all of these come together, we can develop a genuine heart of longing for freedom. Drawing on our own experience, we can clearly see our own precious opportunity, as well as both the truth and origin of suffering in the world in front of us. Only then can we develop a genuine heart of renunciation.

We could compare this experience to being imprisoned: If we were sent to jail, then our first week there would be a particularly raw, naked, vivid experience—one from which we genuinely would want to escape. It certainly would not be theoretical.

However, renunciation does not necessarily mean simply running away from something. It means that we will go into the depths of any such reality to find freedom within it. That is very important here. The desire to free ourselves and others must be balanced with the sense of complete trust in our ability to achieve liberation. We do not see samsara as something that consists solely of unfavorable situations; we also see the possibilities for freeing ourselves from suffering right on the spot. We see that freedom, liberation, and enlightenment are possible within this very moment. Once we recognize this, samsara is no longer seen as something to escape. Freedom is not seen as something that exists outside samsara. Therefore, there is nowhere to run. For example, if you are in Manhattan and you run to a Himalayan cave, you will carry Manhattan with you. It may be even worse for you because the cave is much smaller than Manhattan. In the cave, you will probably appreciate and long for all the good qualities of Manhattan: There are nice subways and it is easy to get around. While the Hinayana notion of renunciation sees the possibility of freedom in getting away from samsara, the Mahamudra notion of renunciation sees the possibility of freedom within that very situation.

In order to develop the first condition, we also contemplate impermanence, which provides us with a deeper realization. Whoever is able to connect with impermanence will understand the true Dharma. The nature of all phenomena is emptiness, shunyata; an understanding of impermanence leads to this realization. The point of contemplating impermanence is not to seek depressing news but rather to find enlightening news, which is the realization of egolessness, selflessness, or shunyata. Although we have many insights, thoughts, and ideas based on discriminating awareness, among all these thoughts, the supreme is the thought of impermanence. It is the thought that makes the deepest impression.

In these teachings on the causal condition, we are instructed to contemplate the four reminders, to think deeply and carefully about impermanence, and then to develop a genuine heart of renunciation. That renunciation will encourage us and engender the effort and wisdom to enable us to see shunyata.

From this instruction, we can see that it is important to develop our own heart of renunciation, abandoning all activities that are not meaningful.

The Empowering Condition

The second condition is called the empowering condition. This term is usually used in reference to a particular component in the process of sense perception. For example, when we see a visual object, the empowering condition is the eye faculty. Unless the sense faculty of the eyes is intact, we cannot have the experience of seeing objects. The eye faculty "empowers" our ability to experience a visual perception, so it is called the empowering condition.

In a similar way, the empowering condition for Mahamudra meditation is the guru. Thus, the principle of devotion is emphasized again: Without the guru, nothing is possible on the path. In his Mahamudra songs, the great yogi Tilopa said that the main characteristic of a guru is the lineage blessing, or lineage transmission. There is no guru without the lineage transmission. Therefore, Mahamudra practitioners are very serious about keeping their relationship with the lineage pure.

Within the empowering condition there are four types of gurus. The first of the four gurus is the individual who holds an authentic lineage—a lineage master. The second is the guru that is the very words of the Buddha. The third is the guru of symbolic appearances. The fourth is the ultimate or absolute guru.

The Guru Who Is an Individual in a Lineage

The first guru is called the guru who is an individual in a lineage. This guru is also called the guru of the oral instruction, or ear-whispered, lineage. The lineage guru is one who holds the unbroken lineage and tradition of the Mahamudra key instructions, meditation, experience, and realization. From the great dharmakaya buddha Vajradhara, the lineage comes down to the nirmanakaya buddha of our own guru. It is the unbroken tradition of the lineage of the mahasiddhas of India, such as Tilopa, Naropa, and Maitripa. There are eighty-four mahasiddhas, each with a different tradition and a different lineage.

The adhishthana of such a lineage can bring the experience and realization of Mahamudra into the mindstreams of disciples through the creation of the right space or the right atmosphere. Thus, instruction consists of more than mere words. The atmosphere—space itself, the ground, the earth—feels different. Such an atmosphere can be created only by an authentic teacher who is a master of the lineage. It does not arise without the blessing of the lineage of Vajradhara, Tilopa, Naropa, and all the rest of the masters.

This first guru is the most important of the four. The lineage guru is one who opens the door to the treasury of oral instructions, to the deeper knowledge or prajna that we all have, and to the deeper knowledge or prajna that the lineage presents. The ability to open the door consists of more than simply pointing someone to the door. It also requires knowledge of exactly what the door is. The guru has already walked through that door and can show disciples how to work with unfavorable circumstances and transcend the reality of pain and confusion right on the spot. Having such insight, the guru shows us how we can gain the greatest benefit from such circumstances. Thus, any circumstance can become absolutely positive. If we know how to relate properly to such conditions, then we can gain a great deal of insight. The guru is someone who can show us that possibility.

The lineage guru is a living human being with whom we can communicate physically and mentally and from whom we can receive proper instruction, clarification, and continuous guidance on our journey. The truest sign of the lineage guru is the quality of transmission that we feel in the presence of such a teacher. Such blessings are not generated through words or through the ritual ceremonies of empowerment. Someone may be very well trained in philosophy, knowledgeable in practice matters, and able to speak clearly about the path. Those skills come from training, and anyone who is sufficiently diligent can achieve them. However, we experience in the guru a palpable quality of presence that goes beyond that and does not come from training.

Having the right contact or relationship with our guru is the most important condition on the path of Mahamudra. In the tradition of the practice lineage, it is said that the pattern of our path is determined by the pattern of our relationship with the guru. Our connection to and relationship with the guru is a model for our journey. It is said that if we relate to our guru as a living buddha, then we receive the blessing of an enlightened teacher. If we relate to our guru as a living bodhisattva, then we receive the blessings of a bodhisattva. It is also said that if we see our guru as a completely ordinary being, then we receive the blessings of a completely ordinary being. If we see our guru as a completely confused, neurotic person, then we receive those kinds of blessings.

If we take medicine with full confidence and trust in the medicine's effectiveness, then we will receive the most benefit from it. However, if we take the same medicine with an ambivalent attitude, thinking, "I will try this. Maybe it will help and maybe it will not," then we will receive a corresponding benefit. Our attitude exerts a strong psychological effect. In a similar way, the success of our Mahamudra journey depends on the level of confidence and trust we have in the instructions we receive from our guru.

The path of Mahamudra depends fully on our devotion. The teachings emphasize that we should be careful, clear, genuine, and frank, without any sense of holding back, in our relationship with our guru. There should be a total sense of openness. That is what we call devotion: totally exposing ourselves to the lineage, to the teacher, and to the teachings.

THE GURU WHO APPEARS AS THE WORDS OF THE SUGATA

The second type of guru is called the guru who appears as the words of the *sugata,* or the scriptural guru. This is the guru of enlightened words. This guru is related to the enlightened teachings of the Buddha, the mahasiddhas, and other great masters of the past and present. When we read these enlightened words, they perform the same function as our living guru. They provide us with instructions, guidance, wisdom, and compassion. For example, when we read the *doha*s, or yogic songs, of Tilopa, Naropa, Saraha, Milarepa, and others, we are relating to the scriptural guru.

However, in order to understand the scriptural guru, we must rely on the lineage master. Through reading, examining, and contemplating, we see that the words of the Buddha are actually nothing other than the instructions we have received from our guru. We see the connection between them. We see that through the simple pointing-out process, the lineage guru has introduced us to the essence of the Buddha's teachings. We come to an understanding and certainty that the meditation instructions that we have received are fully in accordance with all the teachings of the Buddha, whether they are Hinayana, Mahayana, Vajrayana, or Mahamudra. We see that there is no contradiction within the great variety of the Buddha's teachings and that they all constitute one single path.

We need a certain foundation in order to be able to relate with the guru who appears as the words of the sugata. This ground is created through the instructions that we have received from our guru, and it forms the basis for the manifestation of the guru who appears as the words of the sugata. As a result, whenever we read the words of the sutras or tantras of Lord Buddha, we can clearly see the reflection of our own experience.

The Guru Who Manifests as Symbolic Appearances

The third type is the guru who manifests as symbolic appearances, or the guru of appearances. The term can also be translated as symbolic guru. Mahamudra practitioners see all appearances as the enlightened instructions of the guru.

This instruction refers to *all* appearances: outer appearances, such as the five elements of earth, fire, water, wind, and space, as well as anything developed from those basic five, in addition to all appearances in our mind. Whether the appearance is a perception, a concept, the ego, or ego-clinging, it is seen as the guru. Whether we see the five elements individually or in combination, when we look at our own body or at the world outside, we can see the message of enlightenment. Thus all appearances are seen as the guru and the activities of the guru, and as instructions on the path. Our encounters with these appearances may not be very different from the instructions we receive from our guru—provocative instructions, challenging instructions, practical instructions, direct instructions, spontaneous instructions, and nonconceptual instructions.

It is important to understand how to rely on the guru who manifests as symbolic appearances. If we can truly see all appearances as the guru, then all appearances become pointing-out instructions that communicate different aspects of reality to us. We can use all our internal and external experiences to understand shunyata and the selfless nature of all phenomena, whether we analyze those appearances or not. If we can connect with an understanding of shunyata merely through seeing, hearing, tasting, or simply experiencing a thought, then we are relying on the guru who manifests as symbolic appearances.

The Guru Who Is the Ultimate Dharmata

The fourth type of guru is called the guru who is the ultimate *dharmata*. This is the guru of the ultimate nature. It is the experience of the nature of ordinary mind that has been introduced to us by our guru, the flash experience of emptiness, impermanence, or renunciation.

The true understanding and realization of Mahamudra mind and the reality of all phenomena are called the ultimate guru because there is no higher realization that we can achieve through our reliance on the guru. What is the function of the guru? The whole purpose of relying on and following the guru is to achieve this ultimate realization. This realization is basic confidence. Having basic confidence, trusting our own heart, and trusting the nature of all phenomena becomes a first-hand experience—a direct realization.

In that sense, there is no difference between ground, path, and fruition. This is the ground we have been studying for so long. This is the path we have been trying to experience. This is also the result, which we are finally realizing. Ground, path, and fruition are insepara-ble. For that reason, the Essence Mahamudra teachings say that samsara and nirvana are inseparable. We realize that samsara and nirvana are inseparable and that mind and mind's basic nature are inseparable. Any element of mind that may seem to be confused, chaotic, or overcome with disturbing emotions, is in fact inseparable from its basic nature of dharmakaya. Seeing, experiencing, and realizing this reality is the ulti-mate guru—the guru who is the ultimate dharmata.

PREEMINENCE OF THE LINEAGE GURU

Among the four types of guru, the most important is the lineage guru, the human master. This is so because it is only after we have received his or her instructions pointing out the nature of mind, and then, based on those instructions, gained some certainty in our own hearts about the actual nature of phenomena, that we have the oppor-tunity to experience the other three gurus. Without the benefit of the lineage guru, it is not possible to work with the words of the sugata appearing as a guru, nor with the symbolic appearances that manifest as a guru. Of course, it is similarly not possible to work with the ulti-mate dharmata, who is also our guru. These three are dependent upon the first guru. We could say that the guru who is an individual in a lin-eage is a cause or seed that produces a certain result, that is, our abil-ity to experience the other three types of guru.

The Object Condition

The object condition refers mainly to working with the genuine nature of all appearances—all objects that we perceive or conceive—with a true understanding of their reality. In this way, we do not fall into any extremes or wrong views. We begin by seeing the mistakes that we make due to our clinging and fixation—how we hold on to the extreme views of a personal self and of the self of phenomena. Then, through a progressive process of studying the various systems of the view, beginning with the *Shravaka* and followed by the Chittamatra and Madhyamaka views, we finally reach the view of Mahamudra. In terms of understanding the reality of objects or seeing the true nature of objects, it is necessary to have genuine insight into the view of shunyata and egolessness.

The object condition comprises the practice instructions on the Mahamudra view of the ground and the meditation instructions of the Mahamudra path. The term "object condition" is used to describe the third condition because it is similar to a component of sense perception, namely the object that is perceived. For example, if there is no visual object, one cannot generate a visual sense perception. In a similar way, without these instructions on the view of Mahamudra, which is the object, one cannot generate the experiences of the path of Mahamudra. Therefore, the Mahamudra instructions and meditations are called the object condition.

The basic object of our meditation is the inseparability of samsara and nirvana, or the inseparability of the three kayas, in this very nature of mind and in this very moment of reality. That is ground Mahamudra. Developing the right understanding of this ground is essential because if we do not have the right view, then we cannot have any sense of the right object of meditation. Resting in that state of reality, which is the Mahamudra state, becomes the object condition.

The Instantaneous Condition

The instantaneous condition is freedom from hope and fear. To be free from hope and fear means that we do not hope for a "good" meditation to arise. We do not hope for anything *maha* or "great" to happen in our session of sitting. At the same time, we are not afraid that we will fail to connect with the heart of Mahamudra or with the genuine space of reality.

However, as most of us know from our own experience when we sit down to practice Mahamudra meditation, we cannot simply click into the state of ordinary mind right away. When we first sit down, our minds are full of thoughts and concepts. It is difficult to immediately click into the state of no hope and no fear. So, initially, we work with hope and fear on a conceptual level. Then we try to go beyond the labels in order to go into the Mahamudra meditation instantaneously.

On the one hand, realization and experience will never arise if, when we sit, we are dominated by fears such as "I am not able to do it. I have to be a better person, otherwise I will not get it right. I am not able to be free of thoughts. I am not able to be free of hope. I cannot do it; I have to work harder." On the other hand, we may sit with excessive hopes or preconceptions about meditation, experience, or realization, such as "I want my practice to be exactly the way the Mahamudra book says. I want it to be exactly the same as all these teachers have described in their courses and lectures. I want to have exactly the same experience that Milarepa had with Marpa. I want to have exactly the same experience that Naropa had with Tilopa. I want to have exactly the same experience that my guru had with his or her guru." This kind of thinking indicates that we have too many preconceptions. We are not letting our practice be natural and spontaneous. We are not being "on the spot" or in the present. Instead, we are trying to go back to a past experience.

When you do not think in a way that is shaped by hope or fear, you can simply sit and be fully mindful in the space. You can be present in that particular moment, in that particular situation, no matter what it may be. Your life may be in crisis. Everything may be falling apart when you sit on your cushion. If that is so, simply sit without hope and fear. Simply sit in that very moment, in that very situation, in that very state, with a full sense of appreciation for the moment. Similarly, if you are having a great time, enjoying great success, and taking great pleasure in life, you can also sit in that very moment and appreciate it. You do not have to feel, "This is too wonderful, too pleasurable, too rich. I must be poor like Milarepa. I must be miserable in order to experience samsara." You can simply sit without hope and fear, with whatever situation manifests.

When we sit and meditate on Mahamudra mind, we should be totally open. Our mind should be genuinely open to letting any experience arise, to letting the phenomena play and dance in front of our senses and thoughts. We can be open in the sense that we have a genuine interest in knowing the moment without labeling it. In this state of openness, we are being gentle and kind toward ourselves, as well as toward the space and the moment.

Once we have generated the last condition, we are very close to the actual Mahamudra practice.

As students of the Mahamudra path, we are taught that we should remember these four conditions and strengthen our practice of them. If we are lacking any one of the four conditions, we should try to acquire it through effort, diligence, devotion, and kindness. These are the preliminaries that are special to the Mahamudra tradition. They are not taught in the Hinayana-Mahayana path. They are the conditions that bring about the realization of Mahamudra mind.

4

Ground Mahamudra

The Groundless Ground

GROUND MAHAMUDRA is the fundamental discovery of our Mahamudra essence. It is the basic state of our mind, as well as the basic state of the phenomenal world. It is the fundamental nature of reality, which is the ground of our meditation as well as the object of our meditation. The "ground" here is emptiness. Through discovering this ground, we discover our heart of enlightenment. We find that the fundamental nature of Mahamudra mind exists right within our mundane consciousness and thoughts. Thus, at the level of ground Mahamudra, our topic is emptiness, selflessness, or egolessness. We cannot escape the ground or skip to the next level. We are stuck, here, with emptiness.

On the Sutra Mahamudra path, we rest in this fundamental state, which is the ground essence of our mind. We rest without any conceptuality, without any concept of resting and rested upon, and without any concept of meditator and meditated upon.

TWO ASPECTS OF GROUND: EMPTINESS AND EGO

First we will examine the aspect of ground that is the fundamental state or the fundamental reality that we discover. Next we will look at the aspect of ground that is the target, the object at which we are going to take aim.

The Jewel of Emptiness

According to Maitreya, the fundamental or basic state of our mind—what we might call the initial state of our mind—is pure and free from all fetters, all the conceptual chains that tie us down in samsaric existence. This fundamental state of our mind is the state of buddhahood, or fully awakened being. Because this state of mind is totally fresh and pure, it does not contain even a trace of confusion. In the awakened state of mind, there is not even the slightest possibility that one could become confused, defiled, fettered, or fed up.

That fundamental ground is actually the nature of all living beings. From the very beginning of our existence, our nature has been in the state of buddhahood. Therefore, the nature of our minds is not separate from the nature of enlightenment or from the nature of an enlightened being like Shakyamuni Buddha. There is no difference whatsoever. The nature of our minds is totally free from the self-centered view of ego. That nature of mind is great shunyata, emptiness.

When we talk about emptiness in this context, we are talking about mind being empty of all defilements, being free from all the unnecessary garbage that we usually carry. Maitreya said that this mind is like a precious jewel that has fallen into a very dirty place—perhaps something like a medieval toilet. The fundamental nature of that state of mind is as precious, as pure, and as radiant as the jewel itself. Though this precious jewel may become completely covered by temporary dirt or garbage, the nature of the jewel will not be altered. It remains the same whether the jewel is covered in dirt or has been washed. Similarly, according to Maitreya, the full wisdom and all the qualities of a buddha are ever present within this nature of mind, always shining like a jewel and always pure. This wisdom has never been obscured or stained; no matter what states of confusion or defilements have occurred, its nature has never changed.

Although the nature of our mind has always been in the state of buddhahood, it appears to be defiled. For *kalpas*—for aeons and aeons—we have been accumulating layers of karmic garbage around this precious jewel. Now we find it difficult to identify what is under-neath the garbage. When we look at a jewel that is totally enveloped by filth, we might see it merely as an ordinary stone and never recognize its true nature. Similarly, because our initial state of mind is enveloped in countless layers of karmic garbage, we may not recognize its essen-tial purity. That is, we may not recognize our Mahamudra essence. We are likely to find it difficult to identify even the layers that obscure it, not to mention the jewel itself. Because we have covered this precious mind with so many layers, we cannot perceive it or even conceive of it clearly and accurately.

Therefore, it is hard for us to see that the heart or nature of our mind is in the state of buddhahood. If we cannot even see the layers clearly, then how can we have strong trust and confidence that there is a jewel buried within? Suppose someone were to hand you a stone that is covered with layer upon layer of dust and mud, saying, "This is a dia-mond. Do you want to buy it?" Would you be willing to pay what a dia-mond is worth? Or would you be willing to pay only what the layers are worth? It would be a very critical and difficult decision. That is the kind of challenge that we are facing when we say, "The nature of our mind is fully awakened."

Maitreya has given us several other analogies to show that the na-ture of our mind is in the state of buddhahood. He says that the nature of our mind is like the sun, always shining, always there in the sky, no mat-ter what we perceive from the earth. Today we might not be able to see the sun; it might be gray and rainy. However, that does not mean that the sun is not in the sky. No matter how dense the clouds might be, they never affect the sun itself. The sun is always there, shining and unchanged.

In a similar way, the nature of mind or the wisdom of buddha is always shining within our hearts. The only reason we do not perceive this radiance and do not experience this wisdom is that they are cov-ered by the clouds of ego-clinging, the *klesha* mind, and karmic garbage that we have accumulated. Therefore, in order to experience this wisdom, we first need to recognize the defilements that cover it. Once

we have become familiar with these defilements, we can begin to recognize the true nature of our mind, which is the ground itself. Then we
must identify our target: ego and our clinging to it. That target is not
outside us; and it is the major defilement obscuring our fundamental
wisdom.

Taking Aim at the Target

At the ground Mahamudra level, we must find out for ourselves
what emptiness truly means. We must discover the heart of awakening
within our own mind—this seemingly confused, seemingly self-
centered mind. Making that discovery is the groundwork of the
Mahamudra approach.

At first, we may think that the ultimate ground of emptiness is
unconnected to our relative reality, which in this context refers to our
conventional, unexamined experience of the world. It refers to the
relative level of truth, as opposed to the ultimate or absolute level. In
general, relative truth is described as that which is intellectually fabricated. In other words, it arises out of our commonplace experience of
concepts, labels, emotions, and confusion. However, according to Nagarjuna, in order to understand the ultimate nature of the world—the
ultimate nature of shunyata—we must first fully understand the nature of the relative world. Nagarjuna said that in order to go beyond
concept, we must rely on conceptual understanding. We cannot simply
say, "I have had enough of the world of concept and relative truth, and
now I am ready to jump into ultimate truth. I am ready to go beyond
concept." Traditionally, it is said that if we want to see the other side of
the mountain and enjoy the beautiful view of the valley below, then
we must first climb this side of the mountain. Only when we have
climbed to the top from this side of the mountain can we fully see the
other side of the mountain and the whole valley. In other words, in
order to understand the nature of ultimate truth, which is the other
side of the mountain, we must first know how to properly climb this
side of the mountain, which is relative truth, without breaking our

necks on it. If we are to understand the ultimate truth of emptiness, then we must first understand the subtle nature of relative existence, or relative truth.

INTERDEPENDENT ORIGINATION

If we are to understand the nature of relative existence, then we must understand interdependent origination because the relative world arises only through interdependence. Relative truth is that which exists in this nature of interdependent origination,[1] or the coming together of various causes and conditions. We call this *tendrel* in Tibetan and *pratityasamutpada* in Sanskrit. For example, the notion of "cause" relies on the notion of "result," and the notion of "result" exists only in relation to the notion of something called "cause." Therefore, there can be no cause without a result, just as there can be no result without a cause. The whole seemingly solid existence of our relative world arises simply through this interdependent nature and through our labeling processes.

One example often used by my own teacher to demonstrate to students this interdependent relationship was quite simple. He would raise his hand, hold up the pinkie finger and the ring finger, and ask, "Which finger is the tall finger and which is the short one?" The students would reply, "The ring finger is the tall finger and the pinkie is the short finger." This is how we label things. We have a strong conceptual view of the world that leads us to say, "This is tall and that is short." Then we think, "This really is tall and that really is short." We all think in this way. However, my teacher would conclude by raising the still-longer middle finger, so that whichever finger we had previously thought of as "the tall one" became "the short one."

We can see from this example that our strong clinging, fixation, and labeling, which dictate, "This is tall and that is short" or "This is good and that is bad," always exist in relation to other concepts. Our concepts, as well as the phenomena themselves, arise through the coming together of many causes and conditions. Phenomena themselves are interdependent, as well as being dependent upon our labeling thoughts. Our whole world is simply the creation of our concepts. Consequently, we have a world that we call "beautiful" and a world that we call "ugly." We also have a world that we call "good" and "bad." Everyone experiences "reality" differently. Our experiences are actually very individual. For example, the way I experience a particular flower is unique to myself; the way you perceive or experience that same flower is unique to you. However, these experiences exist only in our minds. They do not even exist in some general group mind; they exist only in the form of the labeling thoughts of conceptual mind.

We label someone a buddha, a fully awakened one, and we label someone else a samsaric being, a totally confused one. Those too are relative labels. To give a more mundane example, we label a certain perfume Samsara and a certain rock band Nirvana. However, these labels do not reflect a general truth; everyone experiences things differently. The experience of samsara is not always sweet; one person may experience it as sweet and another as bitter. Samsara is not necessarily sweet or bitter, not fundamentally good or bad. It is simply our own way of perceiving, our own way of conceiving things. These experiences are all dependent on our relationship to that particular world, as well as on our relationship to the karmic layers or karmic links that we have developed.

For example, one person might perceive someone as a Buddhist monk, another person might perceive him as a brother, and yet another might perceive him as a son. This is only one person, yet each observer would use a different label and would relate to him in a different way. Someone might perceive him as a terrible person—as really bad, aggressive, and irritating—at the same time someone else might perceive him as a very gentle, good, nice person. However, neither the terrible person nor the gentle person is inherently existent. There is no self-entity, no one who exists as someone "inherently good" or someone "inherently bad." If the qualities we perceive in objects were truly existent—if they were real qualities of objects, existing in their own essence and nature—then everyone would perceive them in the same way. If this were the case, everyone would perceive a particular person in the same way—as either a terrible person or a nice person—but they do not.

Our relative perceptions and labels all have a very complex relationship underlying their existence. That complex relationship is called "interdependent origination." The relative world exists in the nature of interdependent origination: Phenomena are generated or arise because of a coming together of various things. If we analyze that interdependent origination of the relative world, we will see that it is empty by nature. This means that the good does not exist without the bad, and the bad does not exist without the good. Therefore, there is no inherent quality that makes something fundamentally good or fundamentally bad.

QUARKS, ENERGY, AND LIGHT

We perceive our entire universe—all our relative experiences—in a similar way. We label these experiences and we solidify them. We take these solidified experiences to be actual qualities of particular objects. We try to make our relative experience "real." At the same time, we feel some fear that it might not be real. If we look more closely at our experience, then we begin to see it as it truly is. When we analyze relative truth, we touch its actual nature, which is shunyata, emptiness, or nonexistence. If we analyze relative existence at the level of labels and concepts, we see that they do not truly exist.

We can also apply this analysis to the outer world of physical objects. When we analyze that world, we find it very difficult to locate any solidity or true existence. We can start our analysis by considering one object. For example, if we analyze a table by mentally breaking it down into smaller and smaller pieces, down to the very tiniest part of an atom, we eventually discover that even the tiniest part can always be broken down further. Thus, neither the atom nor the table can be said to have any solid or reliable existence.

While we can do this analysis mentally, scientists have done it physically with modern scientific experiments. For example, quantum theorists say that the atom does not really exist as a solid entity. Instead, they say it is composed of quarks, and that there is some level of existence that manifests as light, energy, or strings. However, they continue to give names to the particles and energy. They stop short of saying, "Everything is empty," since that would mean the end of the world.

We prefer to say that matter is composed of something. If we say that matter is composed of quarks, energy, or light, then we can hold on to the tiny shred of existence that seems to remain. That notion provides ego with a certain degree of relief because it seems to show that self and world are not totally empty. We can continue to think that we are not totally nonexistent, that we do exist even if we are not quite sure *how* we exist. Accordingly, we use terms like "light" or "energy." However, from the Buddhist point of view, when we analyze the relative world, we do not find any such existence. Whether we examine the outer physical world or the inner world of our minds, we do not find any solid or inherent existence.

We can see then that the ground is groundlessness. When we analyze relative truth—when we examine it and meditate on it—we can see how this ground becomes shaky. If we pursue this analysis, then we lead ourselves into the experience of the nonexistent, selfless nature of the world, which is a great experience. That is why there are so many instructions directing us to reflect on the groundlessness of samsara. At times, we might wonder whether the very ground we are standing on can remain there for the next five minutes because when we analyze that ground, we can see truly and clearly that it does not exist. From the absolute point of view, it does not exist, even though from the relative point of view, it does exist. We might say, "absolutely not, but relatively, yes." We have to make a clear distinction between the relative and the absolute. When we talk about emptiness, we are speaking from the point of view of ultimate or absolute reality. We are not talking about relative experience, which does exist but only in the nature of interdependence.

Clinging to an Old Friend

Having discovered that the outer world of relative appearances is empty, we next analyze our own notion of self and our assumption that the self exists. What is this self, which seems so real and so powerfully existent? What is this ego all about? At the level of ground, our task is to discover the actual nature of ego. We have to conduct a thorough analysis and examine what we mean by this "I." Who is it? Where is it? What is it?

In the Buddhist tradition, the self is said to be composed of the five *skandhas*, or aggregates: the aggregate of form, the aggregate of feeling, the aggregate of perception, the aggregate of concept, and the aggregate of consciousness. It is necessary to analyze each of these aggregates. For example, there is the existence of "form" as a physical body, which we call "I." When we say "I," we are generally referring to our bodies. In our analysis of the physical self, we apply the same kind of analysis as we used with the table. We begin by asking where this personal self is specifically located in relation to our body. Is the self our body as a whole, or can it be found in any particular part of our body, such as our hands, our hair, or in any other of these component parts? Where is this self? It is necessary to carry out a thorough analysis, first with the skandha of form, then with the skandha of feeling, and so forth, in order to find out how or in what manner we are clinging to the self or our ego. We must first identify what the self actually is before we can cut through our clinging to it.

This is a difficult practice. When we analyze this ego, the problem we encounter is that our ego has been with us—within our being—for so long. Our ego has become a friend with whom we have had close ties for millions and millions of years. Now we are finding out that this friend has been cheating us all this time—not just for a few years but for aeons. When we discover this, we experience a tremendous struggle within our own minds. One side of our mind still clings to this friend and to this relationship. The relationship is so intimate that ego has almost become one with our own heart, and, therefore, it is very difficult for us to separate from this old friend. Our natural impulse seems to bring us back to that relationship, back to that friendliness with our ego. We still have sympathy and a certain sense of love that we cannot give up. There is still some resistance to letting go; we do not want to sever our ties to ego completely. At the same time, the other side of our mind sees how dishonest this friend has been and how we have been cheated. We realize how much pain and suffering we have endured. We see clearly that there is no benefit whatsoever in continuing this relationship with our ego. We see that we have gained no peace or happiness; in fact, we can see the harm that has been caused by our relationship with this old friend.

CUTTING THROUGH EGO-CLINGING

We are left with this split feeling, not knowing exactly what to do; or perhaps we do know exactly what to do but we cannot seem to do it. Again and again, we find that we cannot put our insights into practice because there are still strong impulses that bring us back to the pattern of our ego relationship. We find that we must put forth tremendous effort to cut through our clinging. Discovering the truth of the egolessness of self is very bad news for ego, and our ego does not want to hear about it. Confronting ego is like confronting a friend with the discovery of dishonesty in our relationship. Of course, our friend's first reaction is to ignore this truth, and our own initial reaction is to try to forget about it because, in some way, we continue to feel good about this relationship. We still have a certain sense of commitment, which ties us down again and again and again. No matter how much or how deeply we recognize the truth of egolessness, we go back to clinging to the self. It seems that we cannot help ourselves. There is a strong karmic impulse that takes us back to this relationship.

At this point, cutting through our relationship with ego requires great wisdom and great knowledge. The first step in discovering the wisdom of egolessness is to acknowledge that ego is selfless. Instead of rejecting or ignoring ego, we acknowledge that the nature of our self-clinging is selflessness. The very nature of our clinging to things as existent is empty. Seeing these truths clearly and then acknowledging them is the initial step in our practice of cutting through ego-clinging. Once we see this, we develop the courage to cut through ego-clinging and the karmic impulses that constantly bring us back to that relationship with our ego. This courage is the first wisdom that we discover on the Mahamudra journey. It is developed through confidence, and confidence is developed through knowledge. Therefore, knowledge becomes the key to cutting through our ego-clinging.

DEVELOPING CONFIDENCE

Courage is born from our confidence in the wisdom that sees the selflessness of ego. However, that courage is very difficult to cultivate unless we first develop confidence. This confidence is not a blind confidence or a blind faith, a simple belief in emptiness, egolessness, or selflessness. On the contrary, it requires that we analyze and examine. We might say it means that we must chew the teachings properly so that we can actually taste them. Then we can say, "Yes, this is egolessness" or "No, this is not egolessness." Confidence, then, requires developing knowledge—the superior knowledge of the truth of emptiness, which in its most developed state is actually the state of wisdom.

We can understand this process by thinking about our ordinary experience. When we walk down the street and we meet someone, we do not immediately say to this stranger, "I have full confidence in you." In order to have confidence in someone, we have to know that person. When we have known each other for a time and have shared various experiences, we develop a sense of mutual understanding. Then we can say with assurance, "Yes, I have full confidence in you."

In a similar way, we have to gain confidence by developing our intellectual knowledge, as well as sharpening our intuitive understanding and insight. That knowledge and that wisdom are the essence of the teachings of Madhyamaka, in particular the Madhyamaka lineage of Nagarjuna. Nagarjuna's wisdom is the key to developing our confidence in selflessness, with which we can cut through our ego and our karmic ties of friendship with it. Such confidence gives birth to courage, and with that courage, we can come to the end of suffering, the end of confusion, and the end of this unhealthy relationship with our ego. No matter how enduring that relationship might seem, it is temporary because ego is a foreign element. No matter how close ego might seem to be to us, it is still foreign to our being. It is a concept that is alien and extrinsic to us. However, in order to have the confidence to cut through our ego-clinging, we must develop the knowledge and wisdom of emptiness.

BREAKING THROUGH OBSTACLES TO ENLIGHTENMENT

Although we might have glimpsed the basic truth of emptiness and our own awakened heart, we will still face obstacles on our three-yana journey. Once we have trained sufficiently in the foundational vehicle of the Hinayana path, we then approach the vast vision of the Mahayana. However, in order to enter the profound Mahayana path and give birth to the awakened heart of a bodhisattva, we must be able to acknowledge and relate with the obstacles we meet along the way. Lord Maitreya described four main obstacles on our path to enlightenment. The first obstacle is attachment. The second is described as self-clinging, or ego-clinging. The third is clinging to self-liberation, or individual salvation. The fourth obstacle is pride, in the particular sense of self-superiority.

Clinging to Samsaric Happiness

The first obstacle or obscuration is clinging to the seeming happiness of samsara, or the samsaric world. This is the sense of constantly falling back into the pattern of grasping at different aspects of samsara. In so doing, we reject the teachings on detachment, which explicate both the nonexistence of the samsaric world and the nonexistence of samsaric happiness. This first obscuration is connected to constantly being trapped by our attachment to happiness. We have a sense of feeling snuggly toward our existence in samsara. Even though we hear about all of these beautiful, pure realms or liberation from samsara, we still feel that this is not really such a bad place. There is still a sense of being chained within our heart to this place called samsara. No matter how well we understand samsara intellectually or how often we hear about different states of liberation, we are still strongly attached to or saturated with samsara. That attachment is the first obstacle on our path of enlightenment. As long as we have this particular attachment, we will have a natural tendency to reject the genuine Dharma that cuts through our attachment. When we reject the Dharma, we cannot see that samsara is a miserable place.

In the Hinayana world, samsara is described as a valley of boiling lava, and the only thing we want to do is escape. We do not want to just sit here and watch ourselves melt in lava. Samsara is also described as a nest of poisonous snakes. No matter how gentle or skillful we are, as long as we attempt to step into this nest of poisonous snakes, sooner or later one of them will bite us—one of the klesha poisons will get us or has got us already. Therefore, without fully seeing and understanding that the nature of samsara is totally pervaded by suffering and fear, we cannot develop any sense of moving ourselves toward the path of liberation.

For example, if you feel comfortable in your present apartment, then you will have no inspiration to move to a better place. You will likely reject the thought of moving, which is a big step that requires a lot of complex tasks and hard work. Therefore, the first thing that you would need to realize is that the place where you are living is making you miserable.

As long as we are attached to this snuggly world, there is a subconscious force at work that causes us to reject the genuine path of Dharma. This subconscious rejection of genuine Dharma is a greater problem than the attachment that causes it, and it becomes a blockage on our path of enlightenment. This is the first obstacle that we have to overcome.

Clinging to the Self

The second obstacle is ego-clinging. Up to this point, we have not touched our ego-clinging directly. We have worked primarily with our attachment, which is a more gross level of clinging. Now we are going to the root of our problem: ego-clinging, which produces all our other emotional disturbances. Because of this clinging, we become engaged in various physical and mental actions called karma. The result of becoming engaged in these actions is that we produce samsara, which is our experience of the world. Whether it is a beautiful world or a miserable world, it is nevertheless a projection—and the result of our previous actions. So, we can see how ego-clinging is the root of all our samsaric experiences. Therefore, cutting the root of ego-clinging is the major breakthrough on the path of Mahayana.

Our ego-clinging manifests in various ways. First, there is the fundamental, innate clinging to one's self as "I" or "me." It does not matter whether one is a human being, an animal, or another type of being: There is a basic sense of "I." Whether we use a human language or an animal language to say it, there is nevertheless this notion of "I" or "me."

In addition to this fundamental self-clinging, we have a secondary level of ego-clinging, which is imputed. On this level, there is a clinging to the label itself, such as "I," which is merely a concept, a word. Then there is another set of labels, such as "I am Tibetan," and additional sets of labels, such as "I am a monk," "I am a great person," or "I am strong." If we become inclined toward dogma, then we will further accumulate all of the religious labels of a self. We might believe that this "I" is created by certain supernatural beings; or we could have the notion of "I" as being an all-pervasive, self-existent "I," as in certain Hindu philosophies. As Buddhists, we have the notion that "I" is the composition of the five skandhas. All of these labels become layers that we add on to our fundamental ego-clinging. At this point, it becomes very complex and interesting—so interesting that we do not recognize ourselves.

Ego-clinging includes this whole set of possibilities. It does not matter whether it is the innate type of clinging or the secondary, imputed level of clinging: All of these are forms or manifestations of clinging to a self. It does not matter whether you give ego a positive label, such as "religious person," or a negative label, such as "selfish person." It is the same: It is clinging to one's self, clinging to the fundamental existence of "I." This is the major obstacle on the Mahayana path.

Clinging to Individual Liberation

The third obstacle is clinging to individual liberation. At the beginning of our journey, which is the Hinayana path, our aim is to liberate ourselves. When we enter the path of Mahayana, our goal becomes the liberation of all sentient beings. If we continue to cling to the notion of working on the path to liberate only ourselves, then our path is not in accordance with the Mahayana heart of bodhichitta. We are still clinging to our ego, thinking, "I want to achieve liberation and enlightenment for only myself." If we are still clinging to individual salvation, then we have not actually cut through our ego-clinging and there will not be much clarity. This is the third obstacle to awakening from the Mahayana perspective.

Clinging to Pride

The fourth obstacle is a particular sense of pride, the pride of self-superiority. It is the idea that we can achieve everything without relying on teachers, scriptures, or other living beings and, furthermore, without helping anyone else. Having this sense of pride hinders us from developing compassion and loving-kindness. It also stops us from developing trust and confidence in others. Without these qualities, we cannot achieve enlightenment. Without having trust and confidence in teachers and teachings, and without developing compassion and loving-kindness for all sentient beings, it is not possible to achieve the state of enlightenment. Even if we have great wisdom and knowledge, we still need to rely on the help of other beings. Without other living beings, there is no way that we can develop our Mahayana practices of relative bodhichitta, which are a cause of enlightenment.

GENERATING PERFECT MIND

On our personal journey, we face the challenge of overcoming these obstacles and, in turn, developing the mature and complete realization of a bodhisattva. For these four obstacles, Lord Maitreya gave four antidotes, which are the direct cause of generating the perfect mind of bodhichitta. The first antidote is the development of strong faith in and aspiration for the Mahayana Dharma. The second antidote is the development of the wisdom of emptiness. The third is the development of *samadhi,* or meditation. The fourth antidote is the development of compassion. All four antidotes are needed in order to give rise to the result—the birth of the awakened heart of a bodhisattva. As a means of illustrating the birth of such a noble heart, Maitreya used a metaphor that describes the birth of a *chakravartin,* or king.

Maitreya compared the first antidote, which is the development of faith in and aspiration for the Mahayana teachings, path, and enlightenment, to the seed that comes from the father. This seed of faith counteracts any tendency for us to reject the genuine Dharma that cuts through our attachment. Faith relates to our confidence and trust in our own potential—our own buddha nature and qualities of prajna and compassion. When these are missing, it is difficult for anything to grow. However, while this seed is a powerful and necessary force, it cannot give birth by itself to the enlightened state.

In addition to a father, a mother is needed. According to Maitreya, the mother represents the development of egolessness, or the wisdom of selflessness, which is the second antidote. Without a mother, no child can be born. In the Buddhist teachings, the notion of emptiness or selflessness is known as the "mother of all the buddhas." The mother of all the buddhas is Prajnaparamita, the Great Mother, the great wisdom of emptiness. This wisdom counteracts our belief in the true existence of a self and thus cuts through our clinging to that self. Without this mother, there can be no buddhas, which means there can be no enlightenment.

Having developed this wisdom, we then apply the third antidote of meditation, or samadhi. Maitreya said that samadhi is like having the right womb, where the seed can be planted and properly grown. The seed of faith and aspiration that is encompassed by great wisdom needs the perfect womb of samadhi in which to rest and grow. The blissful, nondual experience of samadhi is the remedy for the third obstacle:

the desire to escape the fearful suffering of the world through the path of individual liberation. Since it is not based on having the absolute view, this desire leads us to an incorrect path as a means of escaping samsara. Consequently, we experience only additional pain and suffering. Samadhi dispels such desire and its resultant suffering by uncovering the genuine bliss and happiness of the state of nonduality.

The fourth antidote is the development of compassion, which can be compared to a nursemaid. Once the infant prince has developed in the womb and is actually born, the nursemaid attends to and nourishes the child. In a similar way, our infant state of realization cannot survive and grow to full maturity without being nurtured and sustained through compassion—through the tremendous care of the loving element of the heart. The development of compassion naturally counteracts both the selfish view of the path of enlightenment and the pride that is unconcerned with helping others.

Working with these four antidotes makes it possible for us to enter the Mahayana path from the ground level. There is a gradual process of development on the path, from the seed level to the birth of the child, from the nourishing of the child to the actual state of adulthood and the full realization of a bodhisattva. This metaphor describes an evolutionary path, through which we begin to develop an essential clarity about the view of ground Mahamudra: The ego-clinging and confusion that we have been working with are seen to be inseparable from the ground itself. They are seen to be in the nature of wisdom.

THE INSEPARABILITY OF SAMSARA AND NIRVANA

From the perspective of ground Mahamudra, samsara and nirvana are inseparable. There is no nirvana or liberation that exists apart from the state of samsara. There is likewise no samsara that exists as an entity separate from the state of liberation, or nirvana. Between these two states, there is no difference whatsoever. The nature of samsara rests in the nature of nirvana. The nature of samsara is not samsara; it is not confused and it is not as rigid and solidly existent as we perceive and experience it to be. That nature is totally free from all fabrications.

Therefore, the nature of samsara is the nature of liberation. That is why the Kagyu lineage supplication says, "The nature of thoughts is dharmakaya." That nature is in fact the ultimate state of buddhahood.

Because the view of ground Mahamudra is that samsara and nirvana are not separable, we do not see two separate things when we look at these two states from the Mahamudra point of view. We do not see this place as samsara and that place as nirvana. We do not see one state as a place of total confusion, suffering, and misery and think that we will depart from this place for another place called liberation or nirvana. That is a wrong view as far as Mahamudra is concerned. From the Mahamudra perspective, we see that our disturbing emotions are inseparable from wisdom. Not only do we see that the nature of samsara is nirvana, but also we see that the nature of our klesha mind is wisdom. The nature of our emotions and the various expressions of our emotional thoughts are nothing but expressions of our wisdom. The whole experience of samsaric pain and suffering is simply the expression of this ground liberation. Thus, there is nothing to fear. There is nothing to feel bad about because samsara itself is in the state of liberation. For that matter, there are no thoughts to be discarded because the nature of thought is the wisdom of a buddha.

We perceive emotions merely as emotions because we do not have a method for looking at them clearly and precisely. Therefore, we see emotions as disturbing and irritating, and we experience their energy as destructive. That particular view is based on ego's perception of our emotions. However, if we look at our emotions carefully, then they appear as an expression of wisdom. We no longer see emotion as ordinary emotion.

When we realize the view of ground Mahamudra, we see the inseparable nature of the ground, path, and fruition. There is nothing that separates the path from the ground. There is nothing that separates the fruition from the ground. In other words, we begin our journey from this ground level, and we end our journey there. We come back to this fundamental state, in which we see the inseparability of samsara and nirvana.

It is essential to develop the view of ground Mahamudra in order to understand not only the path of Mahamudra but also the path of Vajrayana. There can be no Vajrayana path without this pure, genuine view of ground Mahamudra. It is this view that helps us to develop the sacred outlook of the Vajrayana path. Therefore, before undertaking our journey, it is vital to understand the ground because it is the main focus of the path. Whichever methods and practices we apply on the path, we are actually practicing the ground. We are practicing according to the ground view, which is the view of the fundamental nature of reality. No matter how vigorously we practice on the path, in the future we will come back to this ground. It may seem that we depart from it when we attain the level of path and then the level of fruition. In fact we are going back to the fundamental state, which is the level of ground Mahamudra.

It is absolutely necessary for us to recognize that the resultant aspect of Mahamudra already exists at this very level of ground. In fact, all that we are doing is rediscovering this ground. We could say that we are reuniting ourselves with the ground aspect through the method of path. When we come to the point of actually returning to the ground, fully experiencing it and fully being in it, that is what we call the resultant aspect.

Ever-Present Buddhahood: The Three Kayas

The three-kaya nature of mind is present within the mind of all sentient beings, right now, but we do not see this. Although it is present, we fail to see it because it is obscured by ignorance. Sentient beings are simply drowning in an ocean of ignorant conceptualizations, experiencing waves of concepts, thoughts, and ego-clinging. Samsara is like that.

The actual unborn, nonexistent state of samsara is dharmakaya. That basic space or state of freedom is called the dharmakaya buddha. From this ground, the unceasing appearance of the relative world of samsara naturally arises. However, there is also a lucid and clear aspect of appearance, which is not something that arises just once and then disappears. There is an unceasing play of clarity, of lucidity, and this is what we call sambhogakaya, or sambhogakaya buddhahood.

When we close our eyes and meditate, when we look at our mind, it is not simply blank. It is not merely a big black hole. When we look at that mind, it is full of energy—it is a field of energy. This is similar to the experience of modern physicists examining an object under a powerful microscope. Although they do not find any solidly existing atoms, what they see is full of energy. There is a sense of complete or all-pervasive luminosity at this point. That sense of the basic vividness of luminosity is called the sambhogakaya nature of our mind—"the body of great enjoyment."

The field of luminosity that we see when we look at our minds becomes brighter and brighter and more and more substantial. When we see that continuity of light manifesting in every aspect of reality— not only in the aspect of mind but also in the objects that we experience in everyday life—the nature of that clarity becomes so vivid and intense that we solidify it. It is similar to having a pain in a certain part of our body that becomes so intense that we feel as if there is a piece of stone there. We feel as if there is some kind of solid, disturbing substance in a part of our body. That sensation seems so real, solid, and material. The unceasing manifestation of this unborn clarity, which pervades every level of reality, is called the nirmanakaya, or the nirmanakaya buddha—the "emanation body" nature of our mind.

To say this luminosity manifests unceasingly means that the nirmanakaya continuously arises in different moments and in different forms. The nature of luminosity manifests, appears, or is projected continuously in a variety of forms. This continuity can be suggested or partially represented by the image of an uninterrupted series of links in a chain. However, what is being described is beyond words.

On the Mahamudra path, it is said that the three kayas are ever present in this very state of samsara. Thus, the three kayas are not something newly produced. They are not products of the path. In fact, they are here right from the beginning of the ground of samsara. They are here from the beginning of this very moment of our confused being. Buddhahood is already here.

The Union of View and Meditation

At the level of ground Mahamudra, the Kagyu lineage emphasizes two approaches: the meditation that is realized through the view and the view that is realized through the meditation.

In the first approach, we find the path of meditation through the right view—that is, though our intellectual understanding and process. In the second approach, we search for and find the right view through the path of meditation. Although either approach can stand on its own, it is the union of the two that is strongly emphasized in the Kagyu tradition.

We might think that we do not need intellectual studies on the path of Mahamudra. We might think that by meditating and by following the Mahamudra path of simplicity we have no need for intellectual understanding or analysis. However, if we look to the instructions of all the great masters, we find that both intellectual understanding of the path and meditative realization are emphasized equally.

First, we come to understand ground Mahamudra through a process of intellectual study and analysis. Second, we experience ground Mahamudra through the path of analytical meditation or intellectual contemplation. Finally, we arrive at the stage of full realization of Mahamudra, which arises from the simple resting meditation on the path of Mahamudra.

That is ground Mahamudra. However, our problem is that we usually do not realize the nature of the ground. Even if we recognize it intellectually, we do not recognize it experientially. We cannot be what we think it is. Therefore, there is a need for a path that will lead us through the process of fully developing and manifesting the wisdom, the courage, and the fundamental qualities that we already possess— the three kayas. It is at this point that we move from the ground level to the path level.

5

The Path of Instructions

Mahamudra Shamatha

PATH MAHAMUDRA is the actual practice that generates
the realization of the ground. At the level of ground
Mahamudra, we develop our intellectual understanding. We experience some realization at the conceptual level, but we do not have a
direct experience of realization. At the level of path Mahamudra, we
realize the actual state of our mind, emotions, ego, and samsara as
being in the nature of the three kayas.

We can look to the great yogi Milarepa as our authority on the
subject of Mahamudra meditation. Milarepa gave us a definition of
meditation, as well as instructions about how to meditate. According
to Milarepa, "Meditation is not meditating on something; rather, it is
familiarizing ourselves with the nature of mind."[1] In short, meditation
is not meditating on any "thing"; meditation is familiarization.
Meditation is habituation, or "getting accustomed to."

Milarepa also said:

Son, when you meditate upon Mahamudra
Do not exert yourself in virtuous actions of body or speech;
There is a danger that nonconceptual wisdom will
    disappear.[2]

This means that on the Sutra Mahamudra path we do not concentrate too much on body and speech. In other words, we do not practice many visualizations of exotic deities; we do not place much emphasis on the physical world, either sacred or profane; and we do not place much emphasis on the verbal effort of reciting mantras or liturgies. These activities are not important. The important thing is to simply rest in meditation. That is what we have been learning from the very beginning of our practice. That is the nature of Mahamudra meditation here. These two sets of instructions on what meditation is and on how to meditate are perhaps the most important instructions for path Mahamudra.

After we have worked with the preliminary practices, it becomes possible for the genuine path or experience of Mahamudra to arise through the pointing-out instructions. Such pointing-out instructions become effective only when we have complete devotion—a complete sense of surrendering and letting go of our own pride.

Our pride may be an intellectual or a meditative pride. We may feel pride in our social background, our educational credentials, or simply our psychological state. When we completely surrender that pride in the presence of an enlightened master, then through such opening of our hearts with devotion, trust, and confidence, the pointing-out instructions become very effective. In fact, pointing out makes sense only at that point. Great Mahamudra masters such as Milarepa, Gampopa, and the Karmapas have all emphasized the path of devotion as the means of genuinely entering into Mahamudra meditation.

MAHAMUDRA POINTING-OUT INSTRUCTIONS

When we are ready to enter this stage of practice, how do we receive the actual pointing-out instructions? According to Gampopa, it is not necessary to go through a Vajrayana empowerment in order to receive pointing-out instructions. In the Sutra Mahamudra tradition, our guru can give pointing-out instructions right on the spot. This manner of pointing out may be given with words and through a guided meditation process. The student listens to the words of the guru and generates devotion intensely; then, within that peak of devotion, the pointing-out instruction takes place or "snaps in" very beautifully. Gampopa stressed this method of instruction in the Sutra Mahamudra.

Many Kagyu masters have used this method of transmitting the pointing-out instructions. However, some Vajrayana masters have questioned the style of giving pointing-out instructions without an empowerment. For example, Sakya Pandita, the great Sakya scholar, said that pointing out is not possible except in the context of Vajrayana empowerment. Although this method has been questioned, it has clearly produced many enlightened masters.

Each of these two viewpoints has a purpose. The intention of one is to ensure that the tantric or Vajrayana tradition is continued. Because of the emphasis on the indispensable nature of the Vajrayana empowerment, that tradition is preserved. The intention of the second is to transmit the essence of a lineage of teachings whose scriptural source is the *Samadhiraja Sutra,* the *King of Samadhi Sutra.*

The *Samadhiraja Sutra* is a teaching from the collection of Prajnaparamita sutras, which was propagated by great masters, such as Maitripa and other Indian yogis, and continued by Gampopa through his transmissions in Tibet. When Gampopa began the cycle of transmission of this instruction in Tibet, he had not only realized the nature of Mahamudra but had also experienced a very vivid memory of being in the presence of Lord Buddha Shakyamuni when the original discourse was given. At that time, there were five hundred bodhisattvas listening to the Buddha. At the end of the sutra, Buddha asked, "Are there any bodhisattvas here who will volunteer to carry on this teaching, to continue this lineage into the Dark Age, into the most polluted of times—the *kaliyuga?*" Only one bodhisattva raised his hand and said, "Yes, I will do that."

The bodhisattva's name was Da-ö Zhönu, or Youthful Moonlight. Later, Da-ö Zhönu was reborn in Tibet as Gampopa, and while he was teaching the Sutra Mahamudra he had a vivid memory of this event. Thus, Gampopa said that in transmitting the essence of the *Samadhiraja Sutra* through the Sutra Mahamudra, he was continuing his promise from a previous life.

In the second stage of path Mahamudra, which is the actual arising of Mahamudra meditation, the main path consists of three instructions known as the pointing-out instructions of coemergent mind:

1. Pointing out coemergent mind as dharmakaya
2. Pointing out coemergent thought as the display of dharmakaya
3. Pointing out coemergent appearance as the light of dharmakaya

These are the three fundamental instructions given on this path. The first pointing out instruction, pointing out coemergent mind as dharmakaya, has two aspects: one that relates to the instructions on shamatha practice and one that relates to the instructions on vipashyana practice. The second and third pointing-out instructions relate wholly to vipashyana. Accordingly, this chapter focuses on the shamatha aspect of the first pointing-out instruction, and the following chapter, on Mahamudra vipashyana, presents the vipashyana aspect of all three of these fundamental instructions.

Pointing out may also be understood as being introduced to the reality of mind's nature. Having received these instructions, we begin to practice them through the two techniques of shamatha and vipashyana. No other techniques are involved. In all of the Buddha's meditations from beginning to end, the basic techniques are shamatha and vipashyana. There are, however, slight variations between the earlier and later stages of both shamatha and vipashyana.

Pointing Out Coemergent Mind as Dharmakaya

This instruction points out that the coemergent mind is the dharmakaya, the unborn, basic space or state of freedom. In the context of ground Mahamudra, it is said that the nature of things is the unborn dharmakaya, which is the same statement. The point is that, from the very beginning, the nature of mind—how mind really is—has been inseparable from the dharmakaya. Mind and dharmakaya have always been together; there is no "mind" that exists apart from dharmakaya. This is the meaning of "coemergent mind." If we look at the mind that we take to be a self, then we will see that it is unborn. Furthermore, if we look at the kleshas, which are a basis of our fixations, then we will see that their nature is also unborn.

Of the two aspects connected with the first pointing-out instruction, shamatha and vipashyana, shamatha must come first and is in a sense the more essential. Shamatha is sometimes translated as "tranquillity" or "calm abiding," and vipashyana as "insight." In this context of Mahamudra, *shamatha* has a specific meaning. It is defined as "the natural pacification of the coming and going of thoughts." This means that the mind comes to rest in its natural condition, which is a state of bliss, clarity, and nonthought. Another distinguishing feature of this type of shamatha is that the object upon which we focus in order to develop tranquillity is the mind itself. There is no other object, such as the breath or a statue. We simply rest the mind in its own nature, which is the coemergent dharmakaya.

How do you bring the mind to rest in its own nature?

1. Do not prolong the previous thought.
2. Do not beckon the next or future thoughts.
3. Rest nakedly in the nature of fresh awareness of
   the present moment.

That is the definition of shamatha in the Mahamudra context. Additionally, there are three ways of resting the mind:

1. Rest the mind in freshness without distraction.
2. Rest the mind naturally and expansively.
3. Rest the mind in such a way that it is self-illuminating
   and clear to itself.

Resting the mind in freshness without distraction means that we rest in a state of awareness of the present moment—the present instant of experience—without our mind becoming distracted by either external or internal conditions.

Resting the mind naturally and expansively means that while meditating, we remain in a state free of contrivance or free of effort or exertion. A traditional analogy for this quality of attentive effortlessness is that of a Brahmin spinning yarn. If one spins the yarn too tightly, then it will break. If one twists it too loosely, then its strands will not adhere so as to become thread or cord. Similarly, when we rest our mind naturally and expansively, our three faculties of body, speech, and mind are neither too tight nor too loose.

Resting the mind in such a way that it is self-illuminating and clear means that we do not separate the nature of the thoughts that arise from the nature of the mindfulness and awareness that apprehends them.

This is Mahamudra shamatha as it relates to the first instruction, pointing out coemergent mind as dharmakaya.

Resting in Ordinary Mind

In Mahamudra shamatha meditation, we simply relax and click into the unconditional state of our fundamental mind. In Mahamudra language, this basic state of mind is called ordinary mind, or unborn mind. Ordinary mind is the wisdom of Buddha and the state of liberation. The great yogi Tilopa said, "One should allow the mind to relax in this unconditional state. When the mind becomes relaxed, one achieves liberation."

Resting in that ordinary mind is what we call shamatha. When we click into that unconditional state, we are resting without any sense of hope and fear. We are not hoping to achieve the state of resting, and at the same time, we are not fearful of becoming disturbed, distracted, or agitated by our klesha mind. If we can simply rest without hope and fear, then we are truly resting.

For example, when a pool of fresh spring water is stirred up, the agitated water mixes with the sediment at its bottom, and this causes the pool to appear muddy. If we try to clear up this little pool by stirring the water, then what we are actually doing is making the water even muddier. However, if we leave the water alone and let it rest, it will clear up by itself. The pool will naturally return to its own state of freshness and purity because the dirt that mixes with it when it is agitated never pollutes it fundamentally.

Similarly, natural mind has always been as pure as spring water. Although we see our mind as murky and unclear when it is churned up by potent emotions, the nature of mind has never been polluted by these emotions. It is only because of our constant struggle to clear up and purify our mind that we see it as murky. This is like struggling to clean a pool of water by constantly stirring it up. Our mind never has the chance to clear itself up naturally because we never give it a chance. Thus, the instruction for shamatha meditation at this stage is simply to rest without any hope and fear.

THREE STAGES OF RESTING

The state of resting is described as having three basic characteristics or levels: nondistraction, nonmeditation, and nonfabrication.

Nondistraction

Nondistraction, which is the definition of shamatha meditation, refers to the state of being totally free from all distractions, outer or inner. That is to say, we are not distracted by the outer world or outer appearances, and at the same time we are not distracted by the inner world or by our discursive thoughts. Ordinarily, we experience a variety of states of discursive thinking, such as gossiping, dreaming, fantasizing, and so forth, which may be either conscious or unconscious. We may experience a whole range of distractions without noticing that we are sliding into states of discursiveness. Becoming free from all this is called nondistraction.

Nonmeditation

It is said that when we prepare to practice meditation, we need the simple thought, "Right now, I am going to sit down and meditate." However, we do not need any more thoughts about meditation after that because then we are actually meditating. If after we have sat down and

begun meditating, we are still having thoughts such as, "I have to meditate. I am meditating. I am doing great. I am practicing Mahamudra,"
then we are not meditating. At that point we are still at the level of
preparation—we are thinking about meditation instead of doing it. Sitting meditation has to be totally free of any state of thought; even the
thought of meditation has to be released. It should not haunt us.

Nonmeditation is letting go of the thought of meditation. In
order to let go of the thought of meditation when sitting, we must
know how to rest our body, our speech, and our mind. We must know
the method of entering into the meditative state, not just physically
but with mind and speech as well. In the stage of nonmeditation, there
is a total sense of resting, and this resting requires a certain quality of
relaxation. Our physical posture should not make us feel stiff, irritated, uncomfortable, or different in any way. It should be completely
natural and relaxed and at the same time we should remain in a correct
posture, such as the Sevenfold Posture of Vairochana, which refers
to the seven points of physical posture commonly assumed during
meditation practice.[3] The reason for the emphasis on posture is that
the position of one's body has a direct and powerful effect on the state
of one's mind. Assuming a correct and upright posture causes one's
mind to come to rest naturally in a state of tranquillity, or peace.

Nonfabrication

Nonfabrication is a state of shamatha meditation that is free from
any conceptual labeling. At this stage, there is no process of labeling
our experience as one thing or another, such as thoughts of "resting" or
"not resting" or "This is Mahamudra shamatha" or "This is not
Mahamudra shamatha." We must be totally free from these fabrications. When we rest in that state of mind, there is a great sense of freedom. We are free not only from the states of discursiveness and
distraction, as well as from the thought of meditation, but we are also
unfettered by concepts and fabrications of any kind. We are not bound
by the thought of sitting. There is no sense of pushing and no stress.
There is a total sense of freedom.

THREE METHODS OF RESTING

The great masters of the lineage introduced three different methods that can lead us to the point of resting. When we contemplate and work with these three processes, we discover for ourselves how to actually arrive at that point.

Abrupt Cutting of Sudden Thoughts

The first method begins with developing watchfulness. We begin by simply watching our minds. We are not "meditating"; we are just watching our minds in the same way that we would watch the ocean. When the ocean of our mind is very calm and still, we rest in that state. Then, a karmic wind appears and blows across the ocean. It blows from different directions, creating beautiful waves. We simply watch the arising of the waves without getting caught up in their movements. We watch the arising of each thought and cut right through it. We do not follow it. We cut it and go back to watching. When another thought arises, we cut through it in the same way, at the very moment of its arising. We do not let it go further. We cut it in that moment and then we rest and watch again. We pressure ourselves to cut through the arising of each and every sudden thought. We continue to do this, on and on, with different winds and different waves until we are completely exhausted.

We are going through a process. The first step is cutting through, which brings us to the fundamental state of dharmakaya or nonexistence. We are working very hard to cut through thought at the moment of its arising, which is a very effective method of developing clarity. We develop this clarity through our practice of awareness and mindfulness. There is a strong emphasis on paying attention and concentrating one-pointedly in order to see every movement of thought, recognize it, and cut through it. When we allow a thought to develop, it is difficult to cut through it.

When we practice this method of recognizing and cutting

through, we are not simply sitting there, letting thoughts come and go. It is not as simple as that. We are entering a different stage, one that requires more directness and a greater exercise of energy and power. This level of practice takes us to the peak of intensity—intensity of cutting, intensity of letting go. Simply sitting and letting go of our thoughts is too passive. It puts us to sleep. According to such a method, letting go is like a lullaby for our thoughts. Our thoughts might go to sleep, but they will come back.

When cutting thoughts, we are not suppressing them or regarding them as bad. We are not saying, "I do not want this thought." We are not cutting in that sense, but rather in the sense of recognizing the arising of thought itself. "Recognizing" does not mean labeling, identifying, or following after these thoughts. It is seeing a thought's arising. It is not seeing that there is "something there" or that "something is going on." That would be very vague. Instead, we have to be more clear and precise with each particular experience of thought, no matter how it arises. Whether it is in the form of anger or a label, we have to be with it. Recognizing means just that: being with the thought, seeing it clearly and then cutting through it. Then we go back to being a skillful watcher. The practice of watching is like going to a beautiful cliff and looking out over the ocean. If you know how to enjoy the view, then the arising of thoughts is so beautiful. However, if you become attached to the waves and jump off the cliff to be with one of them, then you are done for. You will no longer be able to enjoy the view of the dancing waves that come after. You will have no time to enjoy that view because you will be fully enveloped in the first wave.

If we follow our conceptual patterns, then we end up in the beautiful world of samsara. When we know how to cut through and how to reach the level of dharmakaya, or the great shunyata, then later we will come to see thoughts and emotions as dharmakaya. We have not reached that point yet. Thus far, we have been considering the first instruction: pointing out the coemergent mind as dharmakaya.

Letting Be Whatever Arises

We apply the second method when we have reached the state of exhaustion. After working very hard, after exerting ourselves to cut through concept after concept, labeling thoughts and gossiping mind, we are totally wiped out and ready to relax. At this stage, we let our thoughts and perceptions remain as they are. We do not let them gain power over us and control our minds, but at the same time we do not stop them. Maintaining the simple awareness of mindfulness, we let them be in their natural state.

At this point, we allow our thoughts a certain sense of freedom. With the first method, we have been trying to catch the arising of every thought with an acute sense of awareness and watchfulness, struggling persistently to catch each thought and cut through it. There is a sense of catching our thoughts with a net, as if we were catching fish. First, we have to collect our thoughts into the net of our awareness so that we can see them with greater clarity and stability. We are trying to develop a sense of direct relationship with our thoughts. However, when it comes to the second point, we are cutting through the idea of the net and the idea of netting our thoughts; instead, we are letting thoughts be in their own wildness.

The method at this point is simply to tell our thoughts to be whatever they want to be. We give our thoughts permission to fly wherever they want to fly, like a kite. There are three elements necessary for flying this kite: the strongly blowing wind of karma; the present arising of consciousness, which is the kite itself; and the string of our awareness that is tied to the kite. When the two opportunities of wind and kite come together, we try to let the kite fly the way it wants to fly, the way it wants to maneuver in space. We let go and give our thoughts total freedom. However, this kite is tied by a tiny string so that our minds do not go completely crazy. What we are trying to do through this method is simply to leave thoughts in their own state, rather than trying to transform them into another state of being.

Thoughts are born with a certain suit or a particular attire. Sometimes we do not like the attire very much, or we see the possibility of improving it or making fun of it. So we exercise our right to change the attire of the kite. We try to dress up our thoughts in different ways, so thoughts do not really remain as they are. At this point, our thoughts become totally fabricated, totally changed. At first, we start out with the basic kite, which is made of paper and which has a natural sense of beauty as it is. However, we want to paint the kite a different color, and as we paint it with our thick brush, the kite becomes heavier and heavier. We end up adding more colors, more paper, dressing our kite up as if we were trying to imprison it, until eventually the kite can no longer fly. It cannot exercise its full energy and power in the sky. Similarly, we do not give our thoughts the chance to exercise their nature in the great space of dharmakaya, which is their right. What we are trying to do with this second method is to let be whatever arises. We are trying to let the kite be in its own state and let it fly as far as it wants or can. At this point of our practice, we let the kite fly in the great space of dharmakaya.

However, there is a simple sense of awareness, which is the string tied between us and the kite. We need this tie of basic awareness in the very moment of flying the kite, in the moment of totally letting go. We can imagine how the kite would fly if we took off all the clothing we have put on it. Letting our thoughts fly in the space of dharmakaya, we can see their lightness; we can see their transparent quality, which has a certain sense of embracing the sky or the space. There is a sense of all-encompassing space surrounding this beautiful kite, no matter how it appears. This letting go is simply letting go of our thoughts without restricting them further, without changing their identity and without following or fantasizing about our thoughts. The instruction here is to simply stop clothing this kite and simply let the kite be a kite. Let it fly in the space where there is no end to be reached.

Letting go is not simply a matter of watching our thoughts, because watching itself has a certain quality of identifying a thought.

We are not only watching our thoughts; we are also letting them be what they are. This method has a greater sense of freeing our minds from our attachment to samsara.

Being Skilled in the Key Points of the Methods of Resting

With the third method, we develop the skill of resting in genuine balance. Various analogies are used to illustrate this method of resting, one of which is a bundle of straw: Not being too tight or too loose, one should relax with full mindfulness and rest like a bundle of straw fallen open. In this example, our discursive thoughts and concepts are like a bundle of straw that is pulled together quite tightly with only a tiny bit of string. When we are tied up this way, we do not have the energy to cut through this little string and fall back into this natural state of resting. The point here is that we have a bundle of straw that is already tied tightly together, and through the process of watching our thoughts, we are constantly adding more and more straws into this bundle. We are stretching the string that binds the straw to the breaking point. At a certain point, the string breaks; it naturally cuts itself. We do not need to use scissors. Then, when the straw falls, it simply falls. It does so effortlessly. The individual straws do not have preconceived notions of how they should fall down; they do not organize themselves to fall this way or that way. The straw falls freely and naturally and comes to rest. Similarly, we have to have a natural sense of falling and coming to rest without any planning.

In this state of resting, we "space out with clarity." We do not simply blank out. There are two different ways of spacing out or being in the state of nonthought. The first is spacing out without clarity, or just blanking out, which is a state of ignorance. For example, we may get caught up in a state of thought and then blank out, after which we recognize, "Oh, for a moment I didn't have a thought." That only shows the extent of our ignorance. The second state of nonthought is spacing out with clarity. This state has a tremendous sense of luminosity and buddha energy. It also has its own self-recognition or self-awareness, without labels or terms. Therefore, we do not have the thought, "I didn't have a thought" because there is already self-recognition.

When we space out with clarity, it is like the bundle of straw fallen open. We finally manage to discover that the string that is binding us together is only a tiny string and that, with a little effort of mindfulness, the string will break and we can fall back into our natural state of resting. The nature of the straw itself has never, from the beginning, been constrained or bound together. It has always been in the state of resting. In a similar way, natural mind has always been in the state of resting, of liberation, without any hope and fear. We are trying to return to that state. With this method, we cut through the string that binds the straw. Then we let ourselves fall back onto our cushions and we rest in that space. We fall back and rest without any sense of effort, without making any attempt to shape our experience. However, we should rest without hope of resting long and without fear of the string coming back to tie us up. This method is related to the stage of nonfabrication.

Through our practice of each of these methods, we are taking further steps on our path of meditation. We are trying to bring ourselves to the great shunyata, the dharmakaya, the ground Mahamudra, by cutting through the conceptual arising of thought. There can be a tremendous sense of clarity, which comes from the luminous aspect of our mind; and then, at that very moment, another thought arises. We need a little power, strength, and courage in order to cut through that thought. We cannot always be so weak—as fragile as the straw. It is not a big deal. It is the cutting of just one little string that leads us to the fundamental state of dharmakaya.

The third method is also taught through the analogy of spinning wool into yarn, which demonstrates a slightly different approach. Brahmins are said to be very clever and cautious and have a skillful way of spinning yarn. They do not waste anything. It is said that our meditation should be like the Brahmin's method for making thread. No wool is wasted, not even a single strand. At the same time, the wool is spun in such a way that the thread is neither too tight, which makes it difficult to weave, nor too loose, which makes it useless. Instead, the degree of tension in the spinning is managed with precision so that the thread is spun very properly. In a similar way, when we practice the methods of shamatha, we have to balance everything. We should not be too stiff in our physical posture, and our minds should not be too focused or too tense. At the same time, our mental concentration should not be totally loose, which would be like not spinning anything at all. It would be like merely taking the wool out of its basket, which would serve no purpose. In a similar way, if we think, "I just have to relax and not do anything," then we will not enter into the actual state of meditation. Thus, developing a sense of balance is a key point in knowing how to rest properly. That is why it is called being skilled in the key points of the methods of resting.

GENERAL TECHNIQUES OF SHAMATHA MEDITATION

In the Mahamudra tradition, the descriptions of the shamatha meditation practices are very detailed, and the actual practices become quite subtle. The three main classifications of shamatha being presented here are shamatha with focal support, shamatha without focal support, and shamatha of essence.

Shamatha with Focal Support

It is important to train in the method of shamatha with focal support so that we can work with sensory objects and sensory pleasures. Working with these objects takes us to a deeper level of shamatha experience and extends our awareness further into the world. This method is the very beginning of Mahamudra shamatha.

In this first type of shamatha meditation, "support" refers to an external basis for the development of shamatha. Supports are divided into two kinds: pure and impure. In either case, supports are external objects of visual perception that are used as a basis for bringing the mind to rest.

Impure supports refer to neutral objects such as a flower, a pebble, or a small piece of wood. We place one of these objects in our line of vision so that we are looking slightly downward, along our nose. Generally, the object would be placed on a table or other surface in front of us. We then relax our breathing and direct our attention one-pointedly to our visual consciousness of the object. When our mind comes to rest, we mix our mind with our perception of the object. This technique brings about the experiences associated with shamatha meditation very quickly and in a very forceful manner.

This can be a very relaxing meditation. For example, you can go to a beautiful park and meditate on a flower, a tree, a lake, or simply on the clouds. You can pick any specific focal object and meditate on that. This can be a very helpful practice because you do not have to remain inside, sitting and watching your breath or a particular object, such as the form of a deity. You can be anywhere in the world and take any object as an object of meditation. This is one way to bring practice into your everyday life. For example, when you are sitting on a bench waiting for a bus or waiting for your date in a restaurant, you can simply focus on any object before you and rest your mind on it.

A pure support refers to an object that is not neutral but instead has a spiritual or positive significance, such as a statue of the Buddha or an image of one of the enlightened masters or bodhisattvas. These supports are considered pure because they usually bring us more vipashyana—more awareness of enlightenment—than do ordinary, "impure" objects. The act of looking at a mundane object such as a pen, pebble, or flower, usually gives rise to some quality of emotion because we are so caught up in dealing with these objects in everyday life.

Place the statue or image in your line of vision, just as you placed the pebble before. You can either direct your attention to a bare, visual perception of successive details of a statue or to the entire statue all at once. For example, direct your attention first to the lotus pedestal or seat, then to the body of the figure, then to the crown protuberance at the top of the head. Regardless of which approach you take in directing your attention, the use of a pure support in this manner also generates a very forceful and particular type of shamatha experience.

The practice of shamatha with a focal object sounds quite basic and not at all profound. However, when you actually engage in the practice, the experiences that arise through such meditation can be quite extraordinary. This method of practice is particularly useful because we live in a world of substantial materialism: There is a substantial material world surrounding us all the time. When we develop a certain level of understanding, insight, and meditative experience based on the shamatha techniques that use a substantial focal object, we have a greater chance of giving rise to a panoramic vipashyana experience of the outer and inner world.

Whether our meditation object is pure or impure, our mind should be totally free from thoughts. We simply blend our mind with the breath and with the object of our perception. We become one with that space and that experience, and we rest in that space without conceptualizing. We do not analyze the object in front of us. For example, we do not say, "Well, this is a black stone from the Rocky Mountains" or "This is a white stone from Kathmandu." We do not analyze an image of Buddha by thinking about how good the artist was or how colorful the painting is or whether or not we like it. We must remember that the purpose of using the focal object is simply to rest our mind.

Shamatha without Focal Support

The second type of shamatha meditation is shamatha without focal support. Rather than relying on an external, physically present support as a basis for directing our mind, here we rely on the support of an imagined image or a visualization, which may be external or internal.

EXTERNAL VISUALIZATION

As with the earlier method of shamatha with focal support, there are two principal variations used in this method. In the first of these, we direct our mind to a particular aspect of an image; in the second, we direct our mind to the entire image. Developing a clear and stable visualization may take some time—an hour, days, or months.

In the first variation, we imagine the form of the Buddha in the space in front of us, progressively generating the full image from the ground upward, starting with the lotus seat. The first step is to establish the lotus clearly. Then go on to each part, focusing separately and clearly. Continue to visualize individual aspects until you can generate the whole image of the Buddha clearly. In the second variation, direct your attention to the entire image all at once; for example, the overall image of the form of the Buddha. However, this is difficult in the beginning, so start simply and focus on a single detail, such as his hand or his begging bowl. It is not necessary to visualize the whole body at once.

The most common visualization used is the form of the Buddha. However, in this technique, additional methods are used to train one's mind. These are applied once the basic visualization of the Buddha becomes stable. For example, we gradually reduce the size of the image until it becomes as small as a sesame seed. Once we have visualized this, we make sure that all the details of its appearance, such as the eyes and ears, are as clear as they were when it was larger. Then we make the image very large—as large as a mountain—while maintaining the whole image in our mind. These are methods for enhancing the clarity and stability of the visualized image.

INTERNAL VISUALIZATION

In the preceding descriptions, you visualize a form external to yourself. For example, you may be seeing an image of the Buddha as if it were in front of you. Another variation of this method is to visualize an image inside your body, such as a sphere of light in various colors, or an emblem such as a vajra. You might also visualize your own body in an enlightened form. The image of the Buddha is often used for this practice. For Vajrayana Buddhists, it is especially important to meditate on an image of the Buddha because there is a tendency to become fascinated by colorful deities and gurus.

To practice this method, choose an image that makes you feel comfortable or that brings a sense of peace to your heart. Use an image that really generates some feelings. There are many beautiful images of Buddha in Indian art. Some of these images are livelier and more human than the Tibetan paintings. First, concentrate on looking at an actual image for some time, and then create the visualization in your mind, following the instructions for building the visualization from the ground upward and for reducing and enlarging the size of the image while maintaining the clarity of detail.

There are a number of other methods of visualization within the overall category of shamatha meditation without a focal support. However, what we are doing in all of these practices is training our mind to focus, to relax, and to experience the quality of space.

Shamatha of Essence

Shamatha of essence is simply resting in the basic continuity of mind. That resting is explained as the subsiding or dissolving of the waves of thought into the ocean of the all-basis, or the basic mind, which is neither virtuous nor unvirtuous. "Waves of thought" refers to the dualistic concepts of subject and object, or experiencer and experienced, that agitate our minds. The subsiding of thoughts of subject and object is significant here because at this level of shamatha there is no object of meditation. Up to this point, we have been describing techniques in which there was an object toward which the mind was directed—that object being considered separate, to some extent. Here, the concept of a subjective cognition being directed to an object that is separate from it is relinquished. This act of relinquishment leaves the mind in a state similar to an ocean without waves. The ocean remains calm, and in that calmness there is an experience of profundity—one that is regarded as a bridge between shamatha and vipashyana meditation.

There are further practices of Mahamudra shamatha, which are generally communicated within the context of one's individual guru-disciple relationship.

Nine Stages of Resting the Mind.

NINE STAGES OF RESTING THE MIND

There are basically nine stages of resting the mind, or nine set-tlings of the mind, in the practice of shamatha meditation. The illus-trated chart on page 99 can help us understand these stages and their relationship to our practice.

The nine stages of shamatha meditation are translated here as fol-lows, with Tibetan in parentheses—the Wylie transliteration first, fol-lowed by the phonetic spelling:

1. Placement (Tib. *'jog pa/jogpa*)
2. Continuous placement (Tib. *rgyun du 'jog pa/gyundu jogpa*)
3. Repeated placement (Tib. *bslan te 'jog pa/lente jogpa*)
4. Close placement (Tib. *nye bar 'jog pa/nyewar jogpa*)
5. Taming (Tib. *'dul bar byed pa/dulwar jepa*)
6. Pacification (Tib. *zhi bar byed pa/shiwar jepa*)
7. Thorough pacification (Tib. *rnam par zhi bar byed pa/nampar shiwar jepa*)
8. One-pointedness (Tib. *rtse gcig tu byed pa/tsechigtu jepa*)
9. Even placement (Tib. *mnyam par 'jog pa/nyampar jogpa*)

The first stage is shown at the bottom of the illustration, where we see a monk, who represents the meditator. He is carrying two things. One is a hooked stick, such as an elephant handler usually carries in India. In his other hand, he has a rope with a hook at one end. The stick symbolizes watchfulness, and the rope mindfulness. The elephant, sym-bolizing our dull mind, is being guided by the monkey, which represents agitation—the wild, distracted, restless aspect of mind. The large fire flaring up from the first stage of the path represents the effort that we put into our meditation. From here until the seventh stage of resting the mind, the tongues of the flames grow progressively smaller as the effort required in mindfulness and watchfulness lessens.

Stage One: Placement

The first way of resting the mind is called placement. We place or concentrate the mind on an object, which may be a physical object such as a buddha statue, a visualized image, or simply the breath. At the start, our mind is very wild, like a feather blown here and there by the wind. So, first we try to put our mind in one place, focusing or placing it. Normally we are distracted by objects outside ourselves, or else we are distracted internally, and our mind becomes unaware. Placement consists of resting the mind in a state of peace that is neither distracted externally nor made oblivious by something internal.

The instructions for this first meditation are the same as for basic shamatha meditation as it is most commonly understood. The practice of settling the mind consists of bringing our mind back from outer distractions, bringing our mind back from outer dullness, and bringing it back to inner concentration. In contrast to this state of inner concentration, our mind often runs wild with thoughts about the external world—for instance, thoughts of surfing or bullfighting. Alternatively, we might feel completely dull and lazy, wanting to do nothing. We might feel a sense of mental thickness. When we bring our mind out of either of these two states and back to a state of inner concentration by means of focusing on the breath or other shamatha methods, we are bringing our wild or dull mind back to the state of ordinary mind. That is the first stage of the meditation: settling the mind.

At this point in the illustration, there is a fairly great distance between the meditator and his mind. We can see that the monk is chasing after his mind, which is represented by a completely dark elephant and a completely dark monkey. The darkness here represents a mind that is completely out of control in relation to its experiences. This is the stage where we go straight into a full state of dullness or a full state of agitation or wildness. As a result, there is a big distance between the meditator and the mind.

Stage Two: Continuous Placement

When we have some sense of how to place our mind, how to be one-pointed, we move to the second stage of meditation, which is called continuous placement, in which we are placing our mind over and over again.

At this stage, we can see that the gap is closing a little. The monk is getting closer to the elephant and the monkey. The fire is becoming smaller, which means that the meditator's mind is becoming less agitated, less intense, although there is still some degree of effort needed. We can also see that the elephant and the monkey are beginning to turn just slightly lighter. There is a touch of lightness on their heads.

However, at this stage, the monkey is still leading the mind. Agitation still leads our elephant mind, but the pace has slowed. In the illustration, we can see that the two figures are not running as much as they were in the first stage, where both the elephant and the monkey were almost flying. Here, in the second stage, they are not really running, just walking at a fast pace, like New Yorkers or people from Hong Kong. At this point, we can see that dullness and agitation are decreasing a little bit.

Stage Three: Repeated Placement

The third way of resting is called repeated placement, which again refers to placing the mind over and over. The difference at this stage is that when our mind becomes distracted, we try to bring back its focus. It is sometimes called "settling firmly." This refers to the ability to bring the mind back to a chosen object when it has become distracted. One way of doing this is to first recognize the distraction, then determine which of the mental afflictions has produced it, and finally apply the remedy for that particular mental affliction.

We can see from the illustration that the meditator and the mind are now engaged in some kind of communication. They are now face to face, rather than one chasing after the other. The elephant has turned its head back to look at the meditator. The monkey is also turning its head to look back. Thus, at this point, the monk has begun to develop a degree of contact with his own mind. There is a communication that has developed between the mind and the meditator. They are now looking each other directly in the face. That kind of contact or communication is developed through mindfulness. In the illustration, we can see that the rope carried by the meditator is now hooked to the elephant. The rope of mindfulness has caught the elephant mind. Although the monkey is still leading the elephant, and a gap remains between the meditator and the animals, the gap is lessening. Also, the monkey is now walking at a comfortable pace.

At this point, a small rabbit appears, which represents subtle dullness. This indicates that the meditator's dullness is not as great or as coarse as it was in the beginning stages. The elephant projects an image of enormous dullness that is solid and thick, but the bunny suggests a lighter, softer, more delicate kind of dullness.

The elephant, the monkey, and the rabbit are all slowly turning white. Their heads are entirely white, and the elephant's trunk is also white. This indicates that both the dullness and the agitation are decreasing. We can also see that the fire is becoming a bit smaller, which illustrates that less effort is required of the meditator.

Stage Four: Close Placement

In the fourth stage, close placement, we are going more deeply into the state of meditation, making an effort to arrive at a more subtle level of focusing the mind; here, we reach a level of concentration in which we cut off any vagueness about focusing. In other words, this is the ability to rest the mind one-pointedly on an object that is subtle or precise rather than coarse or vague.

We can see from the illustration that the gap between the meditator and the three animals is closing. In addition, the elephant is turning whiter, as are the monkey and the rabbit; and the fire is now smaller.

At this stage, the picture also shows a tree with fruit. The monkey, who is collecting the fruit, is almost white. The tree itself is dark, but the fruit is white. The bright fruit symbolizes virtuous activities or actions. These are the "virtuous fruits of the two benefits," which are the benefit for oneself and the benefit for others. That is what the monkey is collecting. Although virtuous activities are a distraction from the meditative point of view, we still need to collect them. The tree is dark because it is still dualistic and therefore is also a distraction.

Stage Five: Taming

The fifth method of bringing the mind to rest, or settling the mind, is called taming. Traditionally it is said that watchfulness does not permit the mind to be distracted. One gives rise to confidence and is led to samadhi at this point. Taming consists of subduing the impediment that can arise at this stage, which is a dislike of meditation—becoming hesitant, tired of or discouraged with, meditation. This obstacle is tamed by reflecting once again on the benefits and qualities of samadhi.

Interspersed throughout all of the stages, we find images representing the five sense pleasures. These may vary in different illustrations depending on the particular artist's rendition; however, the basic meaning remains the same. The five sense pleasures are the objects of agitation, and here they are symbolized by cloth, fruit, a conch of scented water, cymbals, and a mirror. The cloth is shown at stage one, above the elephant. Three white fruits and a conch of scented water are shown above the elephant and monkey at stage two. The fruits are also found on the tree at stage four. The cymbals, represented by two circles appearing beside the elephant and monkey with their heads turned back, are shown at stage three. Finally, a mirror is shown between stages five and six above the monk, who now leads the elephant. The cloth represents the sensory pleasure of touch; fruit symbolizes the sensory pleasure of taste; the conch of scented water symbolizes the sensory pleasure of smell; the cymbals represent the sensory pleasure of sound; and the mirror symbolizes the sensory pleasure of sight.

Stage Six: Pacification

The sixth stage of meditation is called pacification, which means pacifying distractions and discursive thoughts. This refers to the pacification of torpor and wildness by means of the application of their appropriate remedies. At this stage, we are recognizing our thoughts and trying to get rid of distractions, but we are not yet applying the antidotes thoroughly.

At this point, we no longer have any genuine interest in entertaining our mind with wildness and agitation or with dullness. There is a genuine and total flip in our attitude. We now take complete delight in samadhi and meditation. Ordinarily, when we go to our meditation cushion intending to practice, we experience a struggle. We struggle to get to the cushion; we struggle to sit. That is because we still find some entertainment in our thoughts—we enjoy this wild and crazy mind, as well as the dullness of mind. We also experience a sense of regret. For example, we may think, "I am not doing anything! I am just sitting—doing nothing! I could have finished this or that project." That is why we do not experience complete delight in sitting. However, at this sixth level, we do develop a complete delight in sitting, without the sorts of regret that we ordinarily experience whenever we sit. Now, in contrast, these kinds of thoughts no longer arise. Instead, we feel a complete sense of delight. The fire, representing the meditator's effort, is extinguished at this point.

Stage Seven: Thorough Pacification

The seventh stage is called thorough pacification. At this stage, the kleshas, or mental afflictions, are fully pacified through the application of the antidotes. Not only do we recognize the arising of mental afflictions, but we are also able to pacify them or cause them to become dormant. It is said that it is difficult for even subtle dullness and agitation to arise at this point; but even if these were to arise, they could be discarded immediately with a little effort.

Stage Eight: One-Pointedness

The eighth stage, one-pointedness, is defined as an effortless and natural state of resting the mind. If we rely on mindfulness and watchfulness at the beginning of our journey, then the dullness, agitation, and distance are incapable of creating obstacles at this stage, where we enter into complete samadhi. Here, the elephant, which symbolizes dullness, is free or almost free from all darkness. In some representations of the stages, the tail is still a little bit dark. The meditator is very tame now and simply walks with the elephant, who gently follows. The monkey, which represented agitated mind, is completely gone. When we analyze dullness and agitation, we can see that dullness is more subtle than agitation, which is a very rough or unprocessed state of mind. It is a coarse sort of defilement. We can tame that agitation and free ourselves from agitated mind through meditation, but dullness remains for quite a while. There is a quality of ignorance or delusion in that dullness.

Stage Nine: Even Placement

The ninth method of resting is called even placement. At this final stage, whenever we enter into meditation, our immersion or absorption in it is thorough and complete. We no longer have to struggle; we can rest in one-pointedness as long as we wish, without any conceptual discursive thoughts and without any obstacles. It is completely effortless.

At this point, we experience a complete sense of taming, or meditative equipoise (*nyom-jug*). We can see that the elephant and the meditator are now simply resting together without effort. Beginning with the sixth stage, where the fire is extinguished, there is no effort. It is called effortless meditation, effortless resting, or effortless samadhi.

At this stage of evenly resting, we see the monk sitting down with the elephant. The path emerges from the meditator's heart, which indicates that it is coming purely from the heart, or mind. However, there is still a sense of journey, of one who is taking the journey, and of the meditation, which is the threefold situation. Therefore, there is still a state of duality, which is not completely free or enlightened. Accordingly, the path remains dark in the illustration. The stage of evenly resting, where the path flows out of the heart, is the point where we begin the subtle path of vipashyana.

The Attainment of Shamatha

The path continues until the completion of shamatha meditation, where we achieve the first tranquillity, or *shin-jang* of the body. This is the suppleness, pliancy, and complete processing of the body, through which we attain shamatha. Complete shamatha is attained at the ninth stage of samadhi, along with tranquillity of the mind—the suppleness, pliancy, and complete processing of the mind.

After this accomplishment, we continue the journey of meditation with vipashyana meditation. At this point, we unify shamatha and vipashyana meditation on emptiness and cut the root of samsara. From here onward, there is no solid path, so to speak. It simply comes from the mind. It comes from our heart as we continue our journey, riding on this elephant mind.

At the end of the journey, the monk is holding a sword and a book, which together symbolize wisdom, or prajna. The book alone is not a very active image. However, the sword symbolizes the sharpness or cutting quality of prajna. It is the action aspect of wisdom—it is what wisdom does. When we have this sword, it shows how the sharpness of wisdom manifests in the activity of cutting the root of ego and cutting the root of samsara.

In the final image, there are two lines emerging from the heart of the monk. These seem to be related to the sword, and they are connected with the wisdom of the two truths: relative truth and absolute truth. As a result of the arising of vipashyana, we realize the nature of the two truths. We cut through ego-clinging and we realize the absolute truth, as well as the relative truth and the relative nature of cause and effect. The final illustration seems to represent the realization of the two truths arising from prajna. In addition, there is another fire, which appears at the end of the path. This fire is no longer representative of the effort of the meditator; rather, here it is symbolic of the strength and power of mindfulness and awareness, or watchfulness, arising at the time of fruition.

We can also see that the monk and the elephant are now turned around and appear to be walking back down the path. This may symbolize one of two situations. First, it might represent a sense of searching for the view through meditation. If we have not accomplished the view before going through the stages of meditation, then searching for the view is, in a sense, coming back to the ground. The view is the ground. Second, the image may indicate that there is nothing beyond this stage, that there is nowhere further to go. There is nothing beyond this basic state. No matter how far we go on our journey of meditation, we will always come back to the state of our original mind, which is ordinary mind, *thamal gyi shepa*.

When we search for the view through meditation, we discover the view by developing the power of mindfulness and watchfulness. This is a stage of shamatha meditation. We realize the view through vipashyana meditation. It is the same process in both the common vehicle and Mahamudra practice.

We can see that at this final stage of the nine methods, there is a complete sense of resting. The mind and the meditator are like very good friends—in the meeting of these two, there is a sense of joy, relaxation, and openness.

The illustration provides us with an excellent means to study and learn about shamatha. On a large scale, the picture depicts the complete process or path of shamatha. On a smaller scale, it illustrates the process that we go through in almost every shamatha meditation session. First, there is the stage of placement or resting, in which we bring our mind to the point of settling. Then we continue the struggle with the stage of continuously settling. We move on to repeated settling, closely settling, making tame, making peaceful, making completely peaceful, making one-pointed, and finally, evenly settling. By the end of a particular practice session, we may be comparatively settled.

These are general guidelines created for every meditator among the thousands of people practicing meditation. Of course, when it comes to a particular person, it is an individual journey. The instructions represented by the illustration can be viewed as being similar to the horoscopes we read in the newspaper every day. The daily reading for any one astrological sign will not be equally accurate for everyone born under that sign. There is a degree of common ground, but if we really want to understand our own horoscope, it has to be based on the details of our particular birth time, location, and so forth, and we would need to consult with an astrologer in order to develop an individualized chart. Meditation instruction is similar. We can begin with the general images of the shamatha illustration but if we want our own personal chart of the nine stages of shamatha, then we have to work with our teacher, who is familiar with the particularities of our individual situation.

Before we begin our practice of vipashyana, it is very important to develop the basic ground of resting. This point is frequently emphasized. During this time, we can continue with our studies and contemplations on vipashyana. Our theoretical understanding can be developed, but the actual practice of vipashyana cannot begin until the mind is fully settled. There is a difference between vipashyana meditation and the development of the view of vipashyana. Once we have some background and experience in resting the mind, we can develop the view intellectually and theoretically through contemplation. However, the real sense of resting in that view cannot happen without a full sense of resting in shamatha. For this reason, there is a great emphasis on going through the shamatha levels stage by stage with a master.

Khenpo Tsültrim Gyamtso Rinpoche, a great master of Vajrayana Buddhism.

6

The Path of Instructions

Mahamudra Vipashyana

WHILE IN THE PATH STAGE, we are trying to internalize the view of Mahamudra that we have ascertained by studying the ground and to bring that view into the reality of the path and our experience. As described earlier, there are three basic ways of entering path Mahamudra: the preliminary practices, the pointing-out instructions, and the enhancement practices. Following our discussion of Mahamudra shamatha, we will now examine the three pointing-out instructions and methods of practice in relation to Mahamudra vipashyana.

VIPASHYANA POINTING-OUT

From the Mahamudra point of view, the term "vipashyana" relates to the insight that directly realizes the nature of ordinary mind. Additionally, it refers to meditations that are applications of prajna, which are practiced after we have cultivated some degree of meditative stability through the practice of shamatha. In Tibetan, the word for "vipashyana" is *lhagthong*. The first syllable, *lhag,* means "superior." It is the same term that we find used in "superior training," a term that is common to many Buddhist traditions. *Thong* means "seeing" or "sight." Therefore, *lhagthong* means "superior seeing" or "superior sight."

The term *vipashyana* is often misunderstood in western Buddhist communities because it is used differently in different meditation traditions. Theravada, Mahayana, and Vajrayana Buddhists, as well as some Hindu schools, all speak of "vipashyana meditation." Even among the various Buddhist schools it is used to mean somewhat different things. However, in the Mahamudra context, vipashyana is connected with the superior realization or experience of the basic nature of mind. Any other understanding of vipashyana is irrelevant to the subject of Mahamudra. Thus, the realization of this ordinary mind is what we call "superior sight" or "superior insight."

The term "ordinary mind" can be confusing if we understand "ordinary" to mean "mundane." If that were the case, then "ordinary mind" would mean mundane consciousness, confused mind, klesha mind—a mind that is totally caught up in this world of samsara. However, in this context, "ordinary" means "unfabricated." When we experience this ordinary mind, we experience buddha mind. Buddha mind is not some special mind that we always seem to be searching for elsewhere. It is simple and ordinary in the sense of being totally free from elaborations, from fabrications, and from all conceptual thinking. It is the best part of mind. Usually, we think of buddha mind as something extraordinary, extra-special, but at this point, we cut through all of these concepts and go back to the fundamental nature of mind, which is the mind of buddha, or the heart of buddha mind. It is ordinary because it is so simple.

Great yogis, such as Milarepa and Gampopa, have said that most people do not or cannot believe this because it seems so ordinary and so natural. Instead, we are searching for something very elaborate, perhaps something like a Tibetan shrine. However, the nature of our mind is not that elaborate or complex. The term "ordinary" itself conveys this sense of naturalness and simplicity. When we say that the nature of our mind is ordinary and basic, this suggests that it is not something that exists outside of us. On the other hand, when we say that the nature of mind is extraordinary or special, this makes us feel that mind's nature is something external. When we realize the fundamental nature and very simplicity of our mind, we realize ordinary mind.

COEMERGENT MIND: THE DHARMAKAYA

Generally speaking, the practice of vipashyana begins with the pointing-out instructions. There are a number of ways to present this; however, we will look at instruction on Mahamudra vipashyana through the following three stages:

1. Showing the essence of the nature of mind
2. Developing certainty in the nature of mind
3. Receiving the instructions pointing out the true nature of mind

During all of these stages of meditation, we simply rest the mind in a state of freshness. That is the basic characteristic or nature of insight. We are resting in a state of mind that is fresh and without any distractions. We are resting naturally and expansively, in complete comfort, so to speak. We are not trying to generate something fresh or some natural or expansive state. We are simply resting and there is a sense of natural comfort. In contrast, if we are trying to do something, if we are trying to make our meditation natural or fresh, then there is a feeling of tension. There is no sense of comfort or of freely resting. Therefore, in all of our meditation, we should rest naturally and expansively, in such a way that our mind is self-illuminating or self-clear. We are not relying on generating a light from outside. We are not relying on "making" our mind luminous. It is naturally in that state of luminosity and clarity. It is through these methods that we receive the pointing-out instruction that coemergent mind itself is the dharmakaya.

COEMERGENT THOUGHT: THE DISPLAY OF DHARMAKAYA

Through the Mahamudra meditation methods, we are introduced to a progressive path of instructions. Whereas the first instruction points out the nature of mind itself as being the nature of the dharmakaya, the second instruction points out that thoughts themselves are the display of dharmakaya. There is a direct transmission that points out the nature of mind through stillness and through movement. We train by practicing in both situations: the mind at rest and thoughts in motion. It is here that the vipashyana, or insight, aspect of Mahamudra becomes of foremost importance. We also work with the method of cutting the root of ego-clinging.

The first method is the development of stillness, which means resting in the state of nondistraction. In the Mahamudra tradition, nondistraction is known as meditation. When we define meditation as nondistraction, we can see the difference between the quality of ordinary Hinayana-Mahayana shamatha and vipashyana meditation and the quality of Mahamudra meditation. From the Mahamudra point of view, if we are undistracted, then it does not matter whether our mind is still following our breath or whether it is in a state of conceptual thought or is producing emotions. If our mind is undistracted, then we are in the "gap" experience of meditation.

The second method involves working with mind's movement. We practice with the full occurrence of thoughts, as well as with the undercurrent of thoughts and thought-chasing thoughts.

The third method is the process of cutting the root of ego-clinging. It is cutting the root of ego self-centeredness through a combination of the direct pointing-out experiences, the direct blessings of the lineage and the guru, and our meditation. At this point, cutting the root of ego-clinging is not very difficult because we are not working alone. We are working with the blessings of the guru and the lineage.

The primary practices are the methods for coming to recognize or apprehend the clarity aspect of the mind. When we have accomplished a state of stillness through the practices of Mahamudra shamatha, then, within that stillness, a thought will arise. When that thought arises, we apply the second practice of vipashyana, which is to look directly at the nature of that thought. If we recognize the nature of that thought—or the nature of mind—directly, then insight, or vipashyana, will arise.

Practically speaking, this means that when we are resting, relaxed in a state of tranquillity, we will need a thought to arise in order to practice this. Either a thought will arise naturally, or we should intentionally generate a thought. It could be any kind of thought, such as a thought of aversion or attachment. Once the thought has arisen, we look directly at its nature and try to see if there is any difference between our awareness within a state of stillness and our awareness within a state of the occurrence of thought. This scrutiny of a thought does not last very long because the scrutiny itself will cause the thought to return to a state of meditation.

Our mind is like the ocean, and the occurrence of thoughts is like the movement of waves on the surface of the ocean. The state of shamatha, or tranquillity, that we cultivate is similar to the depths of the ocean, where there is no motion. Therefore, just as waves are an ornament of the ocean, when a practitioner of Mahamudra can meditate within the arising of a thought, the thoughts and kleshas become an ornament of their practice. In fact, an ocean without waves is quite dull and boring, and waves make an ocean all the more beautiful. However, if we cannot meditate using the arising of a thought, then the waves of thought become dangerous. We might dive into them and drown.

Just as waves arise from and return to the ocean, the thoughts that arise in our mind arise from the mind itself and dissolve back into the mind itself. Even while waves are present, they are nothing other than the contour of the water that makes up the ocean and therefore are nothing other than the ocean itself. In the same way, the thoughts that arise in the mind are nothing other than that mind itself—the coemergent dharmakaya. The nature of these thoughts is no different from the nature of mind itself.

There are two aspects to the occurrence of thought, known as the full occurrence and the undercurrent. A full occurrence of thought is a fully manifested thought. It is a coarse or obvious thought that is easily apprehended. The undercurrent refers to the movement of subtle thought that is very difficult to apprehend because, once apprehended, it has usually disappeared. Both the full occurrence and the undercurrent of thought need to be closely observed.

A part of this process of examination involves the scrutiny of our thoughts of "I" and "mine." Scrutiny means pursuing our analysis, trying to find out if this "I" and these instances of "mine" actually exist. Through the direct, experiential scrutiny of thought, we come to determine that this imputed "I" and this imputed "mine"—that which pertains to the imputed "I"—have never existed. We determine that mind in its nature has never been an "I" or a self and therefore has never possessed anything that can be claimed as "mine." In this way, thoughts come to mix with the dharmakaya. This means we recognize that from the beginning, the nature of mind and the nature of thoughts has been the coemergent dharmakaya. There has never been a self; there has never been something called "mine."

COEMERGENT APPEARANCE: THE LIGHT OF DHARMAKAYA

The third instruction is the pointing-out that appearances are the light of the mind and in that sense are also coemergent. They are coemergent in the sense that they are the display or projection of the mind. Therefore, they are called the light of the dharmakaya, the idea being that appearances are the gleam or glow of the mind. The instruction involves a two-step process of working with the recognition of unfabricated mind.

The first step of this process is to understand the self-display or self-manifestation of the unfabricated nature of mind, which is to say ordinary mind. We recognize the appearances that arise from unaltered or unfabricated mind. This is called the "self-appearance" or "individual appearance," which is a pure appearance.

The second step of the process is to recognize the appearances of confusion that arise from grasping mind.

While we experience both the pure and the impure or confused aspects of these so-called outer appearances, there are some differences between the two. In working with these two aspects of appearance, the principal practice is to scrutinize appearances so that we correctly distinguish between the self-appearance of an uncontrived or unaltered natural cognition and the confused appearances or bewildered projections of a fixated cognition. By means of this scrutiny, we come to recognize that all appearances are the natural play of dharmata. This practice involves meditating upon appearances by directing our awareness to those appearances without fixating on them. This enables us to recognize the nature of appearances as the gleam or glow of the mind.

The specific methods for this technique are given when we receive detailed Mahamudra instruction. At that point, we do not limit our practice to working with conceptual cognition, such as occurs in the arising of thoughts. We also work with the nonconceptual or direct cognition of appearances themselves.[1]

Essentially, with this practice, we use a sequential application of this technique to look at the appearances that arise for each of the sense consciousnesses. We begin by looking directly at the forms that are experienced by the visual consciousness, then at sounds as experienced by the auditory consciousness, then at smells as experienced by the olfactory consciousness, and so on.

Although our sense consciousness is directed toward its object—visual form and so forth—we are not looking outward. We are looking inward at the experience of that sense consciousness itself. Perhaps even the word "looking" is misleading, since it implies some kind of outwardly directed attention. Our attention is actually directed at the mind's experience of a form, sound, smell, and so forth. We are looking or gazing inward, with the condition of an unblocked or unimpeded sense consciousness. However, what we are essentially doing at this stage of the practice is learning to recognize the self-appearance of an unfabricated cognition and thereby dispel the confused projections of a fixated cognition.[2]

WORKING WITH THE POINTING-OUT INSTRUCTIONS

Pure and Impure Appearances

In order to make a genuine Mahamudra journey, we must commit ourselves to going through the earlier stages of the pointing-out instructions and the preliminary practices. If we travel on this path diligently and wisely, then we will see the self-expression or self-manifestation of mind, which is an experience of pure appearance. This introduces us to the notion of pure vision. We might say that "the sacred business," the sacred vision of the Vajrayana world, slips into the picture. We see outer appearance as nothing but a manifestation or expression of this ultimate mind—that is, of emptiness, egolessness. Thus, this expression should be an egoless expression; this manifestation should be a selfless manifestation.

Although these pure appearances do manifest in certain forms, they are nevertheless selfless. When we experience this selfless expression, there is a great sense of spaciousness, unity, and totality. In contrast, if we are not familiar with or successful on the path of meditation and the spiritual journey, then we are stuck with the second aspect of appearance, which is confusion—the manifestation of grasping mind. That expression is an egoistic manifestation; it is a narrow, claustrophobic experience. There is no sense of space because we are clinging to an experience, trying to freeze it and make it permanent. That experience is what we call the experience of mundane consciousness, samsaric consciousness, or samsaric mind—which is right here.

The third pointing-out instruction—appearances are the light of the mind and in that sense are also coemergent—refers to these two very subtle ways of working with appearances.

Working with Mind's Clarity

Previously, we described the nature of mind as the unborn dharmakaya; the display of the creative energy of mind as the nonabiding sambhogakaya; and the light of mind, or mind's radiant appearances, as the unimpeded nirmanakaya or the nirmanakaya that can appear as anything. To understand what this means, we can contemplate the analogy of a crystal and the displays of rainbows that are produced from it. A rainbow that emerges from a crystal is not simply one thing. It is a sort of fluctuating variety. In the same way, thought is not unitary, nor does it remain. Even as a thought is arising, it is already passing out of existence. In fact, thought by itself, as the display of mind, exemplifies the qualities of being without birth, without abiding, and without cessation. Therefore, we would have to say that all three aspects of mind—its nature, its display, and its light—perfectly contain the qualities of the three kayas.

That is the whole point in Mahamudra—it is so profound because just one, simple thought is in the nature of the three kayas. We do not have to say, "Okay, this is dharmakaya, so now where is the sambhogakaya? Okay, we have found the sambhogakaya, so now where is the nirmanakaya?" In the general Mahayana presentation, such a reality seems so distant, whereas in the Mahamudra or Dzogchen approach, all three kayas are present in one simple thought. The nature of that thought is the dharmakaya. The luminosity or the vividness of that thought is the sambhogakaya. The continuity of that vividness is the nirmanakaya.

There is a constant creative energy to the mind, which is the basis for the arising of mind's radiant appearances—just as the sunlight that reflects through a crystal and creates a prismatic display is always there. Sometimes we actually can experience this cognitive lucidity in a direct way, rather than in what we would normally consider a cognitive way. For example, you may hear a continuous undercurrent of sound, a humming sound, which is called the sound of dharmata.

In the Mahamudra teachings, not much detail is given about what is meant by this lucidity or clarity. It is simply said that there is a clarity or lucidity to the mind, which is extremely intense and becomes the basis for confusion. More detail is given in the Dzogchen presentation, in which this clarity is referred to as the appearances of the ground or the display of the ground. In the Dzogchen presentation, the way in which this clarity arises or develops is divided into what are called the eight gates of the appearances of spontaneous presence. Dzogchen texts also give a more detailed presentation of exactly how this clarity becomes so intense. Nevertheless, from a Mahamudra point of view, the basic idea is that when we look at our mind's nature, we will perceive an extremely intense cognitive clarity. It has been said by many teachers that we need to look again and again at this cognitive clarity in our practice. While the emptiness of mind is important, there is a sense in which the cognitive clarity is more important as a basis for practice. This is so because confusion begins when we fail to recognize this clarity for what it is. Therefore, in order to break the chain of confusion, we need to work with the cognitive clarity in particular.

The precise method by which we look at the cognitive clarity of mind is a topic within the context of path Mahamudra. Nevertheless, among the practices of path Mahamudra are two techniques that are particularly helpful for working with the cognitive clarity of mind. One is looking at the mind within appearances, and the other is looking at the mind within the movement or arising of thought. These are important because both the mind experiencing appearances and the mind experiencing thought are situations in which the cognitive clarity of the mind is evident and therefore easily apprehended. For example, when a klesha arises in our mind, there is a greater intensity to the cognitive clarity. In that situation, if we look at the klesha, then we will be looking right at the cognitive clarity. In this case, "looking at" means looking at the klesha or appearance nakedly or directly—without any kind of conceptual overlay or analysis based on discursive thought. We can do this not only when we are looking at kleshas and other thoughts, but also when we are looking at the experience of appearances. For example, if the six senses are directed at external objects, then we look directly at the experience of that object. We do not "think about" or discursively analyze the experience; rather, we look directly at the experience itself.

These two methods, looking at the mind within appearances and looking at the mind within thought or the movement of thought, are methods for working with the cognitive clarity.

If we do this effectively, if we look at this clarity with clarity, then we may be able to actually see the development of the split between the apprehending subject and the apprehended object. This recognition is very significant because, from a Mahamudra point of view, the split is something that is always developing in the present and not something that developed at some point in the past. While we are not par-

ticularly trying to look for this split, it will sometimes appear naturally. What we are doing with our practice is looking directly at the cognitive clarity itself. We are not splitting up the clarity; we are not
trying to divide it into a subject and an object. Paradoxically, it is
because we are not dividing it that we will see the division.

The cognitive lucidity that is spoken of in the Mahamudra context
is the same thing as wisdom, or primordial awareness. If we can rest
without fabrication in the experience and recognition of the mind's natural cognitive lucidity, then the display of wisdom will arise within that.
This is the very reason that in the Mantrayana in general, and in
Mahamudra and Dzogchen in particular, emphasis is placed on the lucidity aspect of mind more than on the emptiness aspect. In the Vajrayana, we practice the visualization of deities, which is really a way of
cultivating or familiarizing ourselves with this cognitive lucidity. In Mahamudra, emphasis is placed on the practice of looking at the mind
within the occurrence of thought and within appearances. In Dzogchen,
we cultivate the practice of *thogal,* or "leap-over." However, all of these
practices work with the cognitive lucidity aspect of the mind.

Morning Mist and Space

When we work with these teachings, we are working primarily
to gain a sense of confidence—in ourselves, in the teachings, and in the
teacher—so that we can click our mind into the gap experience. This
experience is not newly produced. It is not produced by any teacher,
any buddha, or any power of our own. The gap experience exists in the
nature of our mind at all times. That is why, in one of his songs,
Milarepa said that between all moments of discursive thought there are
gaps of nondual wisdom. Between one moment of thought and the
next, there is always a gap experience; it is happening all the time. In
our practice, we are trying to "space out" within this gap with a full
sense of clarity. That is what vipashyana is all about: clicking into this
experience.

Out of our shamatha and vipashyana meditation, we produce experience. That is what we should look for. That is our goal. We should not

look at the amount of time we sit. Sitting for longer and longer periods is not our objective. We should not be concerned with the amount of time we sit nor with the type of feedback we get from people who may say, "You have been sitting really well. You are a great meditator" or "You are a great meditation instructor." That does not mean anything. We should be very clear about why we are sitting and what we are we look- ing for. What we are looking for on this path is experience, which is the product of our meditation and inner development.

When we sit properly, various states of experience naturally arise through our practice of shamatha and vipashyana meditation. When we practice meditation, the criterion for determining whether it has been a good or bad practice session is whether we are really doing it— whether we are really sitting in order to meditate or for other reasons, of which we may not even be conscious. Why are we sitting? We may be sitting to pass time, or we may be sitting because we think, "I have to sit one hour every day because my teacher told me to." That type of sitting is very good and it will help us to accumulate merit, but it will not produce the desired states of experience. Therefore, we will not fulfill our fundamental desire, which is our wish to free ourselves and all other sentient beings. When we sit, we should sit with a sense of absolute clarity about our motivation. If our goals and reasons for sitting are very clear, then our meditation will be clear; and if our med- itation becomes clear, then the various experiences will arise.

Nevertheless, working with these experiences is very tricky. They may appear as very pleasing experiences, such as bliss, clarity, and emptiness, or nonthought. These three experiences and countless oth- ers can be produced through meditation. However, we must avoid becoming trapped in these experiences. The great yogi Milarepa said that these experiences are like the morning mist. What does this mean? It means that when the sun comes out, the mist will disappear. Before the sun comes out, the morning mist looks very thick and we think, "Oh, it is going to be cloudy all day"; but when the sun rises, the mist slowly disappears.

Milarepa said that these mistlike experiences are not the ultimate goal of our meditation because as soon as we think that we have gained something, it will disappear. It is often said that when we need these experiences, they will not be there. It is when we really feel depressed and lost and we think, "Now I need the experiences of bliss, clarity, and nonthought," that we will not have them. They are gone, just like the morning mist. Therefore, what is the point of clinging to these experiences? There is no point.

The real project of meditation is realization—the direct realization of ordinary mind. Milarepa said that realization is like space, which rests in the state of the unchanging nature. That space never changes; therefore, realizations never change. Our realization is the ultimate achievement of our experience and meditation practice.

Inviting Awakening

These three pointing-out instructions are the skillful means that we use to try to wake ourselves up from this sleepy, dreamy state of samsaric mind. At this point, the Mahamudra instructions are not suggesting that we use an alarm clock to wake ourselves up. They are suggesting that we use a bucket of water. However, in order to do this we need to rely on a friend who is already awake.

When traveling on this path of Mahamudra, through the different stages of profound instructions, methods, and paths of meditation, we must understand that our journey is a mutual effort of the student and the guru. As students, we must exert a certain amount of effort in order to wake ourselves up and to let our spiritual friend wake us up. We must exert a certain amount of effort in order to develop a sense of trust and spaciousness and a willingness to surrender our own ego. We do this by giving our spiritual friend the key to our apartment. Then there is the effort of the guru, who takes the steps of coming into our apartment, opening the door with the key that we have provided, and carrying in a bucket of water in the early morning.

While we are asleep and dreaming, our trusted spiritual friend comes and tries to wake us up by pouring the bucket of water onto our beautiful, samsaric bed and into our samsaric dream. Consequently, we wake up with a certain sense of shock. At the same time, we totally wake up. This method does not give us a chance to play around by pressing the snooze button on the alarm clock. We cannot say, "I was just kidding." Whether we like it or not, and whether it worked fully or not, the water is already there, in our bed and on us. We are already awake, and we cannot go back to sleep in that state. Our samsaric bed is no longer snuggly, and so we are left with no choice but to get up and take a hot shower. This is not the same as relying on an alarm clock to wake up. When we use that method, we can still go back to our snuggly sleep because the bed is still warm and we think, "Ooh, I can sleep five or ten minutes more." So we press the snooze button.

Before we can make use of the bucket of water method for waking ourselves up, we must trust our friend. We must trust that he will not use something, such as a knife, that will kill us as it wakes us up. That is one way of waking up, but it is a very difficult one. We must trust fully in our companion, who is awake and with whom we have a mutual under-standing. Such a spiritual friend will know the right time and will say, "Yes, it is four o'clock in the morning now, time for you to get up." Then he will throw the bucket of water. However, it can happen only when we have opened ourselves fully and can say, "Please wake me up. I would ap-preciate being awakened by any method at all as long as I totally wake up." It cannot happen in any other way. The teacher does not kidnap us and wake us up every morning with a bucket of water; we are not hostages. We have total freedom. We express our full confidence and trust by removing any barriers. We give our friend the key to our apart-ment because otherwise, how can our guru get into our room to pour the bucket of water? However, the moment of handing over the key is determined entirely by our readiness.

Waking up does not have different stages. Waking up is waking up. The problem is that after we wake up, we go back to sleep. That is our habitual problem. There is no problem with waking up. Once the teacher has done the job of waking us up, then it is up to us to stay awake. Do we want to get up from that bed, take a shower, and walk into the world with its fresh scent of morning air? Or do we want to get up, wipe our body with a dirty samsaric towel, and go lie down on a sofa or some other snuggly place where we can go back to sleep? If we are really lazy, we might even fall back asleep while we are still totally wet.

There is an unfinished dream that we want to continue, so we go back to sleep to dream again. We see no alternative to falling asleep in order to finish the whole story of our dream. It is like seeing one half of a very exciting movie on TV and then being disturbed by a phone call from our friend. Throughout the phone conversation, our mind keeps going back to the movie because we want to watch it through to the ending. That is the kind of thing that is happening here. We feel a strong urge to return to our samsaric dream, which seems so interesting. The strength of that urge pulls us back. Thus, it is our habitual pattern to fall back asleep. Diligence, which is one of the qualities of a precious human birth, becomes very important. We must make an effort to remain awake.

Waking up begins with the pointing-out instructions and continues up to the ultimate level. It is the same process, the same technique, and the same state of waking up. The waking-up process is the heart of the Mahamudra teachings. It is a process that is accomplished through the vipashyana meditation practices and through all of the pointing-out methods. However, determining the most effective methods of waking up is a very individual matter. We cannot generalize. The teacher might appear with a flip-flop sandal, with a bucket of water, or with any number of surprising methods to wake us up, as we can see from the history of these teachings.

We can look, for example, at the relationship of Tilopa and Naropa. Naropa received pointing-out instruction—on and off, on and off, on and off—for many years from Tilopa. Finally, Tilopa said, "You still do not get it, my son!" He took off his flip-flop and whacked Naropa on his forehead. Tilopa was a fisherman on the Ganges in India, so you can imagine how dirty his flip-flop probably was. The whole scenario must have been quite crazy. In any case, at this moment, when Tilopa took off his flip-flop and gave Naropa a really good hit on his forehead, Naropa got it. At that point, there was no longer a need for words or for any explanation. Naropa did not have any more questions. For example, he did not say, "How did you do that?" He did not question why Tilopa used his sandal instead of a golden vase, which would have looked much more sacred. It is difficult for us to imagine Mahamudra instruction being given with an Indian sandal; nevertheless, that is how the pointing-out instructions work.

From this story, we can also see that pointing-out instructions are repeated again and again. However, it is recommended that students do not receive them too often—for example, every month or every year. That does not work because the experience loses its quality of freshness. We can become jaded by pointing-out instructions, and at that point nothing will help us. In the Dharma of the Practice Lineage, we have a saying: "If your mind is distracted by ordinary, mundane disturbances, that is very easy to work out through the Dharma, the path, and with meditation. But if your mind is jaded by the Dharma, then there is no antidote." That is a very dangerous situation and the reason there is so much emphasis on avoiding spiritual materialism.

The Mahamudra path is a very individual path, and the connection to the teacher is a very individual connection. Whether or not we want to be woken up with a bucket of water, we must trust in the awakened person. That trust is our devotion. Whether or not we have that trust is what determines whether our friend will take the initiative to wake us up. The bucket of water does not come at the beginning of our relationship with our friend. It comes only after teacher and student have developed a sense of confidence in each other, and only after we have given away our key. The Mahamudra path is a very profound journey that is based on our individual connection to the spiritual friend, the method, and our prajna related to the teachings. Accordingly, the instructions that point out mind's nature must be received from one's own teachers. What they are pointing out is the ordinary mind, and how they will point that out—you will see.

Our spiritual journey is a mutual effort. We cannot say that it is only the guru's job, even if we have handed over our key and the guru has used it to transmit a certain method of awakening. We must put effort into awakening our own enlightened heart that has been within our own mind from beginningless time. Ultimately, enlightenment is not something new that we gain through the teacher, through the path, or through any outer wisdom. It is something we discover within our own hearts.

7

The Path to Enlightenment

The Four Yogas of Mahamudra

THE YOGA OF MAHAMUDRA develops through four
stages that are known as the four yogas: the yoga of one-
pointedness, the yoga of nonfabrication, the yoga of one taste, and the
yoga of nonmeditation. Each level is both the fruition of the preceding
level and the path to the next one. These stages reflect an increasing
recognition of the three-kaya nature of our mind. The state of nonmeditation is the final achievement of this realization. At that point, all
of our obscurations, all of our emotions and ego-clinging become part
of the experience of enlightenment. There is nothing to be discarded.

ONE-POINTEDNESS

The first stage of traveling on this path of enlightenment through
the four yogas is called the yoga of one-pointedness. This yoga is our
first recognition of ordinary mind. It is the "first click" of genuine
awakening. We can compare it to the very first time we were woken up
in the morning by a bucket of cold water. There is tremendous power
and energy in this form of awakening. It is very different from hearing
the buzzing of our alarm clock. There is a greater sense of bravery,
courage, and certainty when we use the bucket-of-water method.
When we use an alarm clock to wake up, there is a sense of weakness
and trembling; even the sound of the alarm is a shivering sound. Ego

feels that it has the full power to reject the call of the alarm clock by simply pressing the snooze button with one tiny finger and going back to sleep.

At this first stage of recognition of ordinary mind, our focus is one-pointedly directed toward the awakened state. We are fully concentrated on the process of awakening. At this point, we begin to experience various positive states of meditation. These are generally called bliss, clarity, and nonthought. They are not continual experiences, but they do arise from time to time in our meditation. At the stage of one-pointedness, we also develop a sense of power in our meditation. We can go straight into one-pointed meditation at any time without becoming distracted by any outer disturbances.

NONFABRICATION

The second stage of the four yogas is called nonfabrication, or simplicity, which refers to the experience of completely cutting through ego-clinging. It implies a complete understanding and experience of certain stages of egolessness, selflessness, emptiness, or shunyata. At this level, our mind is not being fabricated by any trace of ego-clinging or conceptual clinging. Consequently, we actually see the nature of mind as emptiness, the nature of ego as egolessness, and the nature of self as selflessness. This is the view extensively taught by teachers such as Nagarjuna, and this yoga relies on an understanding and study of Nagarjuna's lineage. Therefore, in order to gain such experiences, we must understand the view of Mahamudra, which is the view of Nagarjuna.

Generally, we regard "appearance" as one thing and "emptiness" as another. On the one hand, we think that there are such things as forms. For example, we think that there are solid tables and solid chairs. We think that the ground is solid ground and that there are solid people to whom we are talking. On the other hand, we talk about emptiness and we vaguely think, "This emptiness is the nature of these forms." We think of this "nature" as something that exists behind these forms. When we think in this way, we create a distinction between the form and its emptiness. At this stage, however, we cut through the state of conceptuality that distinguishes between appearance and emptiness.

The *Heart Sutra* is well-known for its presentation of fourfold emptiness. This sutra states, "Form is emptiness, emptiness is form. Form is no other than emptiness, and emptiness is no other than form." The fourfold emptiness actually communicates a genuine sense of emptiness as the real nature of outer appearances, rather than emptiness as something else called "a nature." Thus, form and emptiness are not separable. Form cannot be separated from emptiness, and emptiness cannot be separated from form.

This is what is realized at the stage of the yoga of nonfabrication: We gain a direct experience of the union of appearance and emptiness. We arrive at the realization that we cannot separate the two. One aspect expresses the quality of emptiness and the other expresses the quality of form or appearance.

ONE TASTE

The yoga of one taste refers to the experience of appearance and mind. At this stage, there is no difference between outer appearances and the inner consciousness that perceives these forms. There is a sense of penetrating the depths of duality, transforming it, and seeing the nondual nature of our minds. That is called "one taste." There is not one taste for whatever is designated as an "object" and a different taste for whatever is designated as a "subject." There is not one taste for something called "appearance" and a different taste for something called "emptiness." The experience of one taste is like eating a giant Snickers bar. No matter which side you bite into, the taste is the same. In the same way, whether you meditate from the side of emptiness or the side of appearance, from the side of the subject or the side of the object, there is no difference in taste. There is only one nature and you experience that genuine nature.

This is very basic Buddhist philosophy, which is explained by the great Indian master Aryadeva of the Madhyamaka, or Middle Way, school. From this point of view, there is no difference between the emptiness of a cup and the emptiness of a table. There is only one emptiness. We cannot say, "This is the emptiness of my mind and not the emptiness of your mind" or "This is my ordinary mind and not your ordinary mind." At the fundamental level of ordinary mind, the basic level of emptiness, there is no difference. If we truly realize that everything has one taste, then there is no difference in the realization of the nature of emptiness for any phenomenon. When we realize the emptiness of a cup, we realize the emptiness of the whole universe. That is the logical argument presented by Aryadeva. Once we have realized the emptiness of self, we realize the emptiness of all phenomena. There is one taste because there is only one emptiness, one reality—one absolute truth.

Because there is only one taste in the ultimate sense, different practices or paths will not result in different tastes. We will not find ourselves saying, "When I practice Mahamudra, I experience emptiness in this way. When I meditate on Madhyamaka, I experience emptiness in that way. When I meditate on Dzogchen, I experience emptiness in another way." No such distinctions can be made because the ultimate reality of the phenomenal world is simply one reality. The nature of ordinary mind is only one fundamental nature. Therefore, no matter which path we undertake, if we reach the level of the realization of one taste, then we will experience sameness, which is actual reality. In the Mahamudra lineage, it is often taught that Madhyamaka, Mahamudra, and Dzogchen are absolutely one. This is sometimes expressed by saying that Madhyamaka is the ground, Mahamudra is the path, and Dzogchen is the fruition. Since achieving the result or fruition is actually the experience of the ground, there is no difference among these traditions. Thus, the yoga of one taste refers to the one taste of the nature of ordinary mind and the nature of the phenomenal world.

NONMEDITATION

The fourth yoga is called the yoga of nonmeditation, or no more learning, which is the state of complete exhaustion of our samsaric garbage. It has all been recycled and totally processed. Furthermore, because there is no garbage left, there is also no sense of purity left. These two notions of "garbage" and "purity" are completely dependent upon each other. When we perceive something as pure, there must be something else that we are calling "impure"; and when we perceive something as impure, there must be something else that we are labeling "pure." Therefore, neither of these two states actually exists. At this stage, all such notions have been totally processed and exhausted.

This is the point at which we realize or actualize the state of dharmakaya rather than merely thinking about it or meditating upon it. We go beyond all such thoughts, beyond all our struggle and effort, and we reach the point where no more effort is necessary. We realize the nature of ordinary mind and the nature of dharmata or the phenomenal world. This is the stage of buddhahood, in which all of the habitual tendencies and samsaric emotional patterns of our life are exhausted.

Here, we are reaching the resultant aspect, or fruition, of Mahamudra. Our journey began with developing the view of ground Mahamudra, which is seeing our mind and the fundamental nature of samsara as existing in the nature of the three kayas. At this point, we are reaching back to that level of ground. We are actualizing the nature of the three kayas and discovering them within our very own mind— this mind of our confused samsaric being.

The yogi Milarepa said, "If you are searching for something called enlightenment outside your own mind, you are like the great wrestler who searched the countryside for a precious family jewel." Milarepa's example tells the story of a particular son in an Indian wrestling family who became one of the greatest known wrestlers in that century. According to the traditional custom, he had inherited a precious stone from his father. When he was about to begin his career as a wrestler, he tied this precious jewel in his hair, as was customary. During one wrestling match, he received a large cut on his forehead. At that time, most people were very afraid of being cut, and so they would apply some medicine to the outer surface to help it heal, but they rarely probed such wounds more deeply.

At the conclusion of this match, the wrestler realized that he had lost the precious jewel that was his family's emblem. He searched everywhere for it, going all over the stage and the wrestling grounds. He could not find it, although he continued to search for months and years. Finally, he went to consult a wise Brahmin. Today we might regard such a person as a psychiatrist, but at that time the role was filled by those who were considered "wise men." The wrestler went to this wise Brahmin to ask for advice about how to cope with losing the jewel, as well as to seek advice about how to regain it. The wise Brahmin listened closely as the wrestler told his story. Then the Brahmin asked, "Did you have that bump on your forehead before you became a wrestler?" The wrestler touched his forehead and said, "No, not really. I got this cut on my head when I was wrestling." The Brahmin said, "Ah, your jewel fell into the cut. It is still there."

All of the time that the wrestler had spent searching for his jewel was wasted because the jewel had always been within him—a part of his own physical being. Milarepa said that, in a similar way, we search for our enlightenment, which we lost, recently or long ago, in our wrestling match with our ego. It is as though we have a similar wound, which has grown over a precious jewel.

Achieving this level of fruition Mahamudra simply means that we recover our lost jewel; we rediscover the buddha heart that is always within our own mind. There is nothing beyond that. Enlightenment is not and never has been outside our mind. Therefore, to come back to that actual state is what we call the fruition stage, which we likely see as something that will happen in the future. We think that we are taking this journey so that we will arrive at some result in the future, so that we will someday arrive at a destination called buddhahood. However, we are actually going "back to the future" because the state of buddhahood has always been the nature of our mind. It is like the ground, which has always been there. We are trying to go back to that basic buddha mind, which exists in the state of the three kayas. The complete realization of our mind as the three buddha kayas is what we call the fruition stage of Mahamudra.

8

Fruition Mahamudra

The Three Kayas

F RUITION MAHAMUDRA is the point at which we finally discover the true nature of our mind. It is the perfection of the path of simplicity, the point at which we have totally completed the Mahamudra journey, which has taken us through all the stages and experiences of our shamatha and vipashyana meditation. We have finally uncovered all our obscurations and defilements through these practices. When we finally realize the true nature of mind without any barriers, when it becomes direct experience rather than conceptual understanding, we immediately achieve buddhahood—in this very lifetime. Beyond any doubt, it is possible for anyone following the path of Mahamudra to achieve enlightenment in this very lifetime. In the Kagyu lineage, the achievement of this stage is known as the state of Vajradhara, or the state of nonmeditation.

It is in this state that we experience the nature of the three kayas within our basic consciousness. As discussed previously, the three kayas—the dharmakaya, sambhogakaya, and nirmanakaya—are the three inseparable aspects of the enlightened nature of mind. At this point, we are clear that this nature exists within our mind now. It is not just a theory, a myth, or an abstract idea. It is truly present in this very moment.

TRANSCENDING REFERENCE POINTS

Although the three-kaya nature of mind is present within the minds of all sentient beings right now, we fail to see it because it is obscured, covered by ignorance and ignorant conceptualizations. When we free ourselves from our samsaric bondage, we are freeing ourselves from two aspects known as the two defilements, or the two obscurations. These are the klesha defilements and the knowledge defilements, which are obscurations to our liberation from samsara. Klesha defilements are our disturbing or afflictive emotions—wild and unattended emotions. Knowledge defilements are subtle ego-cling-ings—our subtle sense of there being a reference point. Regardless of the kind of klesha activity in which we may be engaged, there is always this basic sense of reference point. Whether the emotions are attended or unattended by mindfulness and awareness, there is a fundamental, subtle feeling or experience of reference point. This sense of a refer-ence point is the knowledge defilement, and this defilement is the basis upon which the whole castle of klesha defilements is built.

If we simply cut through this fundamental reference point, which can be compared to cutting through the pillars of an elevated house, then the whole castle of klesha defilements will collapse automatically and naturally. Once we are completely free from these two defile-ments, we have reached the final, resultant stage of enlightenment. The process of transcending or cutting through these two defilements takes place on the level of path Mahamudra.

THE WISDOM OF THE BUDDHA

The three kayas of the fruition stage are called the essence, the nature, and the display of mind. All three refer to the mind itself: The empty essence of our mind is the dharmakaya buddha. The luminous nature of our mind is the sambhogakaya buddha. The unimpeded dis-play of our mind is the nirmanakaya buddha. The three kayas are always within our heart, always within our mind. When we reach back to the original state of ground Mahamudra, completely and fully recognizing it, this is what we call fruition.

Our basic state of mind possesses the two wisdoms of Buddha: the wisdom of seeing things as they are, which refers to the dharmakaya wisdom, and the wisdom of seeing the extent of things, which refers to the relative world. When we look at these two aspects, we can see that this "wisdom" encompasses not only the complete understanding of duality, the subject-object relationship of the relative world, but also the complete understanding of suchness, of *tathata,* "thatness." Thus, wisdom applies to both ultimate and relative dimensions. For example, when we speak of wisdom in regard to the emotions, we are speaking of the "wisdom of seeing the extent of things" because the emotions have so much character and so much color. When we recognize the nature of the emotions, they become the ornaments of enlightenment.

Our mind possesses these two wisdom-energy aspects of buddhahood right from the beginning. Returning to that basic state is the attainment of buddhahood, which is actually present in three states: the essence, the nature, and the display.

The Dharmakaya

The dharmakaya is the empty essence of our mind; it is the wisdom of seeing suchness. That essence is the essence of egolessness, or the selfless nature of our mind. The basic state of dharmakaya is the nature of all phenomena, beyond all speech, thought, and expression. This suchness is not created or conceptualized by anything; it is, rather, the basic state, which we call dharmakaya buddhahood. Dharmakaya may be translated as "body of truth" or "body of reality." It is the basic ground of emptiness from which all phenomena arise.

The Sambhogakaya

Dharmakaya buddhahood is not simply blank, empty, or colorless. It has a tremendous energy and power of manifestation, which we call clarity or luminosity. The luminous nature of mind is the sambhogakaya. When this energy manifests further, beyond the simple expression of clarity, it appears in the form of a sambhogakaya buddha, which is beyond ordinary physical existence. The existence of the sambhogakaya buddha is not perceived by ordinary beings because the sambhogakaya manifests in a totally different state from that of our dualistic mind. This aspect has a permanent quality, which is a basic sense of continuity or the uninterrupted manifestation of that clarity. That unchanging, ever-present continuity of clarity manifests in the lucid appearance of a physical buddha, who turns the wheel of the profound Mahayana Dharma for the most highly realized bodhisattvas in Tushita Heaven. These bodhisattvas exist in the same state of clarity. In fact, the whole sambhogakaya realm itself is a manifestation of that clarity. *Sambhogakaya* literally means "body of enjoyment" and is so called because it exists as the manifestation of the energy of the luminous nature of mind.

The sambhogakaya buddha is described as having five permanent qualities, which are called the five certainties: the certainty of the teacher or the body; the certainty of the teachings; the certainty of the place; the certainty of the retinue or disciples; and the certainty of the time.

THE CERTAINTY OF THE TEACHER

The certainty of the body or teacher is the sambhogakaya buddha, which is the self-luminous energy of the dharmakaya buddhahood. That self-luminous energy exists as an expression of the dharmakaya in a pure energy form. The certainty of the teacher means that the one who teaches in that place or at that level is always the sambhogakaya buddha— always that energy of luminosity, that expression of the dharmakaya.

THE CERTAINTY OF THE TEACHINGS

The certainty of the teachings means that the sambhogakaya buddha teaches only the Mahayana Dharma. Buddha presents only the teachings of the greater vehicle to the bodhisattvas on this level. There is nothing else happening. They are going directly into the essence of the Dharma.

THE CERTAINTY OF THE PLACE

The certainty of the place means that the teachings are always given in Tushita Heaven. The samboghakaya buddha always manifests in the pure realm called the Tushita buddha realm.

THE CERTAINTY OF THE RETINUE

The certainty of the retinue means that the students who can communicate at the level of the sambhogakaya buddha are exclusively bodhisattvas who are on the eighth, ninth, and tenth bodhisattva bhumis. Beings who are on the lower levels cannot communicate with such buddhas. Therefore, the certainty of the disciple is established. All of the retinue of disciples who appear as students of the sambhogakaya buddha have the same level of realization and are ready to digest such teachings.

THE CERTAINTY OF THE TIME

The certainty of the time means that the appearance of the teacher and the presentation of the teachings are continuous. This refers to the uninterrupted nature of appearance, the uninterrupted nature of the teachings, and the uninterrupted nature of existence altogether.

Most of us have a great deal of difficulty in imagining such a world. Therefore, as an expression of skillful means, Shakyamuni Buddha gave several examples, such as the pure realms, to explain the state of sambhogakaya buddhahood to ordinary beings. We can see examples of such images in the depiction of the pure palaces and the pure forms of the sambhogakaya deities. The deities are adorned with the most precious jewels and ornaments, and they are wearing the garments of emperors, who were the most revered beings of that time. All the Indian or Tibetan paintings and statues show the sambhogakaya buddhas with the full ornaments and jewels of the Indian emperors or kings. These images provide us with something tangible, which we can easily imagine and easily contemplate. The Buddha gave us these particular examples because they show the richness of the sambhogakaya realm: it is as magnificent and resplendent as that of emperors and their royal palaces. However, these images are simply examples or symbolic forms; they are not literal. For example, the sambhogakaya realm or Tushita Heaven is not located somewhere in India. All the forms that we see are symbolic representations that transmit the richness and the profound and dignifying quality of the sambhogakaya buddha.

The Nirmanakaya

The nirmanakaya buddha is mind's unimpeded display of the dharmakaya and sambhogakaya energies. It is the display of the energy of emptiness and form, appearing in nirmanakaya form, such as the form of the Shakyamuni Buddha. The nirmanakaya buddha appears or manifests as a human being—as a very, very grounded human being. For example, Shakyamuni Buddha appeared as a real human being who walked on our earth. He ate the ordinary food that was offered to him and wore the cotton clothes manufactured in Varanasi. Buddha was not a supernatural being; he was a real human being like us. Compared to the sambhogakaya buddha, the nirmanakaya buddha has a greater sense of reaching out to various levels of beings. As a human being, he or she can reach out not only to those with pure backgrounds and good karmic records, but also to beings with really bad records and impure karmic backgrounds. No matter who we are, we can approach this buddha.

In the time of Shakyamuni Buddha there were great masters like Shariputra, Maudgalyayana-putra, and Buddha's regent, Kashyapa. At the same time, there was a certain individual named Devadatta, who was totally confused. Due to his totally chaotic mind, he constantly messed up everything with which he became involved. Nevertheless, Devadatta met Shakyamuni Buddha, studied with him, and learned the teachings of the Tripitaka. Eventually, Devadatta's knowledge of Dharma became so vast that the Buddha said that the number of scriptures he knew would fill the saddlebags of five hundred elephants.

Because the nirmanakaya buddha can reach out to many levels of beings and manifest compassion in more diverse ways, he or she has a greater role in benefiting sentient beings. Consequently, the nirmanakaya buddha is known as the kaya that has full power over the activity of Buddha. Although the sambhogakaya has great power, it does not extend to confused beings, such as us. Because the manifestation of the nirmanakaya is impermanent in nature, Shakyamuni Buddha endured all of the human pains of birth, old age, sickness, and death just as we do. There is also a greater sense of the impermanence of the teachings given by the nirmanakaya buddhas.

THE THREE KAYAS IN EVERYDAY LIFE

The three kayas also manifest in our everyday experience of the world. Emptiness is expressed or manifests as mind. Clarity is expressed as speech. Unobstructed awareness manifests as body. Therefore, when we experience body, speech, and mind, we can also try to connect with these three aspects of the mind. For example, we can observe the experience of emotions such as jealousy, anger, or passion. When we experience any of these emotions, we can look at the nature of the emotion, which is the nature of mind itself. When we see the spacious, open, and insubstantial quality of mind, we are seeing its dharmakaya nature, which is the true body of enlightenment.

When we experience that space and the insubstantial nature of mind, we see that it is not just empty and flat. We see that it is full of energy, full of arisings, and full of a vibrant radiance. When we see this luminous, radiant nature of mind that possesses all the qualities of richness and great joy, we are seeing its samboghakaya nature, the body of enjoyment.

These two qualities of spaciousness and radiant clarity are not separable. That inseparable nature manifests everywhere and all the time. When passion arises, the inseparable nature is there. When aggression, jealousy, or ego arises, the inseparable nature is there. When any thought arises in our mind, whether it is a thought of a buddha or a thought of harming someone, the inseparable nature of spaciousness and radiant clarity is present. That all-pervasive, continually manifesting quality is the nirmanakaya buddha. The enlightened quality of manifestation is present everywhere. Of course, this is not to say that there are not different qualities associated with the various emotions that we experience. The experience of jealousy has a different quality from the experience of anger or passion. Nevertheless, regardless of the form in which the nirmanakaya manifests, what is really manifesting is the unity of openness or spaciousness and the radiant clarity quality of buddhahood. When we see this unobstructed display of mind, we are seeing the nirmanakaya buddha.

Usually these three basic states, components of genuine mind or pure reality, are trapped and frozen in our ordinary existence as confused samsaric beings. However, through meditation on Mahamudra, the true nature of mind can be realized. At that time, these three components manifest and appear as the three kayas of the Buddha. The empty essence is dharmakaya. The radiant clarity is samboghakaya. The unobstructed awareness is nirmanakaya. When we recognize the nature of mind as the *trikaya,* this is called buddhahood, or enlightenment. It is as simple or confusing as that, depending on our viewpoint.

In the Mahamudra practice lineage, fruition is simply this recognition of the nature of mind. There is nothing more. That is what we call nirvana or freedom from samsara. There is nothing more to add. However, the way in which you individually manifest as a buddha depends upon particular aspirations—the aspirations you make now, while you are on the path. Those aspirations, which include the expression of relative bodhichitta—compassion and love toward sentient beings—with the desire to benefit beings in a particular way, will determine how you will manifest as a buddha when you realize the true nature of mind.

9

Mantra Mahamudra

IN THE MANTRA MAHAMUDRA TRADITION, the spiritual
path is seen as completely unnecessary because the nature of
the mind of all sentient beings has always been enlightenment. In this
sense, evolutionary theory does not apply here. In evolutionary theory,
we begin with something that has a totally savage, barbaric nature,
which then gradually evolves into something with a more civilized, enlightened nature. From the Mantra Mahamudra point of view, this is not
the way things are.

Here, the path actually leads us into the depths of our own neurosis, our own pain, and our own heart. We do not try to get out of
situations in our life that consist of pain and neurosis; instead, the journey is to penetrate the reality of the raw nature of our agony, emotions, and suffering. The basic view in Mantra Mahamudra is not to
look outside these experiences for something called "awakening," since
enlightenment is actually within our seemingly mundane, ordinary
experience. In fact, the Mantra Mahamudra path uses these very experiences of emotions and neurosis as powerful methods for awakening.

Genuinely experiencing the Mantra Mahamudra journey is totally
dependent upon the strength of our trust, longing, and devotion. There
are no other causes whatsoever. Intellectual knowledge is not the cause,
nor is great endurance on the meditation path with some conceptual
hope of realizing buddhahood. The cause of such experience is complete
trust and confidence in the guru, in the lineage, and in our own true

nature, which is the union of bliss and emptiness. This nature is the mind of the guru and the buddhas of the three times. It is enlightenment, and it is beyond concept.

However, the Mantra Mahamudra path is not generally our starting point. We do not just jump in on day one. That is definitely not recommended, and it is not how most genuine Vajrayana teachers would introduce the path, although that is something to be decided on an individual basis between the teacher and student. To enter the Mantra Mahamudra path properly, we need the three qualities of renunciation, bodhichitta, and right view. These three determine whether or not our practice is genuine Vajrayana.

Renunciation is revulsion toward our attachment to samsaric joy and to the experiences that ultimately bring us pain. When we experience renunciation, what does that do to our mind? It helps us develop compassion toward those who have the same attachment as ourselves to these samsaric objects. We not only develop compassion, but we also develop passion for the liberation of other beings, which is bodhichitta, the second quality. The third quality is right view, which is the correct understanding of shunyata, whether it is intellectual or experiential.

NAMES OF THE SECRET MANTRAYANA

The path that we are trying to cultivate within our heart is known variously as the Secret Mantrayana, the Vajrayana, or the Tantrayana.

The Sanskrit word *mantra* has two syllables: *mana,* which means "mind," and *tra,* which means "protection." *Mana* can be seen as the raw element of mind—our basic kleshas and emotions. This rugged nature of our mind has a great deal of energy. It is so powerful—fully charged, yet very raw. The syllable *tra* refers to the skillful means, or upayas, that enable us to leap into this basic state of mind and take it to a different level. Thus, mantra has a quality of transcending. From the tantric point of view, the ruggedness is in the nature of wisdom. When we recognize that nature, then the raw nature of mind itself is a protection.

Mana may also be viewed as prajna, the mind of insight. When mana is being viewed as prajna, the protection of tra is compassion.

There is a sense of the union of prajna and compassion in the basic meaning of *mantra*. The wisdom that realizes emptiness is inseparable with compassion. That is the second way to understand the meaning of *mantra*.

The Secret Mantrayana is also called Vajrayana, which literally means "diamond vehicle." A diamond is indestructible; it cannot be destroyed by other stones. The quality of indestructibility refers to the fundamental nature of mind, which is imperishable. *Vajra* also means "indivisible" or "inseparable." Our basic vajra nature is not only indestructible; it is indivisible and inseparable as well.

In the term *Tantrayana, tantra* literally means "continuity," which refers to the unchanging quality of our true nature. If something is continuous, it does not change. There is no need for evolution or improvement. The indestructible heart of awakening is continuous and unchanging throughout the stages of the ground, path, and fruition. This pure nature of our body, speech, and mind is continuous from beginningless time until we reach enlightenment. In the beginning they are in the nature of buddhahood, and in the end they are in the nature of buddhahood—that does not change. That is why we say that the beginning is the end of our journey.

Secret Mantrayana, Vajrayana, and Tantrayana are the primary names by which this path is known. It is also sometimes called the fruition yana, because the fruition of enlightenment is taken as the path, or as the Vehicle of the Vidyadharas, or awareness holders. *Vidya* means "awareness" or "naked awareness," and *dhara* means "holder." The followers of this path are able to hold the awareness of the true nature.

Intensifying Trust

As practitioners of Secret Mantrayana, we need to develop a sense of confidence, trust, and devotion in the meaning of Secret Mantra. That trust needs to be so intense that it becomes complete space. What is meant by complete space? Complete space has the quality of being liberated in its own self, of complete letting go. What do we let go? We let go of hopes and fears, which arise from the lack of trust. When we develop this sense of complete intensified trust, confidence, and devotion, that space is experienced within every living moment. Whether we are sitting on a cushion meditating, walking down the street, or enjoying a cup of cappuccino, it does not matter because we have no hopes and fears. When we have no hopes and fears, we have no choice but to give rise to enlightenment.

The most important aspect of this trust is trust in our own heart. In addition, trust in the instructions of the lineage is crucial. The lineage teachings say that we may attain enlightenment "right now." That thought might cause us some worry and make us very uncomfortable. The question is, do we really want to achieve enlightenment now? If we really want enlightenment and if we have trust, we are there in any moment.

When we are sitting on a cushion practicing the Vajrayana path, our goal is not to achieve enlightenment tomorrow or in the next session. Our goal is to achieve enlightenment in that session, on that cushion, in that moment.

The Secret Vehicle

The Vajrayana path is called secret, but this does not mean that we have something to hide or that some of its practices are shameful or illegal. There are two reasons that Vajrayana is called secret. First, there is a danger of misunderstanding the view, the practices, and the entire path. That is why the actual practices of Vajrayana are kept secret between an individual vajra master and a dedicated student. Second, the Vajrayana is said to be "self-secret." The literature of Vajrayana itself is naturally secret, because it exists in the form of a secret code. If someone were to simply read through a whole tantra many times, it would not make much sense. That is why it becomes nonsense when translated without a true sense of lineage into English or other languages.

The Vajrayana path can be quite dangerous, because if we misunderstand it, we can destroy our whole journey of enlightenment. For instance, in certain tantras it states, "Kill your parents. Kill your father and kill your mother." If we were to take that literally, then we would do enormous damage to our whole path and accumulate tremendous negative karma. We would not even be following the basic Buddhist path. However, in this particular tantra, the reference to killing one's parents is actually a reference to the notion of transcending duality. In this context, father and mother represent the notion of perceiver and perceived, or duality.

There are many references like this in the Vajrayana tantras, which can be very dangerous if misunderstood. That is why the Vajrayana path was traditionally taught in secret. In fact, the existence of the Vajrayana was not known publicly throughout the entire history of Buddhism in India.

SHUNYATA AND SACRED OUTLOOK

In order to understand the Vajrayana path, it is critical to develop knowledge, experience, and realization of shunyata, or emptiness. The view of shunyata is the basis of the view of equality or one taste. When we recognize that phenomena do not have inherent, solid characteristics, we can see them as equal, of one taste. This view of equality is the basis of sacred outlook, of experiencing all emotions, perceptions, and thoughts as sacred appearances of the enlightened mandala. Without sacred outlook there can be no vajra view. Therefore, sacred outlook is dependent upon an understanding and experience of shunyata. This can arise through both an intellectual process and an intuitive process, which is a basic heart connection. In order to give rise to sacred outlook—the view and experience of shunyata—we do not necessarily need to take a philosophical approach. However, most of us must go through progressive stages, which involves an intellectual process in the beginning, as well as a basic heart connection.

Without shunyata, our view and our experience of Vajrayana become incomplete. They become one-sided and fall into the extreme of existence. When we fall into the extreme of existence, our visualizations become merely a type of egoistic, self-centered clinging to subtle forms of existence. There is no purity, no basic sense of sacredness.

The core view of the Vajrayana teaching is the indivisible union of prajna and upaya, or wisdom and compassionate skillful means. It is the union of luminosity and emptiness. It is necessary to emphasize emptiness here because it is more likely that we will misunderstand luminosity and think that it is easier to connect with. Sometimes we think that the vivid, raw clarity of the mind is easier to experience than its insubstantiality, and that perhaps this luminosity is all we need. However, we need to actually experience the union or inseparability of these two seemingly different aspects of the mind. Shunyata without luminosity is also an incomplete understanding. In Vajrayana, there is a total emphasis on the aspect of union: the inseparable nature of bliss-emptiness, of appearance-emptiness, and of awareness and space.

The view of sacred outlook is the means by which we perceive the vajra world, which is known as sacred world. Sacred world is often symbolized in the paintings and sculptures of Vajrayana deity mandalas. *Mandala* does not have an elaborate or esoteric meaning in Sanskrit or Tibetan, although it sounds very mysterious in English. *Mandala* simply means "center and surroundings." That is what we see in a mandala—a circle that contains a square, in the center of which there is usually the image of a deity. The practice of a mandala is simply to place ourselves in the middle of it and learn to relate with the social structure and atmosphere around us as a sacred environment. To enter the sacred mandala of the deity, we must receive initiation from our guru. Through this initiation process, we are empowered to use the skillful means of Vajrayana visualization practice.

QUALITIES AND MARKS OF THE MANTRAYANA PATH

The Vajrayana journey is quite different from the general path of the Sutrayana causal vehicles. Sutra and tantra have the same understanding of the nature of luminosity and emptiness, awareness and space, appearance-emptiness, and so forth. However, entering the Vajrayana is like getting into a race car or a jet instead of walking or riding a bicycle the whole way. This vehicle is much faster and easier, and it gives us many more options for reaching our destination.

However, it is also much more dangerous. Therefore, the people who drive or pilot such a vehicle must know how to use all of its many options and instruments skillfully.

The Vajrayana is commonly taught to have four distinguishing features that make it superior to or different from the basic Sutrayana path. The path of Secret Mantra is said (1) to be without ignorance, (2) to have many skillful methods, (3) to have methods that can be applied without difficulty, and (4) to require practitioners who possess sharp faculties.

Being without Ignorance

The first distinction between the general Sutrayana and the Vajrayana is that it is intelligent, or without ignorance. In this context, being skillful or intelligent refers to two aspects: not being ignorant with regard to the profound nature of reality, and not being ignorant with regard to the vast or extensive reality.

The methods of the Vajrayana path work with our basic wisdom and are the tools through which we recognize and realize this true nature. The path emphasizes working with the direct, nonconceptual recognition of the fundamental nature of body, speech, and mind. We take the basic ground, which is our very state of physical existence, into the experience of sacred world, right on the spot. It is a very immediate experience. We work in the most direct manner possible with the physical, verbal, and mental aspects of our being. Through these methods, we are able to ascertain the basic ground of our being, which is the nature of buddha wisdom and is not produced by any aspect of relative mind. Then we rest in that nature.

It is said in the Kagyu lineage supplication:

> Awareness is the body of meditation, as is taught.
> Whatever arises is fresh, the essence of realization.
> To this meditator who rests simply without altering it
> Grant your blessings so that my meditation is free from
>   conception.[1]

These lines refer to the actual practice of "resting" in the tantric tradition. We do not simply work with counting the breath, looking at a pebble, or engaging in conceptual analysis alone. Rather, we go directly into the fundamental state and rest in that without altering it. Through that practice, it is said that we can attain buddhahood in this lifetime, in this session, in this very moment. Thus, we are not creating anything; we are not practicing hard to make it happen. It is happening in every state, in every moment.

Once we recognize our enlightened nature, the Vajrayana path takes us through practices that work with the extensive expression and display of relative reality.[2] All the interdependent appearances of mind and phenomena are experienced with sacred vision, without our abandoning or adopting anything. We work with the vastness of relative reality by seeing it in its true state, the state of sacred world. Thus, the relative world is seen as a sacred mandala or buddhafield.

In the sutra tradition, the ground is analyzed and determined through conceptual reasoning, or inferential valid cognition. One puts tremendous effort into the practice of shamatha and vipashyana meditation, trying to rest in the basic nature of the ground, which is discovered through the view. One has a sense of there being a goal, and one achieves the fruition stage only after many, many aeons or lifetimes of hard work. One does not work directly with the nature of one's physical state or with the extensive reality of sacred world and sacred outlook. The sutra practices simply relate with the basic subtle classifications and distinctions of the skandhas, *dhatus*, and *ayatanas*. Their focus remains primarily on the relative subtleties, so it takes a very long time to experience awakening. There are no methods to transform our experience right on the spot. Therefore, from the tantric point of view, the sutra path still contains ignorance because there are no methods by which one can directly recognize the true nature of the ground, path, and fruition.

Having Many Skillful Methods

The second distinguishing feature of the Vajrayana path is that it has many skillful methods. In this context, the notion of not being ignorant—of being intelligent—refers to the availability of the many practical, accessible, and colorful methods that are employed on this path. It is not just one simple path with one simple method. There are four levels of tantra, each with its own precise way to work with experience. Thus, the path has extensive tools and skillful means.

When we work individually with this approach, there are a variety of methods through which we can experience the true nature of our emotions. In general, in the first stage of Vajrayana practice, we transform emotions through the process of visualization, just as we transform the skandhas, dhatus, and ayatanas. Then, through the prajna aspect of the method, emotions are transformed by our recognition of their essence. We jump into that essence fearlessly. There is a sense of self-liberation within every element of emotion: Whether it is passion, aggression, or ignorance, its essence is buddha wisdom. Whatever methods we may practice in the Vajrayana, none of them involves renouncing the emotions. There is nothing to renounce. There is nowhere to run. On the Vajrayana path we work with desirable objects without renouncing them.

On the general Sutrayana path, however, one cultivates the knowledge of what is to be abandoned and what is to be adopted. For example, the method of working with emotions is basically to renounce or abandon them. One develops a certain degree of detachment and then transcends one's emotions through transcending one's basic attachment and grasping. Practices such as the Hinayana meditation on ugliness or the Mahayana practice of generosity are seen as antidotes to be adopted.

In the Sutrayana context, abandonment is dependent on the idea of duality, the subject-object relationship, and on abandoning clinging to the object. The Hinayana path emphasizes renouncing samsaric existence and running away from such objects. The Mahayana path also includes practices of adopting and abandoning. For instance, in the Mahayana practice of generosity, giving is a form of completely letting go of the object to which one is attached. In fact, all of the paramita practices—generosity, discipline, patience, and so forth—are connected to the notion of abandonment and acceptance, or taking up and discarding. One tries to adopt what is positive or virtuous, such as the two accumulations of merit and wisdom, and to abandon what is negative, such as the two self-clingings, the kleshas, and so forth. However, in the Vajrayana approach, we take everything onto the path and work with it through the application of a vast variety of skillful means.

Being without Difficulty

The third feature distinguishing the Vajrayana from the Sutrayana is that it is without difficulties. This means there are fewer struggles on the Vajrayana path. On the Sutrayana path, one goes through tremendous effort and struggle to perform practices that are very difficult and involve a lot of time, patience, and endurance before achieving the fruition stage. These practices reflect the Sutrayana's tremendous emphasis on what is to be abandoned and what is to be adopted—we see things as good or bad, sacred or profane, and so forth. These dualistic divisions perpetuate a sense of struggle that continues for many aeons and is seemingly endless.

However, in the Mantrayana, everything arises as a favorable condition of the path. Emotions and ego-clinging are not transformed by making them into something to abandon. When we think that there is something to be abandoned, it takes tremendous effort and time just to abandon it. In addition, there are many things to adopt, which also requires tremendous time and effort. In the Vajrayana, there is nothing to be abandoned. Everything becomes path; everything arises as an enlightening, awakening experience. We can even transform ego-clinging on the spot by taking ego onto the path as a favorable condition for recognizing the nature of our mind.

When we understand the Vajrayana journey, all of our experiences of emotion are brought onto the path as great joy, great bliss. Even pain is experienced as joy. For a yogi who is training on the path of experiencing all feelings as bliss, even sharp bamboo sticks inserted under the fingernails can be experienced as joy. This may be hard for us to understand, but by using our inferential mind, we can see that all feelings, sensations, and experiences can be taken onto the path as great joy.

Demanding Sharp Faculties

The fourth distinguishing feature is that the Vajrayana is called the path of sharp faculties. The term *sharp faculties* does not necessarily mean having a very sharp intelligence of the sort that leads one to examine, to analyze, to answer questions, and to score the highest in the class. The term refers to those who have a certain karmic connection with this path. A certain sense of ripening is present in their karmic mindstream. Ordinarily, when someone actively engages the emotions, that experience leads to more intensified suffering. However, in the case of a Vajrayana practitioner, engaging the emotions of passion, aggression, and ignorance can lead to the fruition of enlightenment rather than to further suffering and pain. The person who can transform poison into medicine, the kleshas into nectar, is a person of sharp faculties.

As Vajrayanists, one of the most important faculties we need to develop, and for which we may have a karmic seed, is one-pointed, sharp-edged trust. Such trust can cut through any kind of ego-centered doubt and through unending questions. Trust begins with trusting our own vajra heart, and that trust can be aroused by developing trust in the enlightened mandala of the guru. Thus, we develop fearless trust in our own heart, in the lineage masters, and in their instructions.

THE THREE VAJRAS

Vajrayana is known as the path of skillful means because it is the great means that brings us into this vajra state. The term "great means" refers to the path of fruition, or the path that sees all poisons as nectar. Passion, aggression, and ignorance are called vajra passion, vajra aggression, and vajra ignorance. This is a secret path that works with the inconceivable secret nature of body, speech, and mind, which are known as the three vajras.

Body

On the general Sutrayana path, the practice in relation to the body element is quite conventional. It primarily involves engaging in what are considered to be virtuous actions, such as helping a sick person, lighting a butter lamp or cleaning a shrine room. These practices enable one to go so far as to see the physical existence of body in the form of an illusion. However, that is the extent to which one can go in the Sutrayana, in terms of working with the physical body or working with existence. In the Vajrayana, the physical existence of form is seen as sacred world. Our own bodies are seen to be in the nature of luminous enlightened bodies, and our environment is seen as a sacred palace. This sacred view of form is expressed in the Kagyu lineage supplication when we say, "To this meditator who arises in unceasing play. . . ." Thus, there is a distinct difference between sutra and tantra in how each relates to the physical body.

Speech

Within the Sutrayana, virtuous speech is the practice of engaging in recitations of sutras and liturgies or the practice of silence. Silence includes not speaking and not engaging in mundane thoughts. The practice of silence is a very common Buddhist practice that is generally emphasized on the Sutrayana path. The most one can obtain from these practices in the Sutrayana is to see the nature of speech or sound as being like an echo. In contrast, within the Vajrayana, vajra speech is the speech of the mandala of sacred world; it is the sound of mantra. The primordial nature of speech arises and manifests in the form of the upaya and prajna elements of speech, which are the fundamental nature of the sound of speech. When we experience all sound as the primordial mandala of speech, it is clearly not the ordinary chatter of our everyday speech.

Mind

On the Sutrayana path, one uses the method of shamatha-vipashyana meditation to work with one's mind to prevent mundane or conflicted thoughts and states of affliction from manifesting. This is done through breathing techniques, meditation on emptiness, and so forth.

On the Mantrayana journey, our vajra heart is seen as pristine awareness, primordially luminous and self-arising. All phenomena and the nature of all thoughts and emotions are seen as the display of dharmata. They are not just seen through the filters of conceptual mind but are experienced as an expression of dharmata. This means that the samadhi of the yogi is uninterrupted. If we experience every element of thought and emotion as the display of dharmata, samadhi never stops. It is the unceasing continuity of vajra heart.

In bringing us to the recognition of the three vajra natures, the Vajrayana path brings us to a very different level from the level of the basic Sutrayana path. When we speak of the three vajra natures of body, speech, and mind as being continuous from beginningless time, we might wonder when all these things began. How far back do we go in our history of confusion? In fact, beginningless time does not have to do with time. It has to do with nowness. The beginning of samsara is now and the end of samsara is now.

The very moment when we fail to recognize the vajra nature is samsara. The very moment when, with the blessings of the lineage, we recognize the three vajras is enlightenment. From the Vajrayana point of view, enlightenment is here and nowhere else. The end is the beginning and the beginning is the end. There is no contradiction. When we think about beginningless time, it sounds so long, but actually we are talking about a matter of a moment. A moment makes a difference.

THE TEACHER-STUDENT RELATIONSHIP

The guru-disciple relationship is the basis of our entrance into the Vajrayana world, and the most important factor in building the relationship with our guru is appreciation. When we talk about devotion, samaya, and other aspects of the Vajrayana teacher-student relationship, these subjects sometimes sound threatening or scary. However, devotion and the perfect connection of samaya can arise simply from appreciation: appreciating our individual gurus, our connection to the vajra world and the lineage, and our own presence, our own continuity. Appreciation is the key to developing a genuine experience of the guru mind. In one sense, entering the Vajrayana world is a complicated process. In another sense, it is quite simple. It is basically appreciating our own world and the world around us.

How do we connect with a lineage and a lineage master? We connect as individuals with an individual teacher of a lineage. We have to make a personal and real connection rather than a general intellectual one. There has to be a personal experience that connects us with the path and with the presence of the lineage. The teacher-student relationship is very human. A genuine relationship with a guru is openhearted and honest. It is a spiritual relationship that is totally direct and in which there is nothing to hide or hold back.

Longing

If we have any longing to experience the sacred world directly, then devotion to the lineage is extremely important. Our longing is not actually to be with somebody called a "guru." We are longing to unite, to be one, with the mandala of vajra nature. The guru mandala of vajra nature is the nature of our own heart and our own mind.

For ordinary people, however, the physical presence of a guru brings tremendous benefit. It enables us to directly experience the nakedness of the vajra world. When we are in the presence of the guru, that world is there in front of us. What can we do? There is no way to escape it. Generally speaking, the physical presence of a guru has a tremendous effect. Although there is no difference between the blessings of the guru's presence in person and imagining the guru mandala of Vajradhara, as ordinary beings who have not directly realized the profound nature of emptiness, we have a more difficult time connecting with something that is so totally beyond our concept. When our gurus are in front of us, we experience their presence so vividly and nakedly through our perceptions, our senses, and our minds that we experience the vajra world directly. A guru brings us to the path of

Vajrayana and therefore to the direct experience of our true nature. The method that brings us to direct experiences of our vajra nature is called the ripening process. Through the guru's instructions and our own further practice, that ripening process leads us to liberation.

We may think that we cannot have this kind of relationship because our teacher has so many students and therefore it is hard to connect with him or her on a direct, personal level. However, the length of time we spend with our guru is not an issue. All that matters is that we use the moment of connection in the most effective, complete way. In the sutras, it says that the Buddha had an attendant for twenty-five years. At the end of twenty-five years, the attendant left, saying, "I don't see any difference between you and me, except the halo on your head and a few other things." We can see from this story that being with someone for a long period of conceptual time does not mean anything.

Beyond Ordinary Appearances

In the process of relating with our guru, we get caught up in projections from time to time. Each time, it is different. Sometimes we recognize our projections and sometimes we do not. We may recognize them at a later time and work with them then. However, when our projections are gone, we can truly experience our guru—who he or she truly is—rather than merely experiencing our concepts of what we want our teacher to be. Often, we would prefer to order our ideal version of the guru, one who would meet our standards. But our standards are just concepts; they are cultural. We need to break through all of these and simply relate with the path and the teacher in the most direct manner possible; to go beyond our cultural concepts and develop the quality of clarity in the Vajrayana teacher-student relationship.

When we refer to "seeing the guru as Buddha," as a completely enlightened being, we are not referring to how the guru looks. Appearances can be deceptive. We are talking about our own faith and trust in the completely enlightened state of the guru's mind. If you read the history of Vajrayana teachers, none of these gurus ever proclaimed that they were enlightened. None of them ever said, "I am the awakened one and I can give you awakening." In fact most of them did not even appear to be teachers. Tilopa did not have all the signs of a buddha, such as the glowing light, the Dharma wheels, and webbed fingers, because those are the signs particular to the historic Buddha.

We can never tell what methods the gurus will use or how they might appear. The histories of the eighty-four mahasiddhas, the great masters of India, describe how some of them slept among dogs and some of them hunted in the mountains. One of the greatest masters, Saraha, simply made arrows. Whether we understand the accounts of these yogis as symbolic teachings or literal biographies, their life stories can help us to go beyond our mundane conceptual judgments so that we can develop sacred outlook and devotion.

No matter how the Vajrayana masters may manifest, they all have the same quality of completely caring for their disciples. There is a sense of total dedication, whether it manifests in the form of sharp-edged prajna or very mellow compassion. There is always a quality of completely pouring their hearts into the hearts of their disciples. There is a sense of totally giving, of not holding anything back. It is not like pouring water from one vase into another vase, so that one becomes empty and the other one becomes full. Rather, this pouring quality is like lighting a lamp. When you use a candle to light another candle, the flame continues with full strength and full luminosity. Yet there is still a sense of inseparability, of oneness, between the two flames. We can see this process in how the genuine masters of the Vajrayana lineage manifest.

The Heart of the Guru's Lineage

Mantra Mahamudra is the path of intensifying our trust and developing our confidence. Genuine devotion is the key to bringing all experiences and results of Vajrayana practice into our mindstream. You can be assured that there is no enlightenment and no fruition without this trust. Trust in inconceivable truth is the most important factor in our ability to experience the guru mandala, sacred world, and the Vajrayana path altogether. The very reason we cannot experience appearance-emptiness, buddhahood, the deity mandala, or sacred world in our everyday life is that we lack a basic sense of openness.

We do not have to trust completely; we only have to be open-minded enough to say, "Maybe there is a possibility of inconceivable truth." If our minds are not open, then it is nearly impossible for these experiences to arise. We should ask ourselves what we want and what we need. If we want to experience genuine devotion, bliss-emptiness, or enlightenment, then we need to open up.

The path of devotion is a much more effective way for us to work with our experience than using conceptual maneuvering. The ultimate devotion is to our own vajra nature, which is not separable from the vajra nature of Buddha, the vajra nature of the mahasiddhas, and the vajra nature of the gurus. When we have trust in our own heart, the heart of the guru's lineage, and the instructions that unite them, this trust cannot but bring us experiences. There is no choice for us but to have a direct experience of our vajra nature.

Essence Mahamudra

The Mind of Nowness

ESSENCE MAHAMUDRA is regarded as the most profound path of Mahamudra. It is more profound than Sutra Mahamudra and Mantra Mahamudra because it is the path that brings the realization of enlightenment on the spot. This realization is brought about through the blessings of the guru and the sharp mind and one-pointed devotion of the disciple. When these three elements come together, realization can occur instantaneously. From the Mahamudra point of view, there is nothing that is above this path. It is incomparable and unsurpassable.

WILD AWAKENING

Essence Mahamudra is the simplest and most formless path of Mahamudra. It does not rely upon the elaborate methods of Mantra Mahamudra, nor does it require the gradual progression of intellectual training in the scriptures or in the details of the stage-by-stage practices of the Sutrayana. In Essence Mahamudra, the realization of the nature of mind is brought to one's mindstream purely through the blessings of the guru—sometimes through painful or agonizing methods and sometimes through blissful methods. This instantaneous method of transmission is also called "forcefully pointing out the profound essence."

We can see examples of this path in the biographies of the founders of the Kagyu lineage, which include great masters such as Naropa, Marpa, and Milarepa. The relationship of Naropa with his guru, Tilopa, which was mentioned earlier, is particularly well known and representative of the Essence style of transmission. From one point of view, their spiritual journey together was nothing special; it contained no spectacular elements or events. Tilopa was a fisherman. His student, Naropa, lived with him, and together they spent their days fishing along the Ganges River. Of course, Tilopa was a completely enlightened individual in "hidden" form. He was considered something of a misfit and even an outcast from traditional society. Naropa lived with his guru for twelve years, undergoing his training, which included such trials as jumping from cliffs and being beaten for stealing bowls of soup and disrupting marriage ceremonies. There are many stories of Naropa's complete faith in his guru and utter devotion to the path of awakening. Nevertheless, in most ways Naropa's journey was quite ordinary. Throughout these stories, we never see words like "golden throne." Neither Tilopa nor Naropa became the founder of important monasteries that trained hundreds of monks and disciplined *arhats*.

In Essence Mahamudra, all nonessential or pointless activity is cut out. On this path, the point is to go back to the basic state: to the primal state of emotions, life, and appearances. We cut right through to the fundamental nature of all things by working with these very things. For example, in order to realize Mahamudra mind, Naropa did not have to go to an elaborate shrine room to receive the final blessing from a golden vase placed on his head. How did Naropa realize Mahamudra mind? Naropa was simply walking with his guru. He was probably barefoot, and Tilopa was wearing some kind of wooden Indian sandal. As discussed earlier, Tilopa took off his sandal and hit Naropa's forehead with it. That was the abhisheka. How powerful. How simple. Today, in our world, Tilopa would have bought a flip-flop on sale at K-Mart. The world is that simple when it comes to Essence Mahamudra. Realization is brought into our ordinary life through ordinary objects such as flip-flops. This shows clearly that realization does not depend on appearances. Realization can arise within the most mundane and chaotic situation. When Tilopa hit Naropa, he did not say anything profound. He simply said, "You don't get it, do you? How many times have I given this to you?" Whack! That is how Naropa received the full transmission of Mahamudra mind. Therefore, it is called Essence Mahamudra. It is the essence of the essence.

The most powerful path of the Vajrayana world and of the whole Buddhist world is right here in our ordinary life. We can experience complete Mahamudra realization while driving down the interstate, if we are in the proper situation, which is the ordinary world. From the Essence point of view, all these trappings of spirituality that we have—the beautiful and sacred setup of the shrine, the cushions, the banners—can become the very obstacles that prevent us from realizing Mahamudra mind. Therefore, Milarepa often instructed, "When meditating on Mahamudra, do not bother with the physical activities of dharma and do not bother with the verbal activities of Dharma." Those activities are not important. We should simply be where we are and meditate. In the practice of Mahamudra meditation, sometimes even the recitation of mantra is seen as a sidetrack.

From the Essence Mahamudra point of view, it is very simple. A realized master brings the adhishthana—the blessing—or the realization of Mahamudra into our ordinary world, into our ordinary mind. This is called the simultaneity of realization and liberation.

THE GROUND OF ESSENCE MAHAMUDRA

Ground, path, and fruition are also taught on the Essence Mahamudra path. As in Sutra and Mantra Mahamudra, the ground is ordinary mind, which is the mind of nowness. This mind of nowness is not any particular mind per se, but it is the mind of everything. It is the mind that is "all-pervasive yet beyond all." When we say that the mind of nowness is all-pervasive, we do not mean that it is "all." We mean that it transcends all.

On the Mahamudra path, the ground does not abide in the nature of samsara or nirvana. It does not incline toward either of these two. It is beyond all elaborations, beyond all complexities, beyond all artifice, and beyond all expressions. It is the inseparable nature of space and luminosity. It is the union of *ying,* which is space, and *rigpa,* which is awareness. When we have the right understanding of and approach to this ordinary mind, which is thamal gyi shepa in Tibetan, that knowledge is ground Mahamudra. From this point of view, we are not looking for something special, because anything special is not in the nature of enlightenment. That is a very important message in Mahamudra.

The play of our awareness is so vivid and bright that it fails to recognize its own nature, which is ordinary mind. Because of the intensity of the brightness of awareness, we become confused. At the ground level, our confused mind splits the intense brightness in two. This is called duality. This is the point at which we become enmeshed in samsara.

When we fail to recognize this awareness as it is, we take one aspect to be a self: an "I" or a "me," which provides a sense of there being a fundamental reference point. We then see the self-play of this awareness as other: "you," "them," and all the "objects" that exist separately. At this point, duality begins to dominate our mind. Through this duality, we accumulate karma. We engage in positive and negative actions. From these actions, we generate the results of samsara. From a Mahamudra point of view, we could say that the "creator" is actually the failure of awareness to recognize itself.

At the ground level, the basic instruction is simply to look at this ordinary mind in every moment of experience. We can recognize ordinary mind in a single moment of perception. It does not matter whether we are hearing a sound, seeing a visual object, experiencing a tactile sensation, or tasting a Snickers bar. No matter what we experience in relation to these sense objects, the instruction is simply to look at the very nature of these appearances with the mind of nowness. We can recognize ordinary mind even in a moment of conceptual thought. The particular circumstances do not matter. However, once we connect with this experience, once we recognize the nature of the ground, we begin our journey on the path of Mahamudra. In short, ground Mahamudra is the view of ordinary mind.

Essence Mahamudra stresses devotion to the lineage and especially to the guru as the key to realization. Hence, guru yoga is emphasized and is seen as the practice that directly connects our hearts with the lineage and lineage principles.

THE PATH: MAHAMUDRA SHAMATHA AND VIPASHYANA

The path of Essence Mahamudra begins with the practices of shamatha-vipashyana. On this path, recognition and realization of the nature of mind arise from the combination of two things: the blessings of the guru and the ripening of our own karma—our own karmic seed of connection to the guru and lineage of Mahamudra instructions.

At this point, our intellectual views and theories, our theological studies of Buddhism, and the sophisticated reasonings of the logical traditions are seen as husks of grain. If we want to enjoy the pure grain itself, we must have the courage to let go of these husks. On the path of Essence Mahamudra, we shed all the layers of intellectualization that we previously made such an effort to acquire. At this point, the whole path becomes an unlearning process instead of a learning process. We might say that in the essence of the grain, no husks are ever found. From the point of view of the grain itself, there is a natural sense of being free of the husk. There is no effort needed to become free. Therefore, we no longer put any specific effort into developing further intellectual knowledge.

It is said that when we are meditating on the Mahamudra path, we should not meditate. As long as we have an idea that we are meditating, then we are not meditating. Meditation should be free from the thought, the effort, and the idea of meditation. Instead, nondistraction, nonmeditation, and nonfabrication are the key points.

Mahamudra shamatha is simple nondistraction. It is simply the recognition of the ordinary mind that we discovered at the level of ground Mahamudra. This is then practiced in Mahamudra shamatha. This ordinary mind is what is being introduced or pointed out in Mahamudra vipashyana, which is simple clarity.

In relation to shamatha meditation, the basic posture of the body is comfortable, spacious, and relaxed. These are the three main aspects of the physical posture. The mind posture is simply remaining in shamatha. We focus our mind on a certain point, such as our breath or a part of our body, and then we simply relax. Where and how we focus is individual and differs according to our progression on the path of meditation. Once we have assumed the correct posture, the instruction is to freely relax in that spot without anxiety or worry.

The ability to relax within our meditation practice is a key point. The teachings say that the person who can relax the most will have the best meditation; the person who can relax only somewhat will only somewhat experience Mahamudra meditation; and the person who cannot relax at all or whose relaxation is very poor will have poor Mahamudra meditation.

The Six Points

The Eighth Karmapa lists six essential points for developing our practice of Mahamudra meditation: (1) devotion; (2) faith; (3) giving meditation to its owner; (4) entrusting enhancement to supplication; (5) employing mindfulness as a watchman; and (6) entrusting your postmeditation activity to compassion.

The first two points, devotion and faith, are already familiar to us. The owner of meditation referred to in the third point is renunciation. The fourth point demonstrates the importance of supplication as a means of enhancing our experience of Mahamudra. According to the many instructions on supplicating the guru, it does not matter how we sound, whether we are singing, reciting, or just speaking. The point is not to sound a particular way but to supplicate one-pointedly. In fact, it is said that it is acceptable to sing your supplication even if your voice sounds like a dog's cry, which is actually a wonderful, natural cry. In both meditation and postmeditation, we simply post the watchman of mindfulness and relax. We do not strain or strive; a simple thread of mindfulness is all that is required.

Finally, we employ compassion as the main practice of the postmeditation. We leave our minds in a state of compassion. These six points are the practices that will bring the realizations of Mahamudra on the path.

The Three Levels of Capacity

It is generally said that practitioners have one of three levels of capacity on the path. A practitioner may possess basic intellect and basic capacity, sharper intellect and sharper capacity, or utterly sharp intellect and utterly sharp capacity.

The path of the three yanas is taught according to these three capacities. From this point of view, Mahamudra practitioners are expected to have utterly sharp capacity, utterly sharp intellect, and utterly pure devotion. At this highest level of utterly sharp intellect and utterly sharp capacity there is a further subdivision into basic, sharper, and utterly sharp. Here, for example, when we say "basic," we are not talking about the "basic of the basic." We are talking about three more subtle classifications of the capacities of Mahamudra practitioners: the basic of the utterly sharp, the sharper of the utterly sharp, and the utterly sharp of the utterly sharp.

Illuminating an Ancient Darkness

From the Essence Mahamudra perspective, regardless of how long we may want to remain as practitioners on this path, we cannot stay on it. There is nothing more on which to meditate. There is nothing more to obtain or gather except nondistraction.

This quality of the path is often illustrated by the image of a room or a cave that has remained in darkness for hundreds of thousands of years—perhaps for aeons. Because darkness has filled the cave for such a long time, the darkness itself seems very thick to our conceptual minds. As long as we hold on to the notion of the darkness being so thick, it will seem very difficult to eliminate it, as if we might need thousands of years of effort. However, from the Mahamudra point of view, if we enter that dark cave with a flashlight, then the darkness can be eliminated in a single instant. It does not matter how thick or how old the darkness is. Mahamudra practitioners do not care about the history of the darkness; they care only about illuminating it with the powerful light of awareness.

Regardless of how long we have been stuck in samsara with our confusion, ego-clinging, and emotional disturbances—the full contents of our karmic garbage—when we receive pointing-out instruction, it is like pushing the button on our flashlight. At that point, the light shines through the cave and the darkness is illuminated.

When we have this kind of "flash" experience, which emanates from our pointing-out instruction, it becomes the key to our practice. That pointing-out instruction is the beginning. Someone shows us the button and says, "There is a button here. You just press it."

However, because we have been in this darkness for aeons, we find it difficult to bear the light. We "sort of" push this button—but with feelings of ambivalence and great fear. Then, as soon as we see the light, we let go of the button and fall back into the darkness again. The process becomes one in which we must keep pressing the button so as to continuously experience the light—the luminosity, space, and emptiness.

At a fundamental level, there is no difference between the experience of darkness and the experience of light because, in both of these states, there is a sense of great space. That space is shunyata. That space is emptiness. That space is egolessness. When the luminosity joins this space, the space becomes very vivid to us; it becomes completely one with the light. At that moment, we do not first see something called light, which is solid like an ice cube, and then see the space, somewhere outside in the darkness. It is not like that. When the light joins the space, the space becomes light and the light becomes space. They do not have individual identities. Space and luminosity, or awareness, do not care about their identities as much as we do.

At this stage, our experience will fluctuate, which is natural. We have an experience of pressing the button and experiencing the light, and then going back into the darkness. Then we press the button again and return to the light. Although our experience may not yet have stabilized, we are creating more gaps.

Eight Points of Meditation

At this point on the path of Essence Mahamudra, we should meditate by using the following eight points in order to bring our mind fully to rest.

1. Rest in present awareness, which is primordially empty of self and empty of any confusion.
2. Rest in the innate nature of the ordinary state without any specific focus or desire for particular meditation experiences.
3. Rest in the innate state without hope or fear and without altering anything.
4. Rest in fresh awareness, without polluting that freshness with thoughts of the past and future.
5. Rest within clear awareness, free from agitation and dullness.
6. Rest with awareness and understanding of the empty nature of thoughts.
7. Rest within bare perceptions without following after objects.
8. Rest in the continuity of inexpressible mindfulness and awareness of the view and meditation.

What is meant by the instruction to rest our mind in the inexpressible view? We can compare this to pulling our car off the highway into one of those scenic lookouts and then getting out of our car. There is usually a beautiful, scenic expanse. It could be a view of an ocean with waves, a colorful display of trees, or simply an expansive view of space. When we are standing on the lookout, that experience of "view" is so clear, so vivid, so open, and so experiential that it is beyond words. It is not conceptual. Of course, we can have concepts, such as "beautiful ocean," "beautiful colors," or "beautiful trees." However, the real experience is in our heart, and it is beyond words. That is the experience of view.

Some people who stand on such a lookout become so attached to the view that they jump off to get closer to the ocean or the trees. If that happens to us, then we have a problem. If we jump from that spot, then we lose the whole panoramic sense of the view. At that point, the whole notion of the view is gone. We might be left with only one tree with some dead leaves, or we might be stuck with a smelly ocean with a few waves rolling in to touch our feet.

Similarly, if we become attached to any view and hold on to it, then we will lose our panoramic experience of it. In contrast, when we experience the view within the very continuity of inexpressible awareness and mindfulness, it is as though we are gliding. We become like an eagle soaring in space with an extremely beautiful and tremendous view.

When we experience that panoramic view and are not distracted, that is meditation. Our meditation is simply nondistraction. We are still enjoying the view; we are not abandoning it. We are not trying to run away from the experience of view. We are developing the continuity of our experience of view through the simple experience of nondistraction.

In order to sustain these meditation experiences on the path of Essence Mahamudra, the development of devotion is emphasized. We continuously develop our devotion to our principal teacher, who is the basic reference point for our path. It is said that when you have devotion, there is blessing. When there is blessing, there is realization. That is the unfailing truth about the path. In our practice, if our experiences of the pointing-out instructions become purely conceptual—mere words and concepts—then it is important to maintain our realization of Mahamudra mind by emphasizing devotion, trust, and respect for the living master.

There are many stories illustrating these qualities of devotion and trust, such as those that appear in the biographies and commentaries of lineage masters. One particular incident is described in the biography of Gendün Chöpel, a great Tibetan master and translator of the twentieth century. He translated the *Dhammapada* from Pali into Tibetan.

One day, Gendün Chöpel and one of his students were sitting on the balcony of a house in Lhasa, in the Barkhor. Gendün Chöpel was drinking Tibetan beer, *chang,* which the student was offering to him. The student was serving his teacher and was not drinking himself.

They were discussing Dharma, talking about practice, and the student continued to offer chang to his teacher—again and again and again. The student was listening so intensely to all of his teacher's words that, at a certain point, the student began to smell alcohol on his own breath and taste alcohol in his mouth. Then he started to get a little bit drunk. He described his experience to Gendün Chöpel, who said that is how devotion should be. One should be one-pointedly focused, so that what we call "merging our mind with the mind of the guru" occurs. This is a perfect example of devotion. When we intensely focus our mind, we can experience the enlightened mind of the guru.

This path emphasizes that we have to do our own part in working with devotion. We cannot be passive. We have to actively engage in devotion and trust, and penetrate the guru's heart.

Enhancement Practices: Lion's Roar, Hyena's Howl

The enhancement practices that are given for the postmeditation state vary from one individual to another. Particular practices are given in accordance with an individual's recognition of ordinary mind. Therefore, these instructions are not presented in a general way, nor are they presented all at once.

Tiger's leap is different from fox's jump.
Lion's roar is different from hyena's howl.[1]

Using the analogy presented in this poem, we can see that if we are at the level of a fox on the scale of the realization of ordinary mind, then we cannot jump like a tiger. To mimic the tiger's leap would be fatal. Similarly, if we have the realization of a hyena, then the only thing we can do is howl. There is no way we can mimic the roaring sound of the lion. We have to wait until we are born into the lion's state of awareness, realization, and experience.

THE FRUITION: THE STAINLESS TRIKAYA

The ultimate fruition of Essence Mahamudra, which is the complete realization of the three kayas, occurs when the actual realization of the root and lineage gurus suddenly awakens in the student's heart. This is the experience of simultaneous realization and liberation.

There is a saying: "One instant of Mahamudra realization cuts through all the paths and bhumis. Therefore, those who count the numbers of paths and bhumis are stupid." This is from a song sung by old yogis who practiced the Essence Mahamudra path, so the language is quite blunt. However, from this quotation we can see that in the Essence Mahamudra tradition, the paths and bhumis do not matter very much. Although we talk about the four yogas, they are not taught as solid experiences in which we progress incrementally from the first to the fourth. There is nothing solid to uncover or purify on each of the paths and bhumis because ordinary mind is beyond any faults or delusions.

Relative Fruition: The Five Joys

The relative fruition of Mahamudra is the experience of the five joys, which are sometimes known as the five freedoms. From this perspective, experiences such as clairvoyance and other special powers are not seen as actual fruition achievements. Rather, they are seen as temporary, passing achievements. We do not care about achieving these qualities, either on the path or in the resultant stage.

The first relative fruition experience in the Mahamudra path is having a complete sense of happiness and joy. This arises because one is free from the threefold reference points of subject, object, and action. In practice terms, this can be expressed as being beyond the threefold situation of meditator, that which is meditated upon, and the action of meditation.

The second relative fruition is a sense of joy and freedom that arises because one is free of any focus or reference point. When one is free from the threefold situation, there is naturally no reference point. Therefore, Mahamudra meditators feel a joyful, blissful mind.

The third relative fruition is the joy that arises from being free from any effort involved with what is to be adopted and what is to be abandoned. There is no threefold situation of one who adopts, that which is to be adopted, and the action of adopting; nor is there one who abandons, that which is to be abandoned, and the action of abandoning. These do not exist anymore in the meditator's mind. The fourth relative fruition is the joy that arises from being free of laziness, pride, and hope and fear. Finally, the fifth relative fruition is the great bliss that arises from the realization and experience of primordial purity.

These are the basic fruitions of Essence Mahamudra, which are of a temporary or relative nature. Various signs of these accomplishments will arise. There are outer signs that indicate which level of realization of these joys a meditator is experiencing. The particular signs of these joys, realizations, and bliss are explained in the oral instructions, which pass privately from teacher to student.

Ultimate Fruition: The Sovereign of All Reality

The ultimate fruition of the Essence Mahamudra path is the complete realization of the three-kaya nature of the ground. This realization of the ultimate level of Mahamudra arises from the realization of the dharmakaya. In its ultimate stage, it is called the fruition beyond concept, the fruition beyond thoughts, or the inconceivable fruition.

At this point, the inconceivable ground, path, and fruition are realized. From there, the different fruition levels of qualities and activities arise.

> The fruition Mahamudra is spoken of like this:
> The ground is receiving the transmission of the innate
>   trikaya.
> The path is applying the key points of the view and
>   meditation.
> The fruition is the actualization of the stainless trikaya.
>
> Therefore, its essence is emptiness, simplicity, dharmakaya.
> Its manifestation is the luminous nature of sambhogakaya.
> Its strength, manifold and unceasing, is nirmanakaya.
> This is the sovereign of all reality.
> The nature of Mahamudra is unity.[2]

That is the complete realization of Mahamudra mind and of enlightenment. From the point of view of Essence Mahamudra, it is really quite simple. Ultimately speaking, there is nothing on which to meditate because ordinary mind is stainless, luminous emptiness from the beginning. With the blessings of the lineage master, the student awakens to that realization. That is Essence Mahamudra.

Padmasambhava, who tames the rugged mind and brings forth the heart of enlightenment, shown with Mandarava and Yeshe Tsogyal.

PART THREE

The Dzogchen Journey

DZOGCHEN: THE GREAT COMPLETION

*The primordially awake mind, perfect
in its own state,
Completely full of the qualities of
enlightenment.*

Dzogchen

The Nine-Yana Journey

In Dzogchen, we are trying to leap. Ultimately, we leap beyond any concept of the path and formalities of practice and go directly to the nature of mind. However, in order to leap wholeheartedly into the vast, unconditioned nature of our mind, we must go through the entire Dzogchen journey, which is composed of the nine yanas. Finally, we can transcend the notion of journey altogether. There was never anywhere to go. We just did not realize it.

The teachings of Dzogchen contain the supreme views and methods of the whole Vajrayana tradition—there is nothing beyond them. These teachings present the final stage of the path. They are like a giant full stop. There is nothing beyond this full stop but utterly open, vivid space. From the Dzogchen point of view, the nature of our present mind actually contains the wisdom of buddha. The wisdom of buddha is not something we will find in the future. It is right here in the present, not only on this day but in this very moment. We have the heart of buddha. Our basic, fundamental state of mind is completely awake. We have awakening within our whole being, although most of us cannot realize it; we cannot see it right now. That is why we have the desire to search for buddhahood somewhere outside.

THE GREAT EXHAUSTION

Ordinarily, our minds are fettered by various facets of ego-clinging. However, through the practice of meditation, we are able to transcend all of the coarse and subtle habits that seem to bind us, and we can discover our own natural enlightenment. Meditation uncovers our buddha wisdom, which is currently covered by our emotional disturbances, ego-clinging, and narrow self-centered perspective. The nine-yana journey is a process that gives us the precise and skillful tools to progressively uncover our naturally enlightened state. Each yana leads us deeper into that reality, allowing us to shed more and more subtle layers of conceptuality and fear that we previously would not have been able to even recognize. In this way, meditation brings the wisdom of a buddha. Although we use the term "bring," meditation is not actually bringing anything; it is simply uncovering. The whole purpose of the nine-yana path is to uncover. Paradoxically, we are uncovering the uncovered nature. In reality, it has never been covered because ego never truly existed in the first place.

Within the general Buddhist framework of the three yanas—the Hinayana, the Mahayana, and the Vajrayana—the Dzogchen teachings and practices belong to the Vajrayana. In the Hinayana, Buddha taught the means by which we can transcend our personal suffering; and in the Mahayana, Buddha illuminated how to develop the genuine heart of love and compassion that aspires to elevate all beings from the state of suffering to the state of enlightenment. Finally, in the Vajrayana, Buddha pointed out that the true nature of our experience is not the reality of suffering but the reality of joy—great joy and happiness. There is a sense of agonizing bliss in samsara. When we apply the view and instructions of Vajrayana with mindfulness, we can experience great joy right within the experience of tremendous pain and suffering. The only way we will know this is by doing it. If we make an effort, we will have that experience.

In Tibetan, *dzog* means "complete," "perfect," or "exhaustion," and *chen* means "great." Thus, *dzogchen* means "great completion," "great perfection," or "great exhaustion." Each of these meanings refers to particular qualities of both the Dzogchen path and our own mind.

"Great completion" means that within this path, everything is complete—nothing else is needed. On a more personal level, it means that our mind, this very mind, is complete right from the beginning. It is complete because nothing whatsoever is missing. Mind is primordially awake and completely full of the enlightened qualities of great wisdom and compassion.

"Great perfection" means "perfect in its own state." The path is perfect the way it is, and all experience is perfect the way it is. For example, in searching for a method that we can use to work with a painful emotion that we may be experiencing, we do not have to go outside that raw experience. The antidote is already there, within the experience itself; or, as we often say, "The answer lies within the question." Thus, the path is perfect as it is, and the naked experience of emotions is perfectly enlightened right from the beginning. This approach reflects the tone of the Vajrayana, which is in contrast to the Hinayana or Mahayana attitude that might prompt us to say, "Oh, emotions are suffering. They are bad and we need to abandon them." Here, we say that emotions are pure right from the beginning.

"Great exhaustion" refers to the lack of true existence of the afflictive or negative emotions. Right from the beginning, these emotions are primordially exhausted. This is equivalent to the phrases "no arising" and "no birth" in the Mahayana view of shunyata. Because the negative emotions have no birth, they also have no existence. If we look closely, there is no moment that we can pinpoint, when we can say, for example, "This experience of anger started here." In fact, when we look nakedly at anger itself, we cannot find anything solid whatsoever. In the same way, all emotions are primordially nonexistent. From a positive perspective, we refer to this state as primordial purity, while from the point of view of negation, we speak of this as primordial nonexistence.

THE LINEAGE OF DZOGCHEN

According to the Dzogchen lineage history, Samantabhadra is the source of the Dzogchen teachings. He is depicted in paintings in the form of a blue, naked buddha. The color blue symbolizes the expansive, unchanging quality of space, which is the ground of all arisings, the basis of all appearances, and the source of all phenomena. The absence of robes symbolizes genuine reality beyond any dualistic, conceptual, or philosophical clothing. That is the dharmakaya buddha: the genuine body of absolute truth.

The Dzogchen teachings are transmitted from the enlightened heart of the dharmakaya buddha Samantabhadra to the sambhogakaya buddha Vajrasattva. *Sambhogakaya* means "body of enjoyment." This form of buddha represents the qualities of great joy and richness that the enlightened heart possesses. The richness of enlightenment is depicted through the beautiful ornaments of the sambhogakaya buddha Vajrasattva, who is white in color. The color white symbolizes the luminosity and clarity aspects of mind.

Dharmakaya itself is deep blue, like deep space, and sambhogakaya is like the moon or the sun, shining in that space. Thus, within the space we see light; we see the luminosity, richness, warmth, and clarity that is represented by the sambhogakaya buddha Vajrasattva, who continually propounds the Dzogchen teachings from the sambhogakaya realm, the realm of great enjoyment.

The Dzogchen lineage was transmitted from the sambhogakaya buddha Vajrasattva to the nirmanakaya buddha Garab Dorje, who was a manifestation or emanation body of enlightened heart. This nirmanakaya buddha was a human being who manifested in the human realm in the northwest of India in an area known as Uddiyana. Through Garab Dorje, the lineage was transmitted to many other masters in India, finally coming to the Lotus Born, Padmasambhava. Also known as Padmakara or Guru Rinpoche, Padmasambhava was the primary figure who brought the Dzogchen teachings to Tibet in the early eighth century, along with another Indian master, Vimalamitra, and a Tibetan master, Vairochana, who had traveled to India to study. Historically, these three are regarded as the primary masters responsible for transplanting the Dzogchen teachings in the land of Tibet.

Lineage is very important in the Dzogchen tradition because many of these practices and instructions are not written down in words but hidden in the form of oral instructions. Typically, the vajra master discourages students from writing these instructions down, since they are not meant to be read. They are meant to be heard—listened to, practiced, and discovered in your own heart. The instructions need to bloom in your own heart. You must have your own experience; otherwise, the process is reduced to mere scholarly research. For example, you write a thesis, which is read by somebody else. That person makes his or her own assumptions on the basis of your thesis and then writes another thesis. This process results in a lot of speculation. In the lineage of the Dzogchen teachings and in the Vajrayana teachings in general, there is no speculation. There are oral instructions and then there is practice, and through the practice we discover the experience within our own hearts.

There is a continuous lineage of Dzogchen instructions and practice that comes from Padmasambhava all the way to the masters of our day and time. Within the Nyingma school of Tibet, which is the holder of the Dzogchen tradition, there are two great lines of transmission. One is known as the *kama* lineage, the oral instruction or ear-whispered lineage, which is handed down in succession from teacher to student: Each vajra master "whispers" the instructions into the students' ears. The kama lineage is known as the indirect lineage because it is passed down through many generations of oral instructions. The second lineage, the *terma* lineage, or the treasure lineage, refers to the teachings that were written down and then hidden in various places by Padmasambhava, to be discovered or revealed by great masters at a later time. The terma lineage is known as the direct lineage because it is transmitted directly from a *terton*, or treasure revealer, to a student.

NOT LOSING THE WAY

In general, whether we are on the path of Vajrayana Buddhism, Mahayana Buddhism, or Hinayana Buddhism, the main purpose of spiritual practice is to attain a state of inner peace, mental stability, and freedom. Therefore, when we begin our practice on the Dzogchen path, we need to remind ourselves again and again of our main purpose for making this journey. We should be aware of the sort of freedom we are seeking: We are seeking freedom from pain, freedom from suffering, and perhaps freedom from the hope of happiness—all of these together. Without a clear idea of this, we will not go anywhere on the Dzogchen path or any other path of spirituality.

When we start our journey, our motivation is very genuine, clear, personal, and fresh. Then at a certain point, it becomes a little hazy and we lose our sense of what we are doing. We experience passion, aggression, and jealousy toward others traveling on the same path. We develop all sorts of emotional upheavals and disturbances. When we recognize such circumstances arising on our path, we can see that we are no longer following the path of enlightenment.

At that point on our spiritual path, we can fall into the depths of discontent. It is the same old samsaric story of discontent and grasping. We are not happy with what we are doing; we want something more. For example, we may have a good teacher who is instructing us in the practice of shamatha, but we become dissatisfied with our shamatha practice. We feel that shamatha is for beginners, and we want something more. Then perhaps we are given vipashyana meditation and we are still not happy with that. Next, we might be given a Vajrayana practice to do. We do the visualization and recite the mantra, but still we want more and more and more. When we are practicing sitting meditation, we feel that we need to be reading certain books, so we jump from sitting to reading. When we are reading and studying the profound teachings of Vajrayana or Mahayana, we think, "Oh, I'm missing my sitting practice," and we want to go back to shamatha. We jump around among these activities, fueled by our fluctuating desire and discontent.

If we continue with this approach to our spiritual path, then eventually we will end up back where we began our whole journey. In that case, we are doing exactly the same thing in our spiritual practice that we do in our everyday samsaric, neurotic life except that we have a better label for it: spiritual practice. We feel that we are members of a special club, which is called spirituality, and that it is a little better than the regular club, which is called samsara. However, aside from the labels, there is not much difference in our whole being. Nothing is changing internally. If we become caught up in such patterns of activity, then we are not leading ourselves toward any genuine result or achievement. Therefore, before we begin our journey, we should be clear about our motivation for undertaking the path, and we should have a clear understanding of what it means to follow it. We should know what we are seeking from a particular tradition, such as Dzogchen.

THE NINE STAGES OF THE PATH

Within Vajrayana Buddhism, there is a great diversity among the traditions, lineages, and masters, each of which emphasizes a different perspective in regard to the progressive stages of meditation. Nevertheless, many people are drawn toward the practice of Dzogchen because it seems very simple. It might seem like a shortcut, with few prerequisites. However, a general overview of the Dzogchen approach to the progressive stages of meditation shows us that we basically travel through nine different stages of learning and meditation. The Dzogchen journey is not necessarily about simply jumping into the ninth yana, which is the state of Ati yoga. We must go through nine stages of meditation in order to reach the final destination, the state where we exhaust all our unnecessary garbage. This is the point where the journey ends in the giant full stop.

If, in order to reach our destination, we had to walk all the way, then we would have a long and difficult journey. However, with reliable transportation of some kind, such as a motorcycle or a car, our journey becomes much easier. On the Dzogchen journey, the nine

VEHICLE	YANA	DESCRIPTION
I. VEHICLE OF DIRECTING THE CAUSE OF SUFFERING Causal vehicle: Sutrayana teachings that work directly with the causes of liberation	1. Shravakayana (Hinayana)	Yana of the "hearers" —Path of self-liberation
	2. Pratyekabuddha-yana (Hinayana)	Yana of the "solitary realizer," or "self-buddha" —Path of self-liberation
	3. Bodhisattvayana (Mahayana)	"Greater yana" —Path of the bodhisattva and the liberation of all beings
II. VEHICLE OF AUSTERITY AND AWARENESS (ENTRANCE TO THE VAJRAYANA) Fruition vehicle: three outer tantras	4. Kriya Tantra Tantra of activity	Tantra of activity —Purification practices emphasizing the outer activities of body and speech
	5. Upa or Charya Tantra	Tantra of character or behavior —Purification practices emphasizing the activities of body, speech, and mind equally
	6. Yoga Tantra	Tantra of union —Path of transformation emphasizing inner practice more than outer conduct; unifying the extensive relative and profound absolute truths
III. VEHICLE OF OVERPOWERING MEANS Fruition vehicle: three inner tantras	7. Maha Yoga	"Great yoga" —Development stage practice emphasizing the creation of a visualized deity as an expression of the clarity aspect of the primordial mind
	8. Anu Yoga	"After the great yoga" —Completion stage practice emphasizing the dissolving of the visualized deity by means of the wisdom aspect of primordial mind
	9. Ati Yoga (Dzogchen)	"The peak of yoga practice" —The perfection and completion of all qualities of buddhahood

yanas are different types of vehicles that transport us with little diffi-culty from one stage to another.

The nine-yana journey is divided into three sets of three yanas. The first set of three yanas is called the causal yana, or the Vehicle of Directing the Cause of Suffering. This set includes the Hinayana and the Mahayana. The second set of three yanas is called the Vehicle of Austerity and Awareness, and includes the Vajrayana tantras. The last set of three yanas is called the Vehicle of Overpowering Means, and includes the final stages of Vajrayana practice. Since each of these three sets has three yanas, these comprise the nine-yana journey. Each of the nine yanas presents us with methods that allow us to go more deeply into the nature of our own heart and into the very nature of reality. The progressive practice of these instructions can lead us to experience complete enlightenment in this very lifetime.

The Shravakayana and the Pratyekabuddhayana

T HE PATH THAT LEADS to the ultimate realizations of absolute reality is the nine-yana journey. If there were no path leading to such experiences, we would have a really wonderful theory, but how would we get there? With no guru, no teachings, and no path, it would be solely up to us not to get lost. However, in the nine-yana journey, we are presented not only with a clear view of these absolute experiences and realizations of enlightenment, but also with a path that leads to such experiences.

In the progressive stages of meditation on the Dzogchen path, the first set of yanas is known as the Vehicle of Directing the Cause of Suffering, which is the causal vehicle of the basic Buddhist path. This vehicle consists of the three yanas that we ordinarily speak of as the Shravakayana, the Pratyekabuddhayana, and the Bodhisattvayana, or Mahayana. They are collectively known as the Sutrayana, or the sutra vehicles of the common teachings of the Buddha. The three yanas included in this set work directly with the causes of liberation or freedom.

THE SHRAVAKAYANA: VEHICLE OF THE HEARERS

The first yana is the Shravakayana, or the yana of the hearers. *Shravaka* is a Sanskrit word that means "hearers." This yana refers to one of the most fundamental paths of Buddhism, the Hinayana path. *Hina* is typically translated as "lower" or "basic," but, as explained in chapter 1, these terms do not connote a hierarchy. Rather, they refer to a basic sense of the ground or foundation.

The practice of this particular yana emphasizes hearing the Dharma in the sense of learning the words of the Buddha properly. At this stage, we are trying to develop a conceptual understanding of the teachings. At the same time, shravaka also has the meaning of propagating the teachings. We not only hear the teachings, but we propagate what we have heard.

Historically, the teachers of this yana were primarily the ones who heard the Dharma directly from the Lord Buddha Shakyamuni and then propagated what they heard. Once these teachings were committed to written form, they became known as the sutras, or discourses of the Buddha. These teachers did not write commentaries on what the Buddha said but simply repeated his words. The shravakas did not allow much space for interpretation of the teachings of the Buddha. Instead, they took the teachings very literally, repeating them in a verbatim style. It is for this reason that these teachers were called the hearers and propagators.

In this context, hearing becomes a learning process. There is a proper way of learning the Dharma, which involves having proper motivation when we study. If our motivation is not pure while we are listening to, reading, or contemplating the sutras, then the words of the Buddha will not have much impact on our mindstream. That is why there is a strong emphasis on examining our motivation and paying attention to how we listen to the teachings. There are several ways that we can mistakenly or improperly listen to the Dharma.

Listening Like a Hunter Seeking Musk

The first improper motivation is called the motivation of a hunter seeking musk. Such a hunter is interested only in his own benefit while he searches for the prized musk. He is motivated primarily by greed. If your motivation when reading the sutras or hearing the Dharma from a teacher is only to get "the musk" for yourself, then that is the wrong motivation.

Listening Like a Pot with a Hole in It

The second improper motivation is traditionally explained through the analogy of a pot with a hole in it. When one pours water into such a pot, the liquid immediately drains out. Similarly, if you listen to the Dharma and understand what you hear but then do not remember anything, this can be compared to pouring water into a pot with a hole in it. Since you are unable to receive or hold the teachings, you are also unable to put them into practice.

Listening Like an Upside-Down Pot

The third improper motivation is explained through the analogy of a pot that has been turned upside down. When you try to pour water into such a pot, the water cannot enter and fill the pot and consequently will spill outside it. Similarly, when you listen to the teachings with pride, your mind is not open and receptive, and you do not receive any benefit from teachers or books. No transmission that is given actually penetrates your being.

Listening Like a Contaminated Pot

The fourth improper motivation is called the motivation of a contaminated pot. It is said that if you listen to the teachings with great anger, jealousy, ignorance, or other strong emotional fixation, then your mind will be like an unclean or poisoned pot. Whatever food or drink is poured into such a pot will be poisoned. Under such circumstances, whatever Dharma is poured into your mind will not be received as the genuine words of the Buddha. Your understanding of the spiritual path or of enlightenment will be contaminated by your emotional conflicts, ego-clinging, and self-centered view. In this way, the teachings become merely another tool used to "upgrade" your ego.

THE THREE STAGES OF MEDITATION

On the Shravakayana path, Buddha taught the practice of meditation by means of three stages of learning or training. These are the trainings in discipline, meditation, and knowledge, or prajna.

Training in Discipline

The first stage of meditation is taught through the training in discipline. In Sanskrit, "discipline" is *shila.* In Tibetan, it is *tsultrim.* From the perspective of the Shravakayana path, discipline means working with or taming our mind. Discipline is not simply a set of rules that say, "You cannot do this or that." Rather, it is a practice that has two aspects. The first aspect is taming, which is the method. The second aspect is our mind, that which is to be tamed. We need to ask, "What is the mind that we are trying to tame? What is the mind that we are trying to liberate? What is the mind that we are trying to free from suffering?"

Buddha taught that our samsaric mind consists of four basic aggregates. The first aggregate is ignorance. The second aggregate is lack of awareness. The third aggregate is emotional upheaval; and the fourth aggregate is not having devotion or faith. Thus, when we train in discipline, it is these four aggregates of samsaric mind that we are trying to tame.

IGNORANCE: NOT KNOWING THE TRUTH

Ignorance is the first aggregate, or collection of tendencies, to which we apply the discipline of taming. Ignorance is that state of mind that does not know the truth or does not know what is right and wrong. This ignorance is a state of stupidity, an aspect of our mind that is in a sense uneducated. We often feel that whatever we commit through ignorance is okay. We say, "I was not aware of it. I am ignorant about it. I am not the one to blame. It is those guys—the ones who did not educate me—who should be blamed for what I have done." Whenever we search for a scapegoat in this way, we are displaying our ignorance.

However, regardless of our ignorance, we are always responsible for our actions. The wrong actions that we commit are often due to our lack of inquisitiveness. We have not exerted ourselves to develop an inquisitive mind so as to learn what is right and what is wrong. It is not that our minds are not educated. Rather, it is that we do not want to learn. It is the mind that is lazy and does not step forward to learn. Therefore, we cannot say, "My mind, the ignorant mind, is not the one to be blamed." It is exactly the one to be blamed.

The ignorant nature of our mind is the basic cause of all our suffering and pain. Our lack of inquisitiveness is actually a failure of effort on our part. We cannot claim that an action is not negative simply because we have committed it through our ignorance. The action is still negative. The ignorant state of mind is a mind that is not being opened, not being informed, and not being educated properly. In a sense, the stupid nature of our mind is the lazy nature of our mind. The mind that feels very lazy and laid back, that does not want to move forward to learn, and that does not possess inspiration or inquisitiveness is what we call our ignorance. It is not a rational mind.

If our faith is a blind faith, then that is also an expression of ignorance. Buddha encourages us to be inquiring and skeptical about our spiritual path. He encourages us to expand our knowledge about our mind, about how to tame it, and about how to transcend our emotions. Having an inquisitive and skeptical mind is an excellent quality on the path of Vajrayana Buddhism.

However, this skeptical mind must also have a limit. A skeptical or inquisitive mind can carry us for some distance on our journey, but eventually there comes a time when we have to make a decision. We must reach an understanding whereby we can say, "Yes, this is the right path. This is the right thing for me." Alternatively, we might say, "No, this is not the right thing for me." Otherwise, this very good quality of mind, its skeptical or inquisitive nature, can lead us into a state of paranoia. We can spend our entire lives being paranoid about everything, in which case we will achieve nothing on the path. We will achieve no certainty. Therefore, we have to transcend this paranoia through learning the limit of skeptical or inquisitive mind.

NOT BEING AWARE

The second aggregate to which we apply discipline is our simple lack of awareness about the basic state of wakefulness that exists within our own mind. Although our natural state of mind is fully awake and aware, most of us are without any knowledge or experience of that. Our present state of mind in the relative world is totally scattered. Therefore, our minds are always in a state of unawareness and distraction.

Emotional Upheaval

The third aggregate to be tamed consists of our collection of emotional upheavals, which is quite easy to understand. All of us are born with many different and conflicting emotions, such as aggression, jealousy, pride, desire, and passion.

Insufficient Devotion

There are two aspects of the fourth aggregate, which is a lack of sufficient devotion or faith. The first aspect involves not having enough faith in or devotion toward ourselves. We do not have enough trust, confidence, or commitment to our own basic strength and abilities or to the power of our own minds. The second aspect involves not having enough devotion toward the teachings and the teacher. Consequently, our minds are always disturbed.

Training in Meditation

Having established that what is to be tamed is the mind, which consists of the four aggregates, we can now ask how this will be accomplished. The second stage of meditation is taught through the training in samadhi, which is the actual state of meditation. On the Shravakayana path, the first method that we use to tame our minds is the discipline of shamatha meditation. Discipline is the first stage of meditation, and it is through the application of discipline that we develop one-pointedness and an awareness of our surrounding environment. We become fully concentrated in any given situation. Whether we are talking or listening, writing or reading, if our minds are one-pointedly concentrated, then we can communicate fully and properly. However, if we cannot fully or one-pointedly concentrate our minds, then we cannot communicate effectively. Our communications will be scattered. The second stage of meditation, the training in samadhi or sitting meditation, involves working with our physical posture, our mental concentration, and the arising of distracting thoughts in a disciplined way. Thus, there is actually an entire set of disciplines associated with shamatha meditation.

In shamatha meditation, regardless of the life we are leading, we sit alone with our state of mind and with our breath. Whether we are leading the life of a monk or nun or the life of a single, married, or family person, when we practice shamatha meditation, we share a sense of solitude and an experience of inner peace. At this point, the meditative concentration involves simply sitting alone. We are learning how to sit alone, how to work alone with our minds, and how to liberate ourselves without outside help. There are no outer saviors, such as deities, gods, or demons. The Shravakayana teachings make this very clear: There is no outside savior. Not even Buddha himself can save living beings from their suffering, from their samsaric neurosis.

At this second stage of meditation, we are learning how to stand on our own two feet. We are learning how to walk alone on this path of spirituality and how to liberate ourselves. In Tibetan Buddhism, we use a traditional example of a knotted snake. Sometimes a snake will twist itself into a knot, and it is said that the snake has to unknot itself. There is no one who is going to come along and say, "Oh, poor snake, you have curled yourself up into this knot of suffering and so I will untie your knot and liberate you." This does not happen. This is exactly what Buddha is trying to teach us here. Through sitting alone in our meditation, we learn that we have to liberate ourselves by ourselves, with the basic strength of our own buddha nature. In this state of meditation, we cut through our fundamental desire and our basic attachment to the samsaric world.

Training in Transcendental Knowledge

As we develop the ground of meditation and discipline, we begin to develop the third stage of meditation on the Shravakayana path, which is the training in prajna or transcendental knowledge. That transcendental knowledge is the knowledge of egolessness, and we develop it through our practice of shamatha-vipashyana meditation. Through this profound insight, we can transcend our neurotic mind, which consists of the four aggregates. Thus, through our meditation, we uncover the basic state of buddhahood, the natural state of our mind.

THE FOUR NOBLE TRUTHS

The main practice of the Shravakayana path is the practice of the Four Noble Truths: the Truth of Suffering, the Truth of the Origin of Suffering, the Truth of the Cessation of Suffering, and the Truth of the Path Leading to the Cessation of Suffering. This practice is fundamental to all Buddhist traditions. In fact, if we cannot relate to the Four Noble Truths, then we will not be able to relate to any further stages of the path.

The Four Noble Truths are presented as two sets of two: two causes and two effects. The first two truths relate to the cause and effect of suffering or samsara, and the second two truths relate to the cause and effect of liberation, or nirvana. However, we are first presented with the effect and then the cause. Buddha taught that the First Noble Truth, which is the Truth of Suffering, is the result of the cause that is known as the Truth of the Origin of Suffering, which is the Second Noble Truth. The Third Noble Truth, which is the Truth of the Cessation of Suffering, is the result of the cause that is known as the Truth of the Path of the Cessation, which is the Fourth Noble Truth. In order to work with our relative experience of the world, we need to gain a certain degree of wisdom—a higher understanding of the first two truths. We need this wisdom and understanding in order to work with our habitual patterns. Therefore, the nine-yana journey begins with a detailed discussion of suffering: suffering itself, followed by the cause of suffering, then the cessation of suffering, and finally the path of the cessation of suffering. In this way, we move from one stage to another.

The Truth of Suffering

Buddha used one word to describe suffering: fear. Suffering is fear. Fear has many aspects: frustration, separation, attachment, death, and hope. All of these are expressions of fear. Fundamentally, our fear appears in two different guises: First, there is the fear of losing something that we value, such as our precious human birth or a precious teacher or precious jewelry. Because we cling to these things, attachment arises, as do fear and hope. Second, fear arises when we get something that we do not want. There are many examples, from the flu all the way up to something called death. However, there is little difference among these expressions. Suffering is simply fear, whether it is fear of physical pain or fear of mental pain. In our fear of getting something that we do not want, there is perhaps less of an aspect of hope; nevertheless, the fundamental nature of suffering is fear, regardless of the form it takes.

The Three Aspects of Suffering

The basic expression of the fear described by Buddha has three aspects: the suffering of suffering, the suffering of change, and all-pervasive suffering. All-pervasive suffering is our fundamental fear, as described above. When this basic fear becomes more expressive or "artistic," it appears in the form of the suffering of suffering. The suffering of suffering is very simple. For example, in addition to our fundamental fear, we develop a headache, and then a wisdom tooth begins to bother us. That is what we call the suffering of suffering.

Finally, there is the suffering of change. Since every aspect of change is suffering, this type of suffering is a continuous experience. One of the primary reasons why we experience this type of suffering is that our future is unknown to us. Whenever change occurs and we face the unknown, we experience a sense of blankness. That is why we fear death. We do not know what is going to happen after death. It is possible that we will have a wonderful time, but we do not know with certainty what will happen. We do not know the stages of dying, the experience of actual death, or what occurs after death. Therefore, we experience great fear. The suffering of change is connected with the unknown and with ignorance. We experience this suffering more strongly with changes that come as a surprise: when we expect one thing and then get something totally different. That is the suffering of change.

WORKING WITH SUFFERING

The first practice that we must undertake in order to work with our suffering is to learn not to ignore it. In general, our preferred method of dealing with suffering is to ignore it. We cover our eyes in order to shield ourselves from what we do not wish to see. However, that does not change anything that is happening. If we are in the middle of a war or a fight, covering our eyes will not prevent us from getting a bullet in the forehead. It might allow us to ignore the fighting, but we will not be able to protect ourselves.

We ignore the pain in our lives in a similar way. For example, we ignore our greatest fear—death. We do not even use the word "die." When a friend or family member dies, we say "passed away" or "expired," as though the person were a credit card. We ignore our reality—our suffering—in every possible way. However, if we truly want to avoid suffering, then it is very important for us to look at whatever difficulty we may be facing and try to learn its cause. For example, if we have a small family problem, we should face it and ask ourselves, "What is the real problem?" The solution lies in learning what our real problem is and then dealing with it.

Instead, we try to find an exit or an escape from this pain, from our little problem. If we are Buddhists, although we may have taken refuge in the Three Jewels, we totally forget them. We might begin to take refuge in a bar. Perhaps we drink some shots and then go off at full speed in our car. We might end up driving on the wrong side of the road and crash into another car. We get deeper and deeper into suffering just by ignoring our first little pain, which we could easily have dealt with. Instead, simply by using the wrong method to try to escape our pain, we get into the suffering of suffering. We might end up with broken legs, a broken neck, a smashed car, increased insurance costs, and a very high hospital bill for ourselves and others—not to mention a higher "karmic bill."

According to the Buddha, at the beginning of our path we need to examine the truth of suffering in detail. We must go into the depths of suffering in order to understand it. Only then will we develop the wisdom born of suffering that will enable us to cut through our experience of pain. In order to deal with the root of suffering, we have to realize its depths. We have to clearly recognize the true expression and pattern of suffering so that we can cut through the root of that pattern or expression. To deny or ignore our suffering does not help us to overcome it. Instead, we go into its depths. Rather than panicking when fear arises, we develop the courage and wisdom to deal with it.

For example, if someone pushes you into the ocean and you panic, then you might die there. However, if you rouse your courage and make friends with the water, you can begin to relate with it somewhat as a fish does. With courage, you can quickly develop the ability to float. You will not drown and the water will not seem as threatening to you. In a similar way, we learn how to float in this ocean of suffering and pain.

To ignore our suffering does not change anything in our world or our reality. Therefore, we are trying to develop the wisdom of dealing with suffering by looking directly at it, facing it, and seeing its depth. Working with suffering in this way comes from a clear understanding of the First Noble Truth.

The Truth of the Origin of Suffering

The Second Noble Truth is the called the Truth of the Origin of Suffering, which refers to original suffering or the root of suffering. Recognizing the cause of suffering is the second practice necessary for us to work with suffering. At this point, we discover that all our suffering arises from a certain origin or cause. In order to get rid of our suffering, we have to cut through the root of our problem.

The root of our problem is ego—our good old friend. We try to cut this root, this relationship with our ego, using the greater wisdom of the path. Our sense of individuality, of our individual characteristics, is rooted in ego. It is important for us to recognize how ego and our clinging to ego create all of our suffering. We need to recognize this clearly, on our own terms, rather than relying on scriptural theory. Although theories are helpful, each of us must contemplate the relationship of ego to our own suffering so that we come to our own individual understanding of the root of suffering. This understanding is the most important part of recognizing the cause of suffering.

Buddha taught that life consists of great pain and suffering, but he also taught that pain and suffering are impermanent and that the experiencer of this pain and suffering—the experiencer of the truth of suffering—is nonexistent. This is egolessness. In order to understand the notion of the experiencer being nonexistent, we must understand the theory of ego and the kleshas' game.

We can also say that the cause of suffering is the kleshas. *Klesha* is a Sanskrit term that is difficult to translate. One sense of *klesha* is "afflicting emotions." However, it is hard to define *klesha* as emotion because the state of ignorance or delusion is considered a klesha as well. Therefore, klesha is not strictly emotion alone. Another translation is "distractive state of mind," which is quite correct in its meaning but not necessarily a literal translation. The three root kleshas are passion, aggression, and ignorance. When we look at these three kleshas, we can see that they are rooted in ego-clinging. Therefore, ego-clinging is the absolute root of all our sufferings. On the Shravakayana path, the point is to recognize this and to contemplate the kleshas and their distractive energy.

From the Mahayana-Vajrayana perspective on the Four Noble Truths, the basic experience of kleshas themselves is not the real problem; instead, the problem occurs when our mind fixates on the kleshas. From this point of view, the basic problem arises from fixation, clinging, and the development of imputations and so forth.

We contemplate ego because we want to achieve liberation. We want freedom. However, who is it who wants to achieve freedom? It is "I." "I want to achieve freedom—before everyone else. *I* want the best path, the quickest path, and the easiest path to liberation, enlightenment, and freedom." Such thoughts are a strong expression of ego manifestation; yet those very thoughts are a powerful and mysterious experience because what ego is searching for is freedom from ego. Ego is searching for the realization of egolessness, selflessness or shunyata. Although ego plays a very important role in keeping us in samsara, it also plays an equally important role in bringing us out of samsara. If we simply switch its direction slightly, then that shift in view has a great impact on our path.

The Truth of the Cessation of Suffering

The Third Noble Truth is the Truth of the Cessation of Suffering, which is a fruition stage or result. After the root of suffering has been cut, there is no more result of that cause, which is the ego. In other words, the result of ego is pain and suffering, and after we cut through our ego-clinging, there is no more suffering and pain. When we reach the level of the nonexistence of ego, we also reach the level of the nonexistence of suffering, which we call the cessation of suffering—the end of the suffering of the samsaric world. That is also the end of our fear. At this stage, there is a certain sense of reaching a fearless state of mind. When we reach cessation, there is no more fear of suffering.

The cessation of suffering is ultimate peace because it is freedom not only from all the various kinds of suffering that can occur in cyclic existence, but also from all the causes of those sufferings. When we are free from both suffering and the causes of suffering, we experience joy, happiness, and freedom. Imagine that you have been imprisoned in a very small space for a long, long, long time—millions of years—and finally the gate is opened for you. You are free! That experience of freedom from imprisonment is perhaps the closest example of the experience of the Truth of Cessation.

The Truth of the Path That Leads to Cessation

In order to experience the cessation of suffering, we must work on the path that leads to such freedom. This path is the Fourth Noble Truth, which is the Truth of the Path That Leads to the Cessation of Suffering. The main practice on the Shravakayana path is meditation on the notion of egolessness, or selflessness. In this way, we work with our kleshas in order to cut through our clinging to a self.

There are two self-clingings: the self-clinging toward a person, such as "I" and "me," and the self-clinging toward phenomena. On this path, the greater emphasis is on cutting through the self-clinging of persons—the notion of "I." Therefore, we use a method of analytical meditation that goes through a detailed examination of this self. What is this self of persons? What and where is this ego of "I"? This type of detailed analysis is accomplished through the mind of prajna, or wisdom. Where is ego apart from this prajna? Our prajna is the quality of mind, or the method, that cuts through the clinging to self and thus cuts through the root of suffering. It is only after cutting the root of suffering, which is the self-centered view, that we reach the Third Noble Truth, which is the actual cessation of suffering.

Buddha said that suffering is like an illness. If we have a disease, then we also have the symptoms of that disease. We now have the symptoms of pain and suffering. The causes of that pain are discovered in the Truth of the Origin of Suffering. The Truth of the Path is like the medicine that we take to cure our disease. Reaching the Truth of Cessation is like being completely cured. We are cured of both our disease and its causes, and accordingly the symptoms go away. At that point, we feel great freedom and strength. That is the fundamental idea of the Four Noble Truths, which are the main focus of the Shravakayana journey.

PRATIMOKSHA: INDIVIDUAL SALVATION

The foundation of the nine-yana journey is the contemplation and practice of the Four Noble Truths, and our primary discipline is the commitment to work with our own suffering. Both the first yana, the Shravakayana, and the second yana, the Pratyekabuddhayana, are therefore focused on self-liberation or individual salvation. Thus, these two paths are called *pratimoksha* in Sanskrit, and *sosor tharpa* in Tibetan, which mean "individual salvation path" or "self-liberation path." At this point, we have a vision of liberating ourselves from the truth of suffering, from this painful fear of suffering, which is a chain that constantly binds us. This vision of liberation cannot develop further as long as we remain caught in this fear with our ego-centered view. Therefore, we begin our journey by developing the view of self-liberation, which is an essential aspect of our path. Then we work with this view in order to cut through our own neurosis, our own habitual patterns of karmic garbage and our own psychological clinging. This process is essential before we can begin to work with others.

THE PRATYEKABUDDHAYANA: VEHICLE OF THE SOLITARY REALIZERS

The Shravakayana path leads us to the second yana, which is the Pratyekabuddhayana. This yana is not very different from the first. *Pratyekabuddha* means "solitary realizer." Therefore, the Pratyeka-buddha-yana is the vehicle of the solitary realizer, or "self-buddha," referring to one who is self-enlightened. In this yana, practitioners reflect on the Four Noble Truths and additionally work with the twelve *nidanas,* the twelve links of interdependent origination.

The Twelve Links of Interdependent Origination

At this stage of the pratyekabuddha meditation, Buddha taught the notion of interdependent origination, which is an investigation of the nonsolidity of the relative world. All relative experiences are dependent on each other. There cannot be a subject without an object, and there cannot be an object without a subject. Although we have a strong fixation whereby we say that "this is the subject" and "that is the object," such definitions are not at all substantial. They are always interdependent.

The main emphasis of our practice at this point is on finding the root of samsara and then eradicating that root. In order to find that root, we engage in the process of contemplating the twelve nidanas, also called the twelve links of interdependence. We study interdependence through our analysis of the way beings arise in dependence upon causes and conditions. Both causes and conditions are involved in the arising of beings. The causes are the twelve links: Each link is the cause of the subsequent link. The conditions are the five elements: earth, water, fire, wind, and space.

The twelve links of interdependent origination are Ignorance, Formation, Consciousness, Name and Form, the Six Sensory Perceptions, Contact, Feeling, Craving, Grasping, Existence, Birth, and Old Age and Death. When we are on the pratyekabuddha path, we reflect on each of these, as well as on their interrelationship and cause-and-effect nature. Ultimately, we return to the original cause, which is ignorance—ego— and we work on cutting through ego-clinging again. It is the same work as with the Four Noble Truths, except that here we use the method of the twelve links of interdependent origination.

The cycle of the nidanas goes on and on and on, again and again, with each stage leading to the next. Death, which appears to be the final stage, produces further ignorance, which produces further formation, which produces further consciousness, and so on, as a continual and unending process. This is the meaning of the term "spinning," or samsara. The arising of all sentient beings in a samsaric environment occurs through this twelve-link process. We cannot escape. We are stuck in this situation.

This contemplation of the twelve links touches our whole being, our whole existence. It is a powerful practice that effectively joins theory and our personal experience. Traditionally, it is said that pratyekabuddhas practice in cemeteries. When they find a human skull or other human remains, they use these objects as a basis for their contemplations. They ask, "What is this? This is the skull of a human being. Where does it come from? It comes from death. Where does death come from? Death comes from old age, and old age comes from birth." They trace these connections all the way back to ignorance. By contemplating these twelve links of interdependent origination, we can see how our own existence comes from ignorance. We examine each link or stage, from ignorance through the second and subsequent stages, going through the whole cycle again and again. This helps us to understand the nature of the Four Noble Truths in an experiential as well as a theoretical way. Another way to contemplate the twelve nidanas is to reverse that order so that one ends up at the beginning point of samsara, ignorance, and then eliminates that cause.

The Journey of the Solitary Realizer

At this stage of our journey, there is not much emphasis on learning or intellectual studies. Rather, the emphasis is on contemplation, insight, and meditation. Our goal is to achieve the state of liberation through our own contemplation without relying on anyone else—not even a teacher. At this point, there is a tremendous sense of courage because we are starting to see the path through which we can realize the nature of liberation by ourselves. There is a tremendous sense of confidence and trust in our own basic wisdom and ability. We are not depending on any other factors because the real—the ultimate—realizer is our own self. We have to reach the point of nirvana by ourselves, and we need to be brave to make this journey. We tell ourselves, "I must do this myself. I have the full power, the full energy to reach nirvana, the state of liberation." Therefore, there is a quality of courage, which is very positive and important.

At the same time, this yana involves great pride in our own basic awareness and strength, and in seeing that liberation can be accomplished alone. We do not have to rely on any other beings, any other special friends, or any scriptures. We can do this by ourselves. This is a positive type of pride that we should cultivate, an expression of our basic self-confidence and trust. However, if we are carried away by our courage, then we fall into the state of ordinary pride. Such pride and self-absorption can develop to the extreme of becoming completely solid, so that we isolate ourselves from everything. This is dangerous because it can lead us to isolate ourselves from involvement in other activities on the path. Thus, this quality of pride also has a negative aspect.

To overcome that kind of isolation, we concentrate on the inner pride of the pratyekabuddha, which is pride in our own basic awareness, pride in the strength of our ability to achieve enlightenment by our own efforts. We do not have to rely on anyone else; in fact, it is not possible for anyone else to liberate us from our ego-clinging and disturbing emotions. Instead, we work to discover the basic awareness, strength, and positive qualities of our own mind.

At this stage of our meditation we discover that our path and practice are simply ourselves. We take the initial steps ourselves, and we make this journey alone. There is a great sense of loneliness in this realization, and at the same time there is a great sense of relief. Our freedom is in our own hands. We no longer feel the need to acquire it from others. We are confident in our freedom and relieved that we are not always being chained to or bothered by other people. There is no Big Brother watching us, and there are no other people interfering with our path. It is none of their business, and there is nothing they can do for us on our path.

Underlying our sense of freedom and loneliness is the realization that the possibility of "being saved" does not exist. There is no salvation. Our path and practice are simply our own journey, into which we must put our own effort. There is no other being who has the power to save or condemn us. That is true whether that being is called Buddha, God, the external energy of nature, or anything else. No such power exists outside us. We hold the key and the power to condemn or save ourselves. That is the journey of the solitary realizer.

However, within the context of the whole nine-yana journey, the solitary realizer is not left completely alone. There is benefit, there is blessing, and there is strong support from the spiritual friend and from the Buddha, Dharma, and Sangha. Nevertheless, there is a great sense of freedom in undertaking our own journey.

THE HINAYANA JOURNEY

The Shravakayana and the Pratyekabuddhayana of the Hinayana use very detailed methods to examine every aspect of our path—every detail of our individual existence, every particular pain and suffering that we experience in samsara. Dealing precisely with every aspect of our lives becomes very important for our nine-yana journey.

For example, if you are taking a trip to meet the president of a country, you start your journey at home. You prepare by first taking a shower; then there is a whole process of getting dressed. You put on your trousers or skirt, you put on a fresh shirt, you put on your belt, you put on a necktie or scarf, and then you put on your jacket and your overcoat.

In one sense, all of this preparation may look meaningless. Putting on underwear may not mean much, but it is a very important step. Without it we cannot get to the next stage. Although it seems so meaningless and such a simple thing to do, it is still very important. For example, we need to wear properly fitting trousers and to fasten our belt precisely so that when we meet the president and he shakes our hand, our trousers will not fall down in front of a television crew. The whole process of relating to these small but essential details starts right in our own home. Attending properly to these little details is precisely what prevents our trousers from falling down. Working with these two yanas is like working with every detail of our attire. The next step that we will be taking is to move onto the Mahayana path, which is like going to meet the president.

From the point of view of the nine-yana journey, engaging in the Shravakayana and Pratyekabuddhayana practices does not mean that we have to enter into and complete the Hinayana path fully. We do not have to go to the extent of isolating ourselves and working on individual salvation. However, we do participate in learning the words of the Buddha and developing a conceptual understanding in the first stage, and in the profound contemplations of the second stage. Through contemplation and meditation, we rediscover our basic awareness and strength. We discover that on this path of enlightenment, salvation comes only through our own efforts.

13

The Bodhisattvayana

To enter the Bodhisattvayana, we need to develop our courage, a heart of daring that is willing to penetrate the experience of suffering. This heart of daring is filled with curiosity and inquisitiveness. It is not afraid to deeply explore the nature of our pain and suffering. Once we have touched the basic heart of suffering, then we delve further into our experience of agony and pain until we reach the point of experiencing joy, compassion, and the awakening of our heart. This occurs right within the experience of suffering itself. Genuine love and compassion do not come from anywhere else. Within our shared experience of suffering and pain, we discover how to communicate with all types of sentient beings and liberate them. Those beings who have generated such a connection with others through love, compassion, and wisdom are known as bodhisattvas.

The attitude of the bodhisattva is not to look for enlightenment or freedom for oneself alone, but to seek freedom and enlightenment for all sentient beings. This enlightened attitude comes from the understanding that all beings have the same goal: freedom and happiness. Every sentient being is looking for freedom from pain and suffering. We are all racing toward happiness.

THE GREATER VEHICLE

The Bodhisattvayana is the third yana, following the Shravakayana of the hearers and the Pratyekabuddhayana of the solitary realizers.

This yana is also referred to as the Mahayana, which means "greater vehicle." One could say that, in comparison with the previous two vehicles, the Mahayana engine is more powerful and capable of greater speed. In the old Indian concept of society, the image given was similar to a chariot or bandwagon. A chariot could travel faster than many vehicles, while simultaneously carrying many passengers. Often, forms of transportation that are capable of transporting greater numbers of people are slower. However, this vehicle is not. With its powerful engine, it moves like a sports car. It is a very fast form of transportation, and the journey we are taking on the path of Mahayana is a rapid one. That is why it is called the greater vehicle.

This great vehicle starts with great vision, as opposed to the vision of self-liberation found in the earlier two yanas. Those vehicles were primarily focused on individual salvation, on freeing oneself from suffering and attaining the stage of cessation. However, as far as the Mahayana is concerned, simply attaining the stage of cessation for oneself is a very narrow vision. We begin the Mahayana journey by developing the greater vision that seeks liberation for all beings.

After recognizing the universal quality of our own desire to be free of suffering, we can infer that all beings are looking for enlightenment, for great awakening—the direct antidote for the causes of suffering and the suffering itself. We can see that we all share the same goal. In an ordinary sense, we share the same view; we enjoy sitting together and watching our favorite shows or going to our favorite restaurant. We enjoy doing things together. The Mahayana logic here asks: "Why don't we do the same thing on our spiritual path?" We should all come together and walk on the path with this enlightened attitude, the attitude that says, "I want all sentient beings to attain enlightenment." We have a passion for all beings to attain enlightenment, complete freedom from pain and suffering. This wish is called bodhichitta.

Bodhi means "enlightened" or "awakened," and *chitta* means "mind" or "heart." *Bodhichitta* is translated as "enlightened attitude" or "awakened heart" because our heart has awakened to the vaster perspective of wishing to free all living beings. When we come to the stage of Mahayana, we discover that the path of cessation, of individual liberation, is a very lonely journey. Therefore, we cut through this narrowness and enter into the expansive vision of universal enlightenment.

Loving-kindness and compassion begin as thoughts or concepts. To develop these qualities, we simply need to make a slight shift in our way of thinking and in our motivation. Because they are thoughts and concepts, loving-kindness and compassion are not very difficult to develop. The mental shift we make is from holding a self-centered view to a view of caring for all sentient beings. This is a shift that moves us from a concern for our own benefit and welfare to a concern that includes all living beings. However, this is possible only through understanding our own suffering and pain. We may possess a basic sense of love and of compassion, but we do not possess the genuine loving-kindness and compassion that are required for the path.

THE FENCE OF "MINE"

Our ordinary love and compassion exist within a fence called "mine." We have love and compassion for whatever is within this fence of "mine"; we have love and compassion for our friends, our family and our pets—"my pet," "my family," "my friends." We practice generosity, discipline, patience, and all the other virtues towards whatever is within this fence of "my-ness." However, beyond this fence, our love and compassion often freeze like water turning into ice. If we throw an ice cube at someone, it can be very painful, whereas if we shower the water of compassion and love on someone, it can refresh and awaken them. To develop the refreshing water of genuine love and compassion, we need to break down our sense of territory and generate a greater vision that includes all living beings.

We should really question our hearts by asking, "What do I mean by love?" and "What do I mean when I say that I have compassion for beings?" For example, when we shed tears over the death of a pet, we must question whether those tears are for the being that has died or for ourselves. Are we crying because we miss the companionship of our pet? If so, then we are shedding tears of selfishness, which are based on our self-centered view—not tears of compassion. By analyzing our minds and questioning ourselves, we can see how much genuine compassion and loving-kindness we actually have developed.

According to the scriptures, a practical way to develop genuine compassion is to begin with those beings for whom we naturally feel compassion, such as our close friends or family. Next, we expand those feelings of sympathy and concern to beings for whom we have neutral feelings. Finally, we can include even our "enemies"—those beings for whom we feel strong hatred—inside our circle of compassion. Ultimately, we are able to develop compassion that is unbiased and has no territory or limit whatsoever.

NURTURING THE SEED OF ENLIGHTENMENT

If we aspire to give birth to bodhichitta and to travel the path of great enlightenment, we must develop this limitless heart of compassion. Buddha taught this through the example of a flower. If we want to have a flower, we must first have the seed. At the beginning of our path, compassion is like a seed—the seed of enlightenment. In the middle of our path, after we have planted the seed, compassion is like the water that makes our seed of enlightenment grow. Finally, once the plant is growing, we need the warmth and heat of compassion in order to ripen the fruit of our enlightenment. Without compassion, we have no seed of enlightenment, no water to nourish the seed, and no heat to ripen the fruit. Without compassion there is no bodhichitta; without bodhichitta there is no bodhisattva path; without the bodhisattva path, there is no fruition of buddhahood. Therefore, without compassion, there is no Mahayana path. If we are claiming to be Mahayanists or Vajrayanists without the genuine heart of compassion and loving-kindness, then we are simply fooling ourselves. We are not walking toward any fruition of enlightenment. For this reason, the Mahayana path emphasizes generating compassion at the beginning of our journey.

RELATIVE AND ULTIMATE BODHICHITTA

The awakened heart of bodhichitta is divided into two classifications: relative and ultimate. Ultimate bodhichitta is the realization of the empty nature of reality united with the heart of compassion. The realization of the inseparability of these two becomes the ultimate nature of a bodhisattva's heart. The relative heart of enlightenment is a type of desire: the desire to bring all beings to the state of enlightenment. Relative bodhichitta is simply this positive desire or thought: I want all sentient beings to attain the state of buddhahood.

It is said in the Mahayana scriptures that there is one aspect of desire that bodhisattvas do not give up until they attain enlightenment because without it, they cannot come back to samsaric existence. Therefore, in order to be able to return again and again to samsara to help sentient beings, bodhisattvas retain the desire of relative bodhichitta.

We usually think of generating bodhichitta as reciting lines such as "I want to achieve enlightenment for the benefit of sentient beings" or "I want to work on the path of liberating all sentient beings." We think it is that simple. After all, there are only two or three lines to recite when we take the bodhisattva vow. However, the practice itself is not simple. In order to become a Mahayanist, we must cultivate a genuine heart that cares for others, regardless of the circumstances. Even if we have to go to hell to help someone, we are willing to jump right into it.

This enlightened attitude is usually described as having two stages. The first stage is called aspiration bodhichitta and the second is called application bodhichitta. Aspiration bodhichitta is simply generating the aspiration toward this greater vision of enlightenment. It involves developing a certain sense of courage and warriorship. Later, we develop the actual wisdom of the techniques. The way in which we become great warriors or great bodhisattvas is through the practice of application bodhichitta.

Three Ways of Generating Aspiration Bodhichitta

Aspiration bodhichitta is the enlightened attitude, the pure motivation and intention to awaken and liberate all sentient beings. It is traditionally taught that one can generate this aspiration in three different ways.

KINGLIKE BODHICHITTA

First, we can generate an enlightened attitude that is like the attitude of a king. A king wants first to strengthen the wealth of his kingdom; then, if he is a good king, when the kingdom has enough wealth and the country is strong enough, he shares that wealth with all his subjects. In a similar way, when we adopt kinglike bodhichitta, we say, "I first want to attain enlightenment for myself and then share my wisdom, compassion, and enlightened power with all sentient beings. I am going to benefit all sentient beings through the wisdom and compassion of my own enlightenment." That is the first type of intention, which is called the kinglike attitude of bodhichitta.

CAPTAINLIKE BODHICHITTA

The second way of generating aspiration bodhichitta is called captainlike bodhichitta. We envision ourselves guiding a boat or plane full of passengers to the other side of the ocean of samsara. We say, "I would like to travel the path of enlightenment with all living beings so that we all reach the final destination together." It is not "me first" and the others later, nor is it the others first and me later. Rather, everyone travels together to the same destination. Whatever effort we put into our path and practice, we put into materializing this vision. This is called the captainlike attitude because a captain travels with his crew and passengers on the same ship or plane. The captain does not go before or faster than the others. Similarly, we have a wish to share this great vision with others right from the beginning and to arrive with them at the other shore of enlightenment.

Shepherdlike Bodhichitta

The third way of generating aspiration bodhichitta is called shepherdlike bodhichitta. Like a shepherd with his sheep, we put everyone else in front of us. A shepherd guides his flock to the pasture in the morning, walking protectively behind them. He keeps the sheep together and leads them to good pasture, which is also a safe place. At the end of the day, he brings them back home in the same way, walking behind all of them. This attitude of bodhichitta is a vision that puts all sentient beings in front of us on the path of enlightenment. We say, "I want all sentient beings to attain enlightenment first; therefore, I want to be the last person in samsara." This is the greatest and most difficult attitude among the three types of bodhichitta. It is known as the vision of Avalokiteshvara, who is the bodhisattva of compassion, and is praised by the Buddha as being supreme.

We can see why the vision of shepherdlike bodhichitta is superior by examining our own life experiences. For example, when we are in a big, stuffy supermarket and we are ready to check out, we want to be first in the line. We do not want to stay there one extra minute, so we all usually find the shortest cashier line and rush out as soon as possible in order to breathe fresh air. From the Mahayana perspective, we are in a great big samsaric supermarket, with a long line of beings rushing out to breathe the fresh air of liberation. With shepherdlike bodhichitta, the commitment that we make is to let all of these other beings go first. When we see someone come up behind us in the checkout line, we say, "Please go ahead." We move back in the line again and again. We keep doing this even if it gets to be late—even if it gets to be midnight or two in the morning. From this example, we can see how precious, how profound, and how difficult it is to generate this last type of bodhichitta.

Although shepherdlike bodhichitta is the most powerful, it is not necessarily the best for everyone. We should look at these three in terms of which one best suits us. We should ask ourselves honestly which attitude would truly help us to generate the heart of enlightenment in a genuine way.

All three ways of generating bodhichitta are included within aspiration bodhichitta. We might say, "I want to achieve enlightenment for all sentient beings" or "I want everyone to attain enlightenment at once" or "I want all other sentient beings to attain enlightenment first," but at this point, we are not actually doing anything. We are simply having a good thought. It is like saying, "I will give some money to the panhandler on the street." It is a good aspiration, but it does not actually benefit the person at that moment.

Nevertheless, even though we are not yet acting, this intention is very important. From the Mahayana point of view, all physical actions are directed by our minds, so positive and negative actions are defined not solely by the physical actions themselves but also by our mental attitude. For example, it is said that if you try to help someone but you have a bad intention, then that action is regarded as negative, even if outwardly it seems very genuine and very nice. Consequently, before beginning our actual practice of application bodhichitta, we emphasize training our mind in the intention and attitude of bodhichitta.

Pure Vision: Penetrating the Depths of Suffering

Aspiration bodhichitta involves working with pure vision, which arises from our experiences of pain and suffering. From our basic heart of daring, we develop the courage to further penetrate the experience of suffering. That heart of daring is aspiration bodhichitta, which is also the source of the pure vision of bodhisattvas. Unless we accept our pain, acknowledge our agony, and are willing to discover what these experiences are all about, the heart of bodhi cannot arise.

Aspiration bodhichitta should not be too conceptual, impersonal, or theoretical. It is not a theory of enlightenment, and it is not somewhere far away, outside our own experiences of Dharma, of life, and of path. To develop aspiration bodhichitta we have to approach the basic heart of suffering and pain with courage and curiosity. We are all afraid of this experience, and because of our fear, we have difficulty developing the basic vision of enlightenment. Giving birth to aspiration bodhichitta involves fearlessly diving into our experience of agony. We discover bodhichitta right within our ordinary experiences of painful emotions, as well as within our experiences of compassion, love, and kindness. From this perspective, we can see that the vision of enlightenment begins right here within our own ordinary life. It may sound very good to say, "I am going to help all sentient beings achieve enlightenment and the causes of enlightenment," but if there is no heart in it, then from the Mahayana point of view, it is just rubbish.

Compassion, love, and kindness are not some kind of "sacred heart" or external grace that we are trying to extend to someone who is suffering. The fundamental state of compassion goes beyond the conceptual idea of being compassionate. The acts of a bodhisattva are spontaneous acts of compassion and are not based on preconceived notions of how or what they should be. They are spontaneous, natural, on-the-spot experiences of the heart. Many sutras compare these experiences to a mother's love.

When a mother sees her only child suffering, the spontaneous heart of compassion arises without any preconceptions or preparation. A mother does not have to plan her compassion; when she sees her child, compassion is right there. Similarly, the bodhisattva's heart of compassion is very spontaneous. The nature of aspiration bodhichitta and the vision of enlightenment itself are beyond any concept of formulating love or compassion.

Application Bodhichitta

When we practice application bodhichitta, we seek to fulfill the promises that we have made in our practice of aspiration bodhichitta. This involves a certain sense of honesty, because if we do not work to fulfill our commitments, our aspiration bodhichitta can turn into a kind of cheating. Therefore, Buddha taught that we have to be honest with ourselves. For instance, in every practice session we say, "May all beings enjoy happiness and the causes of happiness, and be free from suffering and causes of suffering." However, such aspirations can become a merely mechanical process—something that we say without thinking. At that point, they have nothing to do with our heart.

When we generate the two bodhichittas, the result is that we experience a greater sense of synchronizing our body, speech, and mind. It is extremely difficult to achieve anything on the Mahayana path unless we combine the two bodhichittas. Thus, giving birth to genuine application bodhichitta is an essential aspect of our path. We must have the courage and the wisdom to implement our aspiration. We must start to actually apply what we have been saying, what we have been thinking, and what we have been aspiring to accomplish. That application begins with the practice of the six paramitas, which are one of the main practices of the Mahayana path.

THE SIX PARAMITAS

The six paramitas are the practices of bodhisattvas who have connected with the basic heart of compassion and love and who have developed confidence in that heart. The six paramitas, which are also called the six perfections, are the practices of generosity, discipline, patience, exertion, meditation, and prajna, which is wisdom or transcendental knowledge. Among the six paramitas, the most important is wisdom.

Paramita is a Sanskrit term. In Tibetan, it is *parol tu chinpa* (*pha rol tu phyin pa*). *Parol* is "the other side" or "the other shore," *tu* means "to," and *chinpa* means "to go" or "gone." Thus, *parol tu chinpa* means "gone to the other shore." The meaning in Sanskrit is the same. The paramitas are so named because, through these actions, we leap to another state—to "the other shore," the state of enlightenment. Through the attainment of progressive levels of realization, we arrive at the state of being who we are and what we are—the true state of phenomenal reality.

"The other" is also a description that is used to suggest the quality of being genuine, indicating that our usual dualistic thoughts, concepts, and kleshas are not our true state. The paramita practices take us beyond the experience of ordinary concepts, beyond the labeling process, and beyond duality to the experience of the genuine state that goes beyond all of these. The use of the term "genuine" also indicates a realization that the Hinayana path is not genuine in the sense that it does not lead us to the complete, absolute truth. In contrast, the Mahayana practices of the six paramitas lead us to a state that is completely enlightened—the state of full wakefulness. This state goes beyond even the experiences of the arhats of the Hinayana path. Therefore, "gone to the other shore" or "gone beyond" has the meaning of going beyond mundane samsaric confusion, as well as going beyond the nirvanic experiences of Hinayana individual salvation.

The Order of the Six Paramitas

The six paramitas are given in a particular order: generosity, discipline, patience, exertion, meditation, and wisdom. There are three reasons for this order. The first reason is so that we begin with the easier, more accessible practices. For example, generosity seems to be the most accessible, and discipline is a little less so; patience is harder than discipline, but perhaps easier than exertion.

The second reason the paramitas appear in this order is that there are cause-and-effect relationships among them. It is understood to be a subtle relationship, in which each paramita becomes a support that gives rise to the next paramita.

The third reason the paramitas are given in this particular order is so that the coarsest elements of the practice come first. Generosity is the coarsest element of the paramita practices, while prajna is the most subtle. The order reflects a development of increasingly subtle elements in the practice.

We begin our practice of each paramita by first working with its obstructions, which constitute its opposite aspect. Whatever obstructs us from practicing each paramita should be taken into our experience of the path. For example, in practicing generosity, we encounter the basic obstruction of attachment, which involves a sense of holding on to something and not being able to let go. That obstruction of our generosity is its opposite side. From one perspective, situations that provoke these obstructions may seem unfavorable, but from another perspective these situations are extremely favorable. Without them, we would not have any opportunities to practice, and thus perfect, the paramitas. Consequently, obstacles play a very important role in our practice of the paramitas.

Right View: Threefold Purity

The factor that determines whether our paramita practice is genuine is whether or not we hold the right view, which comes from our intention. In the most basic sense, right view is the understanding of threefold purity, which invokes the view of prajna—the insight into emptiness. If we can invoke even a glimpse of emptiness, or shunyata, when we practice generosity or discipline, then our practice will become pure. Threefold purity works with the purity of subject, the purity of object, and the purity of action. For example, in the case of generosity, the first aspect of threefold purity is the recognition of the egoless nature of the self—the one who performs the action of giving. The second aspect involves seeing the selfless nature of the recipient of the action of giving. The third aspect involves the recognition of the shunyata nature of the action itself. If there is no subject and no object, then logically there is no act. In this way, the threefold view purifies the egocentric tendencies that arise in our practice of the paramitas.

Most of us cannot begin our practice with the full realization of threefold purity. However, if we are able to engage in these practices without expectations, we will be moving closer to the practice of threefold purity. It is very difficult for an ordinary being to recognize that there is no self who is giving, no self who is receiving, and no action of giving. That is why if we begin by giving without expectation, then even if we have a sense of subject, object, and action, it will lead us toward the genuine practice of the paramitas. We are not thinking, "I will get a little better because I am being generous and I practice discipline." If we expect these things to enrich our ego, then our paramita practice is not the practice of enlightenment; but if we can practice the paramitas without any notion of expectation, then it can lead us to the other shore because we are directly transcending our ego and our self-centered view. On that basis, we can later practice with threefold purity. However, we cannot accomplish threefold purity without the experience and practice of the view of shunyata.

The Path Quality of Paramita Practice

Although threefold purity is strongly emphasized on the bodhisattva path, we must understand that we are on a path. We should not expect our practice to be completely pure, completely perfect, and completely transcendent right from the beginning. Shantideva, a great master of the bodhisattva path, said that as ordinary persons, we will have many thoughts. First, we may have a thought of giving and then we may have a second thought: "No, no. I do not want to give that; I may need it." Shantideva said that these types of thoughts are natural and normal for ordinary bodhisattvas. However, he also said that we must work with these thoughts by maintaining a certain commitment to our vision of paramita practice. For instance, once we have a thought of giving, no matter what second thought we may have, we should try to give.

It is important to recognize that although we struggle and have a certain sense of impurity in our practice, we are not failing. It does not mean that we are not practicing the paramitas or that we are not being successful on the path. With the aspiration to communicate with every living being, we can develop the vision of awakening sentient beings on the bodhisattva path through any of the paramita practices. We can do this whether our path is the Mahayana or the Vajrayana.

THE BODHISATTVA

Those beings who have gone beyond the limits of suffering and compassion are known as bodhisattvas. Their basic vision is to liberate all beings and to develop a heart connection with them through the experiences of pain and suffering that we all share in this samsaric world. In Tibetan, "bodhisattva" is *changchup sempa. Changchup* means "enlightenment" or "buddhahood." The first syllable, *chang,* means "totally free from all obscurations." The second syllable, *chup,* means "attainment," which refers to attainment of all the qualities of wisdom. It also means "realization," which refers to the realization of the wisdom aspect and compassionate quality of our minds. In the second word, *sempa,* the first syllable, *sem,* means "heart" or "attitude"; this refers to the enlightened attitude or aspiration. The second syllable, *pa,* comes from *pawo,* which means "warrior." Therefore, *sempa* means "warrior," "heroic," or "courageous one." We might translate *changchup sempa* as "a person who has a brave mind that has been purified and expanded." It is only when we have generated both aspiration and application bodhichitta that we can be called bodhisattvas or Mahayanists.

The Three Fearlessnesses

A bodhisattva is someone who possesses three qualities of fearlessness in relation to the path. The three fearlessnesses are (1) not being afraid of the number of beings whom we are trying to benefit; (2) not being afraid of the amount of time it will take to attain buddhahood; and (3) not being afraid of the difficulties that we will encounter on the path. Someone who does not fear these three difficulties is called a warrior or courageous one.

Not Fearing the Number of Beings

When we commit ourselves to working toward the enlightenment of all sentient beings, we must remind ourselves that we are not intending to benefit only one or two beings or merely the beings who exist in this world. We are committing ourselves to a limitless number of beings who live in limitless worlds and universes. Think about it. Consider how difficult it can be to work with one person. Consider the difficulties that can arise between two or three people within a family. If we cannot deal with one person, then how can we deal with limitless beings? That is a good question. Therefore, the commitment we make as bodhisattvas is a very courageous one. We are saying that we will work with not only one or two people but all living beings.

NOT FEARING THE AMOUNT OF TIME

It is said that if one is a being of the highest capacity, such as Shakya-muni Buddha, then it takes only three countless aeons to attain enlight-enment. If one is a being of middling capacity, such as the bodhisattva Maitreya, then it takes only thirty-seven countless aeons to attain en-lightenment. If one is a being of the lowest capacity, then it will take an even longer time. Therefore, when we embark on our journey to en-lightenment in order to benefit all living beings and we say "no matter how long it may take," we are making a very courageous move.

NOT FEARING DIFFICULTIES ON THE PATH

Finally, we have to face how difficult it is to help and benefit beings. We have to confront how difficult it is to satisfy only one other living being. There are times when it might seem as though there is not much possibility or opportunity for us to be of help. For example, if an elderly woman is having a hard time crossing a street and we offer our assistance, she may think that we are trying to mug her or take advan-tage of her in some way. We can face many difficulties in helping sen-tient beings.

In the traditional history of Mahayana, there is a story about a monk who had entered the Mahayana path. This monk had fully gener-ated the heart of bodhichitta. He was a "freshman bodhisattva," walk-ing down the street full of courage and a fresh sense of bodhichitta. On his way, he met a Brahmin on the street. This Brahmin decided to test the enlightened attitude of the new monk by asking him for the gen-erosity of his right arm. The Brahmin said, "Please give me the gift of your right arm. I need it for certain things." The bodhisattva thought about it for a while. He was very inspired by bodhichitta and he thought, "This is my first chance to practice generosity, my application bodhichitta. If I say no, then my whole path is going to be spoiled right from the very beginning. This is a great opportunity for me to practice generosity." Thinking in this way, he said, "Yes, of course, I am very happy to give you my right arm." He took a very sharp knife and cut off his right arm. Of course, he then had only his left hand with which to give his right arm to the Brahmin, which he did, saying, "Here you are. Please take it with pleasure." Suddenly, the expression on the Brahmin's face changed. He became very fierce, furious, and upset. In the Indian tradition, you never give anything with the left hand because it is considered very dirty. Brahmins, in particular, are extremely ascetic and concerned with purity. So the Brahmin said, "No, I will not accept this because you have been so disrespectful. You are giving me this gift with your left hand, which is filthy. I will not accept your generosity." Then the Brahmin walked away, leaving the bodhisattva there, alone on the street, with his right arm in his left hand, feeling that he had failed in his first attempt to practice generosity.

This story may seem very discouraging, but it is a traditional teaching from the sutras. To have such strong, caring compassion is very difficult—almost impossible. We can see that bodhisattvas face extreme challenges on the path, since sentient beings have different mentalities and neuroses, which create various difficulties for bodhisattvas who try to please and benefit all these beings. Therefore, when entering the path of the bodhisattva, we must be well prepared so that we are able to say, "I am ready to face all of the difficulties on the Mahayana journey." When we generate bodhichitta, we should be very aware of what we are generating, and we should pay close attention to every step of the bodhisattva path and practice.

The Five Paths and the Ten Bhumis

The implementation of the path of the six paramitas is traditionally said to have five stages, which are called the five paths. The first path is called the path of accumulation, which consists primarily of the accumulation of merit. The second is called the path of junction. According to the Mahayana teachings, it is the junction between the path of an ordinary being and the path of a superior being, which is someone who has attained the levels of bodhisattva realization, known as the *bhumis*. The third path, called the path of seeing, is the beginning

of the path of a superior being. The fourth path is the path of meditation, and the fifth path is called the path of no more learning or the
path beyond training.

THE PATHS OF ORDINARY BEINGS

The first two paths, those of accumulation and junction, are paths
of ordinary beings. On these two paths, our practice of the six paramitas is necessarily imperfect. In fact, we cannot really say that we are
actually practicing the six paramitas. Rather, we are practicing six
virtues, which are similar to the six paramitas. For example, the perfection of generosity has three main aspects: the material generosity of
things, the fearless generosity of protection, and the generosity of
authentic Dharma. Our practice of these is very partial at these stages.
This is also true of our practice of the second perfection, discipline.
Our discipline is constantly being impaired and repaired. Our practices of patience, diligence, and meditative stability are also partial;
and, of course, our practice of prajna, or full knowledge, which is the
realization of emptiness, is partial until the actual realization begins to
occur at the first bodhisattva level. Therefore, on these first two paths
of ordinary beings, we cannot say that we are truly practicing the six
paramitas.

THE PATH OF SEEING

The actual path of the six paramitas starts with the path of seeing,
which is the third path. The path of seeing is so called because it is the
first moment of the direct, full experience of emptiness. This initial direct experience of emptiness is what is called the generation of the absolute mind of awakening. From that moment onward, our practice of
the six paramitas becomes the direct or actual cause of buddhahood.
This third path, the path of seeing, is the first bhumi, or first stage of
bodhisattva realization, which is called Fully Joyful, referring to the experience of delight that occurs when one realizes emptiness for the first
time. The absolute mind of awakening is a unified experience of the full
knowledge of emptiness and compassion. The reason these two become

unified is that we have already become trained in or familiarized with the generation of compassion. Therefore, our realization of emptiness is naturally informed and embraced by that compassion.

Upon the attainment of the first level of bodhisattva realization we acquire twelve qualities, each of which has a one hundredfold power. For example, from that time onward, we have the capacity to see one hundred buddhas at one time and to receive instruction from all of them simultaneously. We also have the capacity to produce one hundred emanations that perform benefit for one hundred sentient beings simultaneously. There are twelve of these qualities. Among the various paramitas, the practice of generosity is the one that is most emphasized at this point. Through the power of our realization of emptiness, it becomes possible for the first time to do things such as give our body without suffering. In fact, we are happy to do so. This is possible only because of our realization of emptiness. In fact, it is said to be unfitting to give one's body in this way until reaching the first bodhisattva level, because one would likely regret doing so later. We might be happy when the idea first occurs to us. We might find it exciting and be enthusiastic; but when we were actually going through with it, we might start to regret it, which would spoil the act of generosity.

The Path of Meditation

The fourth path is called the path of meditation. It includes the remaining nine bhumis. These nine stages consist of a gradually increasing realization of emptiness. This is often compared to the waxing of the moon from the initial sliver on the first day of the month to the full moon on the fifteenth day.

The Path of No More Learning

According to the Mahayana sutras, there are eleven progressive levels. The eleventh level, which is called Total Light, is the level of a buddha and it is the fifth path, which is called the path of no more learning. At that point there is nothing that remains to be done. In the context of Vajrayana, there are different assertions; however, if you

understand the ten bhumis, then you will also have a basic understanding of the underlying concept.

The Ten Paramitas

From the perspective of the five paths, there are ten paramitas.
The sequence of the practice of the ten paramitas corresponds to the
ten bhumis, the ten levels of bodhisattva realization. In addition to
the first six paramitas of generosity, discipline, patience, exertion,
meditation, and prajna, there are also the practices of skill or method,
aspiration, power, and finally, wisdom. The practice of generosity is
emphasized on the path of seeing, which is also the first bhumi, Fully
Joyful. The practices that are especially emphasized on the remaining
nine bhumis of the path of meditation are the second through tenth
paramitas. Thus, the practice of the second paramita, discipline, is
emphasized on the second bhumi, Stainless, and so on: the practice of
patience is emphasized on the third bhumi, Brilliant; the practice of
exertion on the fourth bhumi, Radiant; the practice of meditation on
the fifth bhumi, Difficult to Accomplish; the practice of prajna on the
sixth bhumi, Actually Brought About; the practice of skill or method
on the seventh bhumi, Far Gone; the practice of aspiration on the
eighth bhumi, Immovable; the practice of power on the ninth bhumi,
Excellent Intelligence; and the practice of wisdom on the tenth bhumi,
Cloud of Dharma.

There is a further division within this progression such that the
first through the seventh levels, from Fully Joyful to Far Gone, are
called the seven impure levels. Of course, they are states of unimagin-
able purity compared with those of an ordinary person. However,
compared to the following three levels and the level of a buddha, they
are comparatively impure. Therefore, the eighth, ninth, and tenth levels are called the three pure levels.

THE TWO MAIN STREAMS OF THE MAHAYANA LINEAGE

The Mahayana path consists of two main streams or lineages: the
one inherited from Nagarjuna and the one inherited from Maitreya and

Asanga. These two lineages represent different ways of showing us the actual path of enlightenment. We can more easily understand these two lineages and their different approaches, which are not contradictory, through the analogy of a map.

The Lineage of the Profound View: Nagarjuna

If we were to ask Nagarjuna, "How can we make the journey on the path of enlightenment?" he would lay out a very detailed map, clearly showing all the streets and highways. Then he would describe every detail of the map, saying, for example, "If you take this street, you will be going the wrong way. This is called the street of eternalism. If you take Exit 21, you will end up in nihilist country." Nagarjuna would continue to point out various streets and avenues that are sidetracks or dead ends. In this way, he would eliminate all the wrong turns and detours of our journey before sending us off.

Having studied the map carefully with Nagarjuna, when we are actually driving our speedy Mahayana automobile on the highway, we see the route very clearly. When we come across Exit 21, we remember, "Oh, Nagarjuna said that this is the exit to nihilism. I will not take this exit." We continue on and when we see Exit 42, we say, "Oh, Nagarjuna said that this is the exit to eternalism. I should not take this exit." That is how we make the journey. We are certain about our path because all of the wrong streets and wrong exits have been pointed out and eliminated. The wisdom that we have developed comes from Nagarjuna's instructions.

The Lineage of Vast Conduct: Maitreya-Asanga

If we were to consult with Asanga, he would show us a very simple map. It would not be marked with every street and wrong exit. It would simply show us the actual route that we should travel, without many details about other streets or highway exits. With Asanga's map, all we would know is the name of the highway that we are supposed to take. Therefore, we would be certain about the right highway and exit, but we might be uncertain about all the other wrong streets and exits.

In driving our Mahayana automobile on this highway, much of the time the name of the highway might not appear, and the names of the other streets or exits might not always be clearly marked. As we come across these various exits and streets, we might not feel as certain or confident about our route. The problem is that we might end up taking a wrong street or exit because we are uncertain about where it leads; we might think it will lead us to the street that we are supposed to take. However, we will not be certain of this because our map is not a detailed one that shows all the wrong streets and exits, like the map provided by Nagarjuna.

Knowing the Roads

The most beneficial aspect of Asanga's approach is that we can feel certain about the route that we are supposed to take. He describes that particular highway in detail: how nice it is, how easy it is, and how to take the right exit at the right time. In contrast, Nagarjuna does not necessarily tell us about the right street. He might not describe the exact road we are supposed to take. We are told primarily about all of the streets and exits that we are not supposed to take.

There is no contradiction between these two maps. In fact, if we study both maps, we will become better drivers and better travelers. We will know exactly which road we want to take and which streets and exits we should avoid. In this way, our minds will be crystal clear about the path. Our certainty about the wrong streets and exits is absolute. After we have gone through the detailed learning processes of the two Mahayana lineages of Nagarjuna and Asanga, there is no risk of going astray.

The Natural State of Liberation

These two lineages lead us to the discovery that the fundamental nature of reality is shunyata, selflessness, regardless of any appearance of phenomenal existence. This reality is called the natural state of liberation. This discovery is not simply an intellectual understanding of shunyata. It is not something to be understood and studied purely from a philosophical perspective. On the Mahayana path, we are discovering that emptiness is both the fundamental truth of our world and the fundamental state of liberation.

At this point, our notion of liberation changes slightly. From the Mahayana point of view, we do not need to leave this particular world to find freedom. In fact, there is nowhere beyond this world where we will find liberation. From the Mahayana perspective, there is nothing that we see as suffering that we need to leave behind in order to find a state of cessation. This understanding represents a leap from the first two yanas to the third vehicle of Mahayana because we recognize that the cessation of suffering is the fundamental nature of suffering, which is the state of liberation itself.

At the same time, we discover that the nature of our emotional disturbances, our ego-clinging mind, and our habitual patterns is also in the state of fundamental liberation. The empty nature of ego, which is the nonexistence of ego, is found right within ego-clinging. We recognize that the true nature of our mind and our emotions is buddha nature—the basic sanity or purity of our mind—and that the true nature of our body is in the state of a buddhakaya, or body of buddha.

THE EMOTIONS: FRIENDS AND ENEMIES

On the Mahayana path, we rediscover our own being through the lineages of Nagarjuna and Asanga-Maitreya. The lineage teachings of Nagarjuna address the shunyata aspect of the fundamental state of liberation, while the lineage teachings of Asanga address this fundamental state of liberation from the perspective of buddha nature. Therefore, on the Mahayana path, no matter which emotions we experience and no matter how strong they appear to be, we do not panic. We do not go into the turmoil of hope and fear, because we recognize their true state. In fact, for Mahayanists, all emotional states become great fuel for the fire of wisdom and for the fire of the path. Although we often look at our emotions as harmful, negative, irritating, and disturbing experiences, from the Mahayana perspective the emotions are a great help to us on the path.

Shakyamuni Buddha taught the Mahayana perspective on emotions through the metaphor of human waste. To those who live in cities, human waste is simply garbage that they want to get rid of as soon as possible. However, to a Mahayanist farmer, human waste is excellent manure with which to grow stronger and healthier crops. Buddha said that our disturbing emotions, which Hinayana practitioners regard as being like human waste, are regarded as excellent fertilizer by Mahayana practitioners. Consequently, as Mahayanists, we do not panic when we get into emotional states.

Getting into the state of egohood is no reason to panic, provided that we have already started our fire of wisdom. However, if we have not already started our fire of wisdom, then we are going to have a big problem. We could say that if we have not started to plow our field, then the manure will not help us very much. It will not penetrate the earth and will remain simple, stinky garbage, even for a Mahayanist farmer. In contrast, once we have started to plow, which is equivalent to starting our fire of wisdom, then the fuel and the manure become a great help. For a Mahayana practitioner, who has developed the fire of wisdom or plowed the ground of wisdom through the blessings of the two lineages of Nagarjuna and Asanga, the emotions can be dealt with as manure. This is a great relief. We no longer have to run away from our emotions. We no longer have to ignore or escape from our disturbing emotions and ego.

On the nine-yana journey, we go through a process of progressively working with our emotions. At the stage of the first two yanas, the Hinayana levels of the Shravakayana and the Pratyekabuddhayana, we approach working with our emotions as though we are going to war. As warriors of the Hinayana, we have the courage to confront the enemy, which is our ego. The disturbing emotions are also seen as our enemy, which we have to destroy. It is for this reason that the result of the Hinayana path is called the state of an arhat, which means "foe destroyer." We have destroyed our enemies, which are ego and the disturbing emotions, or klesha mind. In this context, we are waging war, and wisdom means that we understand how to deal with our enemies.

If we know how, then we destroy them. Alternatively, if we know, for example, that they are wearing bulletproof armor and there is no way that we can defeat them, then we run away from the enemy of our emotions.

On the Hinayana path, our strategy is entirely directed toward learning how to deal with our emotions and ego. Going into a state of solitude can help us to see our enemy more clearly. We might say that all of our enemies are wearing bulletproof armor and helmets with bulletproof visors, through which they can see us and thereby chase us. That is how we view ego at this point—as fully armed and fully armored. Therefore, at the beginning, as practitioners of the Hinayana we try to run away from our enemies. If we cannot destroy our enemies, then at least we will not get hurt.

At the Mahayana level, there is no notion of "enemy" because we have developed a greater vision. With the greater vision of the Mahayana path, we look at all our enemies with the heart of bodhichitta. We see all our emotions as friends rather than enemies because we have the wisdom of shunyata and buddha nature. We might say that we have rediscovered our own self-existing armor. We can never be harmed because we are primordially armored with shunyata and buddha nature. There is no way that this ego or the disturbing emotions can harm us. In fact, they are simply a manifestation of our buddha nature. Therefore, rather than rejecting them or trying to destroy them, we use our greater vision to look at our ego and disturbing emotions as path. We take them onto the path and they become our greatest aid on the Mahayana journey. Indeed, this journey cannot exist without ego and without the klesha mind.

THE CHITTAMATRA AND MADHYAMAKA SCHOOLS

According to the Mahayana tradition, the Buddhadharma is presented through the two philosophical approaches of the Chittamatra, or Mind Only, school and the Madhyamaka, or Middle Way, school.

Chittamatra: The Mind Only View

According to the Chittamatra school, our entire experience and the whole universe are our own individual reflection or perception. There is no existence of an outer world. Whatever we perceive is simply a projection of our own individual mind. The example most often given is that of a dream. If we are dreaming of Mount Everest, the whole mountain fits into our little room. This towering mountain appears to be very solid; the temperature on the mountain can be freezing or hot—anything whatsoever. We can enjoy the struggle of climbing Mount Everest, and we can enjoy the view from the top. In our dream we do not say to ourselves, "This is just a dream. I am making this effort only in a dream." When we climb Mount Everest in our dream, we really climb the mountain and really experience the struggle. We have a vision of the existence of a whole world. However, when we wake up from this dream, there is no Mount Everest outside. There is no "me" who is climbing the mountain. There is no mountain view or freezing temperature. We come back to our heated bedroom. That is a big jump, from Mount Everest to our centrally heated apartment.

The Chittamatrin Mahayanists say that all of our experiences in the relative world are similarly simple projections of our mind. These projections are like a movie. We project the images on a screen, which is primordially pure, primordially empty, and blank. On this screen, which is our basic consciousness, we see various images of nice scenery or frightening nightmares; but we ourselves are projecting these images onto that blank screen. We can project a pure, sacred view or we can project an utterly confused state onto this screen. It is entirely up to us. Our consciousness or mind is totally blank and primordially, fundamentally empty, with no image or form whatsoever. The Chittamatrins call this the "basis of all consciousness." There is the projector of our consciousness, and there is also the film of our habitual patterns that we run through our projector. We project these images onto the screen, and then we may go through a hellish nightmare for two hours.

The problem is that we go through aeons of this. This is a movie that never stops. At a certain point, we almost become a part of that movie because we have been constantly experiencing that projection in the theater throughout hundreds of thousands of years. However, because it has been going on for aeons and aeons, we are growing tired of it, so we try to discover the truth.

What is the truth behind all this, behind this whole nightmare that we are experiencing? The truth is simply that the screen is blank; it is totally empty from the beginning. When we realize that these projections do not exist at the level of basic consciousness and that the basic mind is free from all projections, we realize the state of liberation. Whether the projections are sacred or confused, they are still projections. It does not matter at all what kind of projection they are. Rediscovering that the projections do not exist on the screen, and knowing that the screen is fundamentally pure, blank, and empty, is the state of liberation. At that point, we are free from the aeons and aeons of movie nightmares. There is no such thing as a solid world that exists outside our own perception or mind.

One way we can understand this truth is to reflect on and examine our experiences of yesterday. For example, we can compare our "waking" experience of yesterday with our experience of last night's dreams. From our current perspective, these two are very similar. What is the difference? From the point of view of today, there is no difference between yesterday's daytime experience of a table and last night's dream experience of a table. They are both dreamlike. Furthermore, when we reflect on today's experience from the point of view of tomorrow, it is equally dreamlike. Yesterday was a dream and today is also a dream. This is a dream. We are going through another dream, another illusion. We think we are quite smart, but we are not. We are being fooled again. In brief, that is the Chittamatrin view. It is called Mind Only because everything is a projection of our mind.

Madhyamaka: The View of Emptiness

Madhyamaka has become well-known in Western literature as the Middle Way school. However, the term *madhyamaka* can also mean "not even a middle." There is a difference between a "middle path" and a path that is "not even a middle."

In Sanskrit *madhya* means "middle." However, *maka* can be interpreted either as a term of negation or as a modifier that changes *madhya* into a noun. When understood as a noun, *madhya* becomes "middle way." When *maka* is taken as a negation, *madhya* can be understood to mean "not even a middle." This latter interpretation accords with Nagarjuna's philosophy and path, which cuts through all extreme views of existence and nonexistence, as well as any clinging to those extremes.

Within this tradition, we typically refer to the four extremes, which are four incorrect views concerning the nature of phenomena. These include viewing phenomena in any of the following ways: as truly existent, as utterly nonexistent, as both existent and nonexistent, and as neither existent nor nonexistent. We can summarize the four into the two extremes of eternalism and nihilism. If we totally refute both of these extremes through the intellectual path of reasoning and reflecting, then how can we say, "This is the middle"? For example, if we were to knock down all four walls of a room and entirely take away the ground, then we would not be able to point to a spot as the middle of the room since there would no longer be a room. The concept of "the middle" is dependent on the existence of sides. Thus, we cannot continue to cling to a "middle path" because Nagarjuna's philosophy precludes clinging to any side or extreme. There is no middle whatsoever at this point. Accordingly, there is no reference point at all.

THE GROUND OF THE TWO TRUTHS

Nagarjuna uses the format of the two truths, which are relative truth and absolute truth. Relative truth, also known as deceptive or conventional truth, is defined as being mundane and referential, or conceptual. Absolute truth, also known as actual or ultimate truth, is defined as being beyond the sphere of conceptual recognition. According to the tradition of Nagarjuna, it is important to distinguish between the two truths and to keep them separate. When we look at absolute truth, we should not attend to relative truth right away, and when we look at relative truth, we should not bring in absolute truth right away.

Nevertheless, understanding relative truth is the cause of understanding absolute truth. Therefore, relative truth should not be thought of as being inferior or unrelated to absolute truth. In fact, Nagarjuna said, "There is no way to realize absolute truth except through reliance upon relative truth." Relative truth is seen as a method to bring forth the realization of absolute truth. Although relative truth may be conceptual, there is no way to realize nonconceptual, absolute truth without it. The understanding of either one of the two truths assists in the understanding of the other.

Relative Truth: Mere Appearance

We begin our study of mundane or relative truth with an examination of the conceptual imputations of ordinary experience, such as our experience of objects and reference points: for example "this table," "this vase," and "my name." These are all conceptual labels. While relative reality may be mundane and conceptual, it is also infallibly consistent from an internal perspective. Within relative truth, whatever seed is planted will lead to the corresponding crop. For example, we cannot plant barley and get roses. That is why this is called relative truth. We should not lose sight of this element of truth in "relative truth."

According to Nagarjuna, relative truth cannot be analyzed because once you analyze it, it disappears. We cannot actually find relative truth, relative reality. All we find is absolute truth. Relative truth is that which is present before analysis or when we do not analyze. Such things as "me" and "you," which are valid relative or conventional experiences, are not present when we analyze them. Therefore, relative truth is taught to be that which is in accord with ordinary, worldly usage and understanding—something upon which everyone will agree.

One great Madhyamaka master of twentieth-century Tibet said, "When my fingertips experience the touch of a needle pricking through, then I feel like things do exist. There is no question." However, he also said that when he used Madhyamaka logic, reasoning, and contemplation to analyze his experience, he felt that nothing existed in any kind of solid or real way.

When we analyze, there is nothing solid to be found, yet when we do not analyze, everything is experienced so vividly and sharply. On the one hand, the two truths might seem sophisticated and complicated, but on the other hand, they are very simple. We can see how they function in our everyday experiences. For example, the conceptual, rational mind says, "If you put your finger in the fire, it will burn." Of course, there is a certain validity in that thought and in that logic. We would all agree that on a mundane level, fire burns. That is called relative truth. It is that which is present as an agreed-on experience yet when analyzed cannot be found. To ask, "From where does that fire arise? Is the fire merely a projection of the mind?" is not in accord with mundane usage. While we all agree that fire burns, if we look to find its essence, its "fireness," our relative concept of fire breaks down under analysis and we find that there is nothing there. Thus, according to Nagarjuna, relative truth is that which cannot withstand analysis. The Madhyamaka school teaches that relative truth is simply mere appearance. Relative truth makes no statements as to what these appearances are, or as to why or from where they arise.

Absolute Truth

Nagarjuna's presentation distinguishes between two levels of appreciation of absolute truth. His definitions of these two levels include the situation in which there has been slight analysis and the situation in which there has been thorough or complete analysis.

LEVEL OF SLIGHT ANALYSIS

To discover absolute truth, we engage in analysis and questioning. We might ask, "What is fire? What is a finger?" Through this questioning process, we first find that there is a gap between the basis of the label and the label itself. There is a gap between the word "fire" and the basis of that word. They are two different things. Why do we think that when we say "fire," we are referring to one particular thing? What is the actual connection between the label and its basis?

If we think about the relationship between these two, then we will find there is not much connection except that, in our samsaric education, we have been taught to perceive these two things as one. Usually we perceive the label—the term *fire*—and the basis of "fire" as one. We do not see the gap or the difference between the two. However, what we think of as "fire" with our conceptual mind is merely our idea of fire—it is not the actual basis of that label or concept, nor is it the thing itself.

This label "fire" simply does not exist outside our conceptual mind. There is nothing truly existing outside that is the label "fire." Thus, when we look at such labels, it is easy to see their relative nature. From this perspective, labels are irrelevant. Therefore, the first step of Madhyamaka analysis is to see the difference between the basis of the label and the label itself, or between the basis of the label and the labeling processes of mind. As a result of this analysis, we can see that the basis of the label is not the label. The basis is free from any label, free from the labeling process, and free from any conceptual theory. Our actual experience of the world—for example, our actual experience of the fire element—goes beyond concept, thought, and label.

We can then analyze the basis of the label itself. What is the basis of the labeling process? For example, if we look at the basis of the label "table," what is it? The basis is not a singular entity, not just one thing. It has many parts—a top, sides, and so forth. If we analyze each part, then we will see that each part has different parts; and if we analyze these parts further and further, then we will come to the point of seeing the atoms of the table. If we go even further, then we will discover that the atoms are composed of tiny parts, which in Hinayana analysis are called partless particles. However, if we analyze the partless particles, then we will discover that they too have parts. If we go even deeper with this analysis, then we will discover that we cannot find anything that is solid, substantial, or real. Modern physics shares a similar view: Scientists now say that even atoms do not substantially exist. There are no solid building blocks of reality. Scientists now use terms like "quark" or "energy field." Thus, both modern physics and Madhyamaka reasoning will lead us to similar conclusions. While Madhyamaka logic says that the nature of reality is emptiness, or shunyata, modern science says that nothing exists at the atomic level.

LEVEL OF THOROUGH ANALYSIS

In all Madhyamaka reasoning, we first go through a complete refutation of any notion of existence. We analyze, destroy, refute, and transcend any clinging whatsoever to existence. However, after we reach this point, we must then engage in nonconceptual meditation through which we will experience the nature of emptiness directly. It is very important that we do not become stuck in a complete sense of negation. From the Madhyamaka point of view, we must go beyond negation and find the nature of reality that goes beyond both existence and nonexistence, or eternalism and nihilism. The level of slight analysis, which was described above, is sometimes called "nominal absolute truth," which means that it can be categorized as absolute truth; but it is not really the complete absolute truth.

Eventually, the level of thorough analysis brings us to the state of the actual absolute truth. That basic state of reality goes beyond all conceptualities and beyond all views of existence and nonexistence. It is the state that we call freedom from all elaborations, and it is experienced through the nonconceptual meditation that follows analysis. It is beyond existence and nonexistence; there is no concept of something being empty or not empty. It is not at all conceptual or inferential; it is a direct experience. This direct experience of what we call emptiness is the experience of genuine absolute truth. The Prajnaparamita sutras teach that this state is indescribable and inconceivable. It cannot be signified in any way at all—not with any form, word, gesture, or concept. It is referred to as being without conceptual elaboration or statement. There is not even a real or correct view to which we can cling.

Generally when people are first told about emptiness, the absolute truth, they become frightened because it sounds so difficult to apprehend correctly. In fact, sometimes people do misunderstand it and mix up the absolute truth and relative truth, which leads to mistaken notions such as, "Well, everything is just empty, so there's no karma, and I can do whatever I want," or "I don't exist; maybe I'll disappear." Because of this, Nagarjuna said that if you misunderstand emptiness, then your knowledge will destroy you. To avoid this potential misunderstanding of emptiness, we need considerable accumulation of merit, which serves as the cause for us to experience correct realization of emptiness.

When we develop a clear understanding of the ground, which is the causal vehicle made up of the Shravakayana, Pratyekabuddhayana, and Bodhisattvayana, we are building a solid foundation upon which to establish the next stage of our nine-yana journey. Having laid this proper foundation, we can step onto the Vajrayana path and have a smooth ride on our Vajrayana journey, which consists of the remaining two sets of vehicles: the Vehicle of Austerity and Awareness, and the Vehicle of Overpowering Means.

14

Entering the Vajrayana

The Vehicle of Austerity and Awareness

ENTERING THE VAJRAYANA PATH requires wholehearted commitment. At this stage, we are approaching a point of no return. The Vajrayana journey is a one-way journey. It is imperative that we understand this before undertaking the path. Once we have begun, we cannot say, "Well, I made a mistake. I am going back." There is no going back. Thus, entering such a potent path involves intense determination and profound commitment. There is no rehearsal here. Therefore, preparation and groundwork are extremely important. It is best to take time to study the tantras so that we have a very clear understanding of the path. Only then do we embark on our Vajrayana journey.

TAKING RISKS

Entering the path of tantra is traditionally symbolized by a snake entering a bamboo tube. In this representation, we are the snake who has decided to enter the bamboo tube. It is important to understand that there is no one who forces us to do so. Also, in the Vajrayana literature, it is said that we are proud to be such a snake entering this bamboo tube. The bamboo tube has only two openings. We enter from the bottom end and we begin to climb up. Either we come out through the top, which is enlightenment, or we mistakenly turn our heads in the wrong direction and begin moving downward toward the bottom.

If we continue moving downward, then we will exit from the bottom hole, which opens into hell. There are no sidetracks; there are no other openings in this bamboo tube. We say the Vajrayana is a direct path. It is direct whether we go up or down, which is why it is so powerful.

We could also compare entering this path to boarding a supersonic jet. It is a very powerful but dangerous vehicle. We may travel to our destination very quickly and safely, or we may end up in a disastrous accident. Whenever we want to make use of something very powerful, we have to take a risk. There is no choice. That is what we learn in our lives. Risk is not specific to the Vajrayana. For example, if we want to achieve great financial wealth, we might decide to take a big risk in the stock market, where we might either make a lot of money very quickly or go completely bankrupt. However, becoming bankrupt in a Vajrayana sense is much more serious and painful. Therefore, we cannot afford to simply play around on the Vajrayana path.

ENTERING THE ROYAL BANQUET

Our relationship with our guru is our Vajrayana path; our relationship with our guru is our Vajrayana fruition; and our relationship with our guru is our Vajrayana world. There can be no Vajrayana without the guru. He or she creates the vajra world—our own vajra bamboo tube. On the Dzogchen path, our relationship with our guru is the same as the guru-disciple relationship on the Mahamudra path. This relationship requires the same full sense of confidence and devotion, and it involves a certain aspect of faith—a complete sense of trust in our guru.

When we enter the Vajrayana path, we are actually entering a royal banquet that is hosted by the vajra guru. When we enter this banquet, we must remember that we are not entering a restaurant. We cannot ask for a menu so that we can order the food or drinks that we like. When we enter this banquet, we must accept whatever food and drink are offered by our royal host. It may be junk food or it may be health food, but we must have complete confidence in our host. If we want to be able to choose our food and drink, then we should go to a restaurant, where we can be regular customers. However, if we enter the banquet, then we must be willing to be a guest. We will never know with certainty what is in the drink or in the food. We will be in no position to order, investigate, or examine our food. We need to be very mindful of the notion of a banquet and not mess it up. As a guest, we will take the food and drink that is offered by our vajra host, which will be vajra cuisine. We might have the good fortune to attend the Vajrayana banquet and receive the Vajrayana treatment, but as a Vajrayana guest, we must have a sense of dignity and discipline, as well as a sense of respect and trust in our host.

Therefore, before we enter the banquet, we should get to know our host so that we can imagine what kind of food will be served. We will know his or her particular culinary interests and whether or not that type of food or environment interests us. The Vajrayana instructions emphasize that we should analyze the teacher thoroughly before we enter the realm of the banquet. When we receive the invitation, we should reflect on the opportunity and the commitment. We should consult with our lawyer, our astrologer, our psychiatrist, and any other advisers we may have before deciding whether or not to accept this invitation. This is a crucial point. We should investigate our potential guru carefully and thoroughly, and we should take our time. There is no hurry because in the Vajrayana world there is always a banquet being held. We do not have to worry about missing the banquet or not getting an invitation. We must analyze our host before accepting the invitation. These preparations are very important for the Vajrayana journey.

Of course, it is also possible to take too long in making our decision. Our advisers might give us complex advice, which is no less complicated than our minds. We could end up analyzing for ages and ages and ages. There is a story of a Chinese emperor who was analyzing a teacher. When the emperor was finally ready to accept this teacher, the emperor found out that the teacher was already dead. He had died three years earlier. The emperor was never able to find another teacher. He could not even think of another teacher with whom he could have a comparable relationship. Thus, if we take too long in choosing a teacher, then that can create another problem.

VIEW AND MEDITATION

The Vajrayana is called the fruition yana because we are working with the whole mandala of enlightened being. We are entering into the realm of awakening through our vajra body, vajra speech, and vajra heart or mind. We are taking the whole buddhafield of the three vajras as our path and working with these three elements through the development of the view of sacred outlook, or sacred world, and through the practices of the path of skillful means. We develop both view and meditation through complete confidence—through taking vajra pride in our deity yoga practice.

However, without the proper philosophical training, we may experience a degree of struggle in our practice of meditation. When we have thoughts and experiences that do not accord with our theoretical understanding, we are often left wondering how it all works. Our philosophical training can help us to develop the right view. Such training provides us with a perspective from which to understand both the relative and absolute natures from different levels of the view. Before we enter into meditation, if we have developed a sharp conceptual understanding, then we will see the subtlety of our thought patterns; we will see how our mind relates with the outer world through body and speech. If we have gone through a process of philosophical training and analysis, then our practice becomes very clear. When we look at the lives of the mahasiddhas, it is clear that many of them, such as Naropa and Saraha, were also great *mahapanditas*, or great scholars. There is a great tradition of bringing together the paths of scholarship and meditation. However, the main message of the mahasiddhas' lives is that one-pointed trust is the most important element of our Vajrayana journey.

THE VEHICLE OF AUSTERITY AND AWARENESS

When we enter the Vehicle of Austerity and Awareness, we are truly entering the Vajrayana path. From the perspective of the nine-yana journey, there are three outer tantras and three inner tantras or yogas.

This system is associated with the Old Translation school of the Nyingma tradition. The three outer tantras are the practices of the Vehicle of Austerity and Awareness: Kriya tantra, Charya or Upa tantra, and Yoga tantra. The three inner tantras are the practices of the Vehicle of Overpowering Means: Maha yoga, Anu yoga, and Ati yoga, which are otherwise known as Dzogchen.

Vajrayana is also known as tantra, which, as mentioned earlier, means "continuity." This refers to the basic continuity of our mind and our body. On the Vajrayana path, our physical existence is regarded as very important. In the lower vehicles we look at the existence of our samsaric body and samsaric world as unclean, something to abandon or renounce. However, in the tantras we have an entirely different view of body and mind. Body and mind are the expression of the continuity of the primordial nature of our vajra heart, which we discover through the Vehicle of Austerity and Awareness, which brings us into the vajra world. Our vajra heart can then develop into the fullest state of a vajra master.

Kriya Tantra

The first tantra is called Kriya, or the "tantra of activity." Kriya tantra primarily emphasizes the activities of body and speech, which are outer activities. To a lesser degree, we also become involved in the activity of mind. There is a strong emphasis on the activity of cleansing or purifying. Our practice of deity yoga meditation begins at this stage and is related to our focus on purification. Here, we relate with the deity as being superior to ourselves and, in a certain sense, as a savior. There is a quality of separation between us as a practitioner, as a little guest at this vajra banquet, and the host, our deity, whom we view as other than ourselves and larger than life—something "vajra." We are not yet close. We are not yet embracing the deity, not yet becoming one with the deity. However, that gap contains a tremendous amount of energy, vajra wisdom, and power. Simply creating this gap between the deity and ourselves, and then experiencing that relationship through our devotion, trust, confidence, discipline, and respect, gives us a certain quality of vajra wisdom.

Through the Mahayana path, we rediscover our fundamental state of liberation, our basic nature of tathagatagarbha. This is actually a rediscovery of the existence of our genuine self—who we really are—and this is the basis for entering the path of the tantras. Once we have rediscovered that self, we enter the path of Kriya tantra, which emphasizes purification practices or methods of cleaning ourselves before we enter into the depths of the Vajrayana path—before we enter the Vajrayana banquet. Entering the practice of Kriya tantra is similar to the experience of waking up in the morning. We wake up to beautiful Vajrayana sunshine and discover that our body is dirty. We have bad breath and our eyes are closed with gunk. We are covered with all sorts of grime. At this stage of the nine-yana journey, we discover our whole collection of karmic garbage that we do not want to carry with us. Therefore, what we need is a good cleaning. We need to brush our teeth and take a nice soapy shower.

The empowerment we receive, which includes many cleaning processes and purifications with water, is like stepping into the shower. In this tantra, we discover the power of the water, the power of the deity, and the power of the recitation of a mantra to purify our body and mind. The deity yoga meditation is like the water of tantra, and the mantra that we recite is like the soap. The deity yoga practice includes all the things we need—the toothpaste, the soap, and the shampoo—to clean ourselves up. We are using the processes of Kriya tantra to maintain the basic continuity of the purity of our body and mind. However, it is crucial for us to understand that we are not trying to get rid of our body; rather, we are trying to rediscover the pure nature of our body and mind.

At the same time, we should not become attached to the soap and water of the deity practice, or we will never finish our shower. If the mantra or the deity becomes an ego trip, then it simply becomes another type of dirt. So we have to thoroughly rinse off. We have to transcend even our attachment to the sacred world of Vajrayana deities and the power of mantra.

Charya or Upa Tantra

Upa means "character," "behavior," or "way of being"; thus, this next stage is the tantra of character or behavior. In the Upa tantra there is an equal emphasis on working with the outer actions of body and speech, as taught in the Kriya tantra, and the inner action of mind, which is samadhi, as taught in the Yoga tantra.

At this point we enter into an entirely different level of relationship with our host and into a totally different atmosphere in regard to our relationship with the vajra world. Now that we have had a clean shower and have managed to get out of our bathroom without getting attached to our soap and water, we are ready to further develop our relationship with the host, who is the vajra deity. At the earlier stage of Kriya tantra, meeting the deity was like meeting a king or queen on the street. We felt that we were encountering a very powerful person and that there was such a big gap that we did not know how to relate with him or her. We felt very inferior and in need of this person's blessing. At this point, however, we feel that we can relate with the deity as our friend, as a companion with whom we can shake hands, with whom we can sit and chat. We can gossip with our vajra emperor, which is a much better situation to be in. At this stage, there is a great sense of sharing; we are sharing our neurosis, as well as our friend's wisdom and power to cut through our neurosis. In Upa tantra, we have finished our shower; we are walking out of the bathroom and dressing to meet our friend. How we dress ourselves is very important here, because it determines the development of our relationship with our friend and host.

With the methods of Kriya tantra, we discovered not only the truth of our basic existence as a body, but also the great wisdom of how to clean our body and thus improve our appearance. Now, in Upa tantra, we come to a point where not only can we clean ourselves, but we also have a method for dressing ourselves carefully and beautifully. Having cleaned our body, we do not simply walk naked out on the street. Instead, we beautify ourselves with various articles of clothing, and we also conduct ourselves properly. We discover that we can beautify the fundamental continuity of our body and mind through the various powers of the tantra and the deity. At this stage of Upa tantra, which also means "skillful means," we are able to dress ourselves and adorn our own existence.

When we learn the skill of beautifully dressing ourselves with the clothes of Upa tantra, our whole being becomes Upa tantra. In other words, our whole being becomes the behavior. There is no separation between the behavior and the person who is behaving. There are no longer any such distinctions, nor are there any laws that describe to us the rules and regulations of our behavior or conduct. Instead, it is through our own skill and wisdom that we develop the knowledge of how to dress up, how to look nice, and how to truly be a beautiful person.

Yoga Tantra

The third tantra is called Yoga tantra. In Tibetan, "yoga" is *naljor*. The first syllable, *nal,* means "the natural state," the uncontrived, unfabricated state, or the freshness of all existence. That is the vajra state of our mind. The second syllable, *jor,* literally means "to arrive at," "reach," or "attain" that level of reality. Therefore, *naljor* means realizing or coming back to the uncontrived, unfabricated, natural state of our vajra heart. *Naljor* also means "uniting with" that nature. We reach or unite with this state through genuine knowledge and awareness of profound absolute truth and extensive relative truth. In the Yoga tantra, the main focus is the inner path of skillful means and wisdom, or upaya and prajna, which is taken into our practice of meditation and contemplation.

At this level of practice, there is a sense of unity as we become one with our host. Having come out of the shower, having dressed ourselves well, and having developed the relationship with our friend, we now have a sense of becoming one with the deity, rather than being separated in the manner of an emperor and subject. Even as friends, there remains some degree of separation. In contrast, in Yoga tantra we

ourselves become the host; we become the deity. The deity is not separate from our own being. There is a greater sense of leap at this point.

After we have dressed ourselves in beautiful clothes, we discover
that this is not enough. Clothes are not the only means of making ourselves look beautiful. Having applied all of the available skillful means to
clean ourselves, clothe ourselves, and present ourselves nicely to our
host, we become a full human being—a great being—elegant and richly
adorned. We now beautify ourselves even further with the richness of
ornaments, the richness of diamonds, gold, amber, and rubies. In so
doing, we reach the full state of beauty, dignity, and richness that is symbolized by our jewelry. We visualize ourselves as the deity, and in fact we
become the deity. Through this method of practice, we discover that our
nature is the nature of the deity. At this level of tantra, we completely cut
through our theistic view of Vajrayana reality. We cut through any notion
of the deity as a power outside our own being. We see that all the power,
dignity, and richness of the deity exist within us. All that remains is for
us to discover how we can best express that quality.

At the stage of Yoga tantra, we see that the whole state of our
being as a fully beautified person existed right at the beginning, when
we got out of our bed and walked to our shower. This state is nothing
new. After all, there could be no beautiful person now if there were no
such person at the first stage. That is how we discover that the deity is
within us. Now, when we see the queen or king at the banquet, we are
less concerned, because we see that we can be one of them, that we are
in fact one of those wisdom beings. Thus, we are in a complete state of
unity with the deity, which is a very powerful state.

These three stages of tantra are taught for three different reasons.
Buddha taught Kriya tantra to those who are powerfully engaged in the
klesha of ignorance, Upa tantra to those who are primarily involved in
the klesha of anger, and Yoga tantra to those who are engaged in the
immense klesha of passion. That is why the Vajrayana path is sometimes
known as the path of passion. Unlike the shravakas, pratyekabuddhas,
and bodhisattvas, who cultivate renunciation and detachment in relation to physical existence and the samsaric world, we do not have to

give up cleaning and beautifying our body or further enriching our physical existence with ornaments. In this respect, the Vajrayana path is uniquely daring and fearless.

It is generally necessary to follow a progressive path when engaging in these three yanas. For example, if we do not take a shower when we first get up in the morning, then how can we be truly ready to dress ourselves and put on ornaments? We could still put on new clothes, with our hair sticking out in all directions, but our clothes would soon be dirty and we would look quite odd. However, no matter which stage of tantra we begin with—even if we were to try to skip ahead to a later tantra—we would nevertheless go through all three stages of the outer tantras. There is no escape. For example, if we were to enter at the level of Anu yoga tantra, we would still experience showering, dressing, and adorning ourselves because each of the higher tantras contains all of the processes of purification and enrichment that we find in the lower tantras. Therefore, our practice might not necessarily be confined to practicing Kriya tantra first, followed by Upa tantra and then Yoga tantra, since everything contained in these practices is included, in some form, within the inner tantras or yogas of the final Vajrayana stage, which is the Vehicle of Overpowering Means. Within the progression of these yanas, the higher ones include more and more of the previous ones.

15

The Final Breakthrough

WHEN WE ENTER the final three yanas of our nine-yana journey, we are also entering the absolute or ultimate vehicle, which is the Vehicle of Overpowering Means. In our practice of the first set of three yanas, we discover the basic truth, which is the fundamental reality of the nature of our mind and the phenomenal world. In our practice of the second set of three yanas, we are provided with the methods to completely reveal this fundamental nature and to fully manifest it. With the final three yanas, we begin the most profound part of our journey, which is also its innermost essence. This is where the notion of a giant full stop arises. This part of the path is more restricted, and it is more directly connected to our notion of Dzogchen.

THE VEHICLE OF OVERPOWERING MEANS

When we enter the yanas of Maha yoga, Anu yoga, and Ati yoga, there is a tremendous sense of energy, power, and speed that is difficult to describe or conceptualize. These last three stages of our Dzogchen journey become a little crazy and a little tricky. We are entering a vehicle that is like a rocket; we are approaching that level of speed. If we have properly prepared everything from the ground level up to this point, if we have checked out every feature of the rocket itself, as well as our own skill in piloting it, then it is possible to proceed without great difficulty. If we undertake this part of the journey with both confidence and full knowledge of how the whole vehicle works, then our journey will be much easier. If we have prepared very carefully and thoroughly, then when we take off, we will not have any problems, such as an oil leak or an explosion, which has happened to us before. There is no longer any danger that the snake will turn its head toward the bottom of the bamboo tube and end up in hell. As we enter the final three yanas, it is possible to see more clearly why the notion of thorough preparation has been so emphasized. Ultimately, it is much more important to discuss our preparations for our journey than to discuss the actual journey itself.

THE GURU IN THE DZOGCHEN LINEAGE

Looking back at the history of the Dzogchen lineage, we have the example of Guru Padmasambhava to show us how outrageous this journey can become. At this very interesting and powerful stage of our journey, there is a tremendous sense of the guru minding our business. Not only does the guru mind our business, the guru minds the business of our business. We could say that the guru minds our business 200 percent.

Padmasambhava received the transmission of the profound teachings of Dzogchen from his guru, the great master Shri Simha, and others. One of his gurus conferred the empowerment by reducing Guru Padmasambhava's whole being into the tiny syllable HUM. The little HUM was then placed on the tongue of his guru, who swallowed it. That was the beginning of the abhisheka. Then the letter HUM passed out from the other end, by which time Padmasambhava had received the complete transmission of Dzogchen, including the final three stages. Needless to say, this manner of empowerment is quite outrageous and very direct in the sense of cutting through our conceptual clinging.

MAHA YOGA

Maha yoga deals primarily with the visualization aspect of tantra practice, most particularly with deity yoga. As a Vajrayana deity practice, it is called the Maha yoga teachings of visualization practice, or the

Maha yoga teachings on development practice. Within the general practice of deity yoga, it particularly focuses on developing the wisdom and courage of the deity.

As explained previously, *yoga* means "arriving at the natural state," or "arriving at the uncontrived state of our vajra heart." *Maha yoga* means "great yoga," indicating that we are arriving at the state of the luminous nature of mind—*rigpa*, which is the clarity aspect of the visualization. Visualization becomes the expression of the clarity nature of our vajra heart, which is also called "primordial mind" in Dzogchen.

Visualization practice is a very powerful and immediate way of taking birth in the sacred world of Vajrayana. We do not have to wait for aeons in order to experience a pure buddha realm, as is the case in the gradual paths of Hinayana and Mahayana, where it usually does take aeons to achieve the state of fruition. In contrast, visualization practices are the path that can bring us into the vajra world right on the spot. We can take birth in the vajra world at this very moment with the powerful skillful means of visualization practice. At the same time, the whole process of taking birth in the sacred vajra world purifies the karmic garbage that links us to rebirth in the samsaric world.

The practice of visualization occurs within one's formal meditation sessions. In this process, we first visualize the great space of emptiness, which is the fundamentally pure nature of our mind, our basic stream of consciousness. Within this space, we visualize a lotus seat, which symbolizes our pure stream of being. On this lotus seat, we visualize a sun disk and a moon disk, which symbolize the two reproductive cells from the father and mother. On top of that, we visualize a luminous, flickering syllable, which symbolizes our bardo consciousness. The flickering syllable begins to radiate light, which streams out into space and then returns, dissolving into the syllable, before radiating out again, over and over. The process of the light radiating out and returning represents a process of conception. Through this conception, our consciousness transforms from the flickering syllable into a Vajrayana deity, such as Vajrasattva. Thus, we transform ourselves into one of the Vajrayana expressions of the Buddha and are born into that particular realm of buddhahood. At that very moment, we cut directly through all our ego-clinging and emotional conflicts by simply taking birth in this vajra world, which is a pure world.

By adopting the form of a *heruka,* a wrathful or semiwrathful male deity associated with the transformation of ego, such as those we see in Vajrayana iconography, we cut through our basic duality of good and bad, our basic sense of ego-centered, discriminating mind. We get rid of all of our beautiful ornaments and clothes. Instead of wearing a beautiful silk blouse, at this point we wear something like animal skins. Instead of wearing some kind of brand-name skirt, we wear a tiger-skin skirt. We wear skulls as ornaments. We wear a wild variety of clothing and ornaments and makeup. We go barefoot; we do not need ballet slippers or Birkenstock sandals. At this point, we adopt all of these outer expressions of the Vajrayana. This process is a gradual progression. We cannot enter it at the beginning. It is developed through the first three yanas and the first three tantras. Then, we reach this level where we can completely abandon all conceptual clinging and enter into a certain stage of Vajrayana craziness.

ANU YOGA

After we have developed our visualization of the deity through the Maha yoga practices, we have to dissolve it. The dissolving aspect of the visualization process is the practice of the primordial mind of luminosity, which is Anu yoga, the second stage of the final three yanas. This dissolving aspect refers to the prajna, or wisdom, element of our practice. It is called Anu yoga because *anu* means "after," or "that which comes after" yoga. It is the yoga of dissolving, which is practiced after the development stage of Maha yoga. This dissolving meditation consists of different exercises and inner yogas that relate to the vast and profound methods of the *sampannakrama* teachings. All of the Anu yoga practices are connected to the yoga practices of prana, nadi, and bindu, or inner fire. When we reach this level, we are able to practice the yogas fully and properly because we have laid the groundwork; we have completed all of the necessary preparations.

When we enter the realm of Anu yoga, we are entering a world that has a certain sense of craziness, a certain wildness, openness, and spaciousness. There is no longer any space in which to draw distinctions between good and bad, ugly and beautiful, you and me, and so forth. After the practice of Maha yoga, we break through all those barriers. We take off all clothing and jewelry. We do not need our designer clothes. We even throw off all our beautiful bone ornaments, tiger-skin skirts, and so forth. We cast off all barriers and join this crazy world of Vajrayana. We join the real heart of the Vajrayana teachings—this great sense of space and openness.

The last step of our breakthrough happens here. We are breaking through our clinging to ourselves as beautiful and clean and our clinging to certain other things as dirty, ugly, and inhuman. We are cutting through all of this clinging to separation and dualistic thought and breaking into the reality of nondual equanimity, the great space of the vajra world. It is, after all, a wonderful world.

ATI YOGA

The development stage of Maha yoga practices together with the dissolving practices of Anu yoga lead us to the third stage of the final vehicle, the stage of Ati yoga, or Dzogchen. *Ati* means "peak" or "highest," so Ati yoga is the peak of yoga practice. Dzogchen is the state of great perfection or the great completion; it is the giant full stop that ends our journey. It is called the great completion because we have completed the whole journey, the whole path. It is called the great perfection because we have perfected all the qualities necessary to become a buddha, an enlightened being. There is no further place for us to go. There is no higher yana or goal to achieve.

Up to this point, our journey has taken us through all the levels of the path and through all the stages of cutting through our basic duality. Now we are entering the realm of Ati yoga, where we discover that actually the fundamental state of our being is our physical body—our existence as body. At this level, we go back to the fundamental state of nakedness. We have thrown off all aspects of clothing and jewelry. By the time that we come to the stage of Ati yoga, we have cast off all of these things and gone back to the basic state of our being, which is called "alpha pure." It is pure from the beginning and pure at the end. We discover that, after all, there was never any reason for us to have taken this journey.

In a sense, we go all the way back to the original state of our existence—before we got up and took our shower. Now we realize that all of these steps were not necessary, to a certain extent. We realize that, from the beginning, our whole being has been primordially pure and primordially in the state of buddhahood, or in the state of Samantabhadra.

There is a sense of coming back to square one. We come back to the exact point where we started our journey; that is why the ground level of Dzogchen is not separable from the resultant aspect of Dzogchen. The ground is actually the result, and the result is the ground. Dzogchen is a path of the fruition level, not a path of the causal level, because we take fruition as the ground and as the path, and we reach the level of fruition after all. This level of Ati yoga goes beyond any sense of conceptual boundaries or clinging, beyond clinging even to the conceptual boundary of something called sacred world. We go beyond that world, into the basic space.

There is an example given that shows us how the fundamental nature of our existence is like an eagle. In this example, we are always trying to make this eagle look like a human being, like one of us. So we dress up the eagle. We put a hat on the eagle; we put a coat on the eagle; we put a pair of boots and a nice bow tie on it. We never let the eagle be "eagle." Meanwhile, the eagle feels terrible wearing all these beautiful clothes. It does not feel at all comfortable. However, at the stage of Ati yoga, this eagle takes off from the cliff, first throwing off the boots, then throwing off the coat, and finally throwing off his hat and bow tie. We can imagine how free the eagle feels at this point. Eagle has become eagle at last.

Similarly, the bare nature of our mind, the naked state of our being, does not feel at all comfortable with these layers of conceptual, philosophical, and religious clothing that we are trying to put on it. Like the eagle wearing a hat and boots, the fundamental nature of ego does not feel at all comfortable. When we reach the stage of Ati yoga, ego finally gets its freedom. It gets the courage to take off from the cliff and fly, gradually dropping the boots, coat, hat, and bow tie. It is wonderful—now the ego can join the greater space of primordial buddha, the greater space of primordial awareness. Finally, ego has the freedom to be bare and naked.

At this level of Ati yoga, we are totally free from all conceptual clothing. We have thrown off the hats, coats, boots, and bow ties, as well as all our ornaments, and we are flying in the great space of Dzogchen, the great space of Samantabhadra. At last, we realize how we can experience the redness of red and the blueness of blue without conceptualizing the colors. We have achieved the state of complete fearlessness. At this point we are not afraid to present our naked state of mind because it is the basic truth of our existence. We have achieved the courage to present ourselves in the way we fundamentally exist. Up to this point—during our whole journey on the Vajrayana path and our whole existence in the samsaric world—we have been trying to become something or someone that we are not. Now, having shed all of our conceptual clothing, we can simply be what and who we truly are.

At this stage of practice, many different instructions are required. Various methods for waking ourselves up are pointed out by our individual guru. After we have developed a proper relationship with our guru, we go through the detailed training of the Maha, Anu, and Ati yoga practices. The Ati yoga practices especially are based on a heart-to-heart connection. They are given in the form of a heart-to-heart teaching between student and guru, rather than through a spoken teaching. Therefore, the details of the Ati yoga practices are considered to be extremely private, and the methods themselves are practiced secretly, as are all Vajrayana practices. Certain of these practices are kept secret because there is a great danger of misunderstanding the path, the methods, and the invitation. The invitation to this journey is

254 THE DZOGCHEN JOURNEY

a heart-to-heart invitation, so you will not receive it along with the junk mail that you get in the rest of the spiritual journey; nor will you hear elsewhere about these practices. When the path or invitation is misunderstood, it not only messes up your own path, it messes up the paths of others. Thus, the secrecy is not only for the benefit of students; it is also for the benefit of the whole lineage and the teachings. Therefore, in order to train ourselves on the path of the three higher levels of yoga, it is necessary to go through this process privately with one's individual guru.

Ati yoga is further divided into three sections, called Sem-de (*sems sde*), Long-de (*klong sde*), and Men-ngak-de (*man ngag sde*), which can be translated as "mind," "space," and "instruction." Through these very detailed steps of our yoga practices and the instructions of our guru, we take our journey into the space of primordial Buddha. However, we have to learn how to throw off our boots. We have to learn how to throw off our jackets. We have to learn how to throw off our hats. We have to learn how to be brave and how to be naked. We have to be brave in order to bring out the nakedness of our basic awareness. Developing this courage is the essence of the whole journey.

In the final stage of Ati yoga, we are completely free from all conceptual clinging. We do not even have the thought, "Finally, I am free," or the conceptual label that says, "I am a Dzogchen practitioner," which is perhaps the greatest clinging we could have. We enter this final stage through a powerful wake-up call, which we call the empowerment of rigpa. Receiving the empowerment of rigpa, or naked awareness, is the final wake-up call. We are no longer in the dream state. Whereas we ordinarily want to go back to sleep because we have not finished our dream, whether it is a sweet and enjoyable dream or an action-packed nightmare, here we have completely finished our dream, so we wake up in the state of buddhahood, in the real world. The last stage of Ati yoga, of Dzogchen, is no different from the state of buddhahood that is achieved through the Mahayana path or through the Mahamudra path. The final achievement of awakening is always the same.

WAKING UP

We can look at all the approaches to the process of awakening on the Buddhist path as being similar to the regular methods we use to wake ourselves up in the morning. We might be trying to wake up, but the question is, How do we want to wake up? The general method of Hinayana-Mahayana is like setting an alarm clock. When we hear the beeping of the alarm, we usually press the snooze button and go back to sleep. When the alarm goes off again, we have a choice: We can get up or we can press the snooze button again. Sometimes, we might even kick the alarm clock so that it will never wake us up again. That is similar to the basic Hinayana-Mahayana process of waking up. In contrast, in the Mahamudra and Dzogchen approaches to waking up, the guru comes into our room while we are still sleeping and throws a bucket of ice water onto our bed. That is our wake-up call, and we usually "get it" right away. We have no choice but to get up. We are so irritated— but so awake.

The purpose of our whole journey, regardless of which path we take, is to wake up. Through this nine-yana path we completely wake up to the state of buddhahood. However, that awakening depends on us. If we do not hand our apartment key to our guru with full confidence and trust, he or she cannot enter our room to wake us up. That is why the whole journey starts with building this relationship of trust and confidence with our guru. It is the first and the most important part of our journey in Dzogchen and Mahamudra. Sometimes we get frustrated with our gurus because we really want to finish our dream, and they are waking us up. From the Vajrayana point of view, the primordial buddha is ever present, whether we want to experience that or not. So, on this spiritual journey, the real question is, Am I willing to wake up?

Notes

2. MAHAMUDRA: THE GREAT SEAL

1. *Mahamudra Drop Tantra* (Tib. *Phyag chen thig le'i rgyud*).
2. Dakpo Tashi Namgyal quotes this in *Phyag chen zla ba'i 'od zer*, which is published in English as *Mahamudra: The Quintessence of Mind and Meditation*, trans. Lobsang Lhalungpa (Boston: Shambhala Publications, 1986), p. 95.
3. The origins of Sutra Mahamudra trace back to the words of the Lord Buddha Shakyamuni, mainly the *Samadhiraja Sutra*, and elements of Mahamudra teachings are found in such sutras as the *Sagaramatipariprichchha*, *Maitreyaprasthana*, *Gaganaganjapariprichchha*, and many others. Sutra Mahamudra, according to the tradition of Lord Gampopa, is essentially derived from the *Uttaratantrashastra*.
4. *Samaya* is traditionally translated as "sacred word," and refers to a promise or commitment made by the student at the time of Vajrayana empowerment that in effect binds together the guru, the practice, and the student's own fundamental nature. *Deity yoga* refers to meditation practices that use the support of a visualized enlightened being as a means of connecting with the wisdom symbolized by the deity.
5. The five paths and ten bhumis are discussed in chapter 13.
6. The origin of Mantra Mahamudra is found in the tantras, especially the Anuttarayoga tantras taught by the Lord Buddha. These include *Guhyasamaja* and other father tantras, *Mahamaya* and other mother

tantras, *Kalachakra* of the nondual or neutral tantras, *Hevajra Tantra* of
the essence, *Chakrasamvara Tantra* of the quintessence, *Vajrachatushpi-
tha Tantra,* and many others.

7. The creation and completion stage practices refer to the two stages
   of deity yoga meditation. The creation stage emphasizes the development of the visualized form of the deity. During the completion
   stage, the practitioner dissolves the visualization and meditates
   formlessly. Through the practice of these two stages, the practitioner realizes the inseparable nature of the luminous, appearing
   aspect of mind and its emptiness. *Nadi, prana,* and *bindu* are terms
   referring to the channels, winds, and essences that are the basic
   elements of the subtle vajra body. The nadis are the channels or
   pathways through which the pranas move, and the bindus are the
   essences of the physical body.

8. The origin of Essence Mahamudra is found mainly in the
   Anuttarayoga tantras, as well as in the other sutras and tantras mentioned earlier. Also, there are many *upadesha* (instruction) treatises
   and *doha*s (yogic songs) by the mahasiddhas of India and Tibet,
   which transmit Essence Mahamudra.

3. THE PATH THAT BRINGS EXPERIENCE

1. Quoted in Patrul Rinpoche, *The Words of My Perfect Teacher* (Boston:
   Shambhala Publications, 1998), p. 56.

2. From *Sixty Stanzas on Reasoning,* by Nagarjuna. Unpublished translation from the Tibetan by Tyler Dewar.

4. GROUND MAHAMUDRA: THE GROUNDLESS GROUND

1. This refers to the dependence of causes, conditions, and their results upon one another. It also refers to the interdependence
   of these things and their arising in dependence upon the other
   elements. Further, it also refers to the relativity of causes, conditions, and results as being identified as such in relation to one
   another.

5. THE PATH OF INSTRUCTIONS: MAHAMUDRA SHAMATHA

1. Milarepa, *The Hundred Thousand Songs of Milarepa,* trans. Garma C. C. Chang (Boston: Shambhala Publications, 1999).
2. From a song Milarepa sang to Gampopa, "Instructions to Not Be Attached to the Conventional Provisional Meaning, and to Practice Only the Profound Definitive Meaning." Unpublished translation from the Tibetan by Elizabeth Callahan.
3. The Sevenfold Posture of Vairochana is the meditation posture in which the meditator sits with (1) the legs in a cross-legged position; (2) the spine straight; (3) the shoulders even and relaxed; (4) the neck slightly bent; (5) the hands in the gesture of equanimity, with one hand placed palm upright upon the other, resting four fingers below the navel; (6) the tip of the tongue touching the palate and the lips slightly open; and (7) the eyes half-open with the gaze directed along the direction of the nose.

6. THE PATH OF INSTRUCTIONS: MAHAMUDRA VIPASHYANA

1. Two texts by the Ninth Gyalwang Karmapa, Wangchuk Dorje, provide further explanations of the introduction to mind based on appearances. See *The Ocean of Definitive Meaning* (New York: Nitartha International, 2001); and *Pointing-Out the Dharmakaya* (New York: Nitartha International, 2001).
2. There is considerable similarity between the Mahamudra technique of pointing-out the mind in the context of appearances and the Dzogchen technique of "leap-over," or *thogal.*

9. MANTRA MAHAMUDRA

1. This supplication was written by Pengar Jampal Zangpo, and translated by the Nalanda Translation Committee.
2. Extensive relative reality refers to the skandhas, dhatus, and ayatanas, all the elements that compose the world of interdependent

origination. The five skandhas are the bases of physical form, feeling, perception, the development of karmic formations, and consciousness itself. The ayatanas and dhatus comprise all the elements of the perceptual processes.

10. ESSENCE MAHAMUDRA: THE MIND OF NOWNESS

1. From an unpublished poem by Dzogchen Ponlop.
2. From "The Song of Lodrö Thaye," *The Rain of Wisdom: The Essence of the Ocean of True Meaning*, trans. Nalanda Translation Committee (Boston: Shambhala, 1999), 89.

Glossary

WHERE THE TIBETAN-LANGUAGE equivalent of a term is provided, the Wylie transliteration follows the Sanskrit, and the phonetic pronunciation appears to the right.

ABHISHEKHA (Tib. *dbang/wang*; empowerment) The conferring of authority, commonly by way of ritual, to practice specialized vajrayana deity meditations.

ADHISHTHANA (Tib. *byin rlabs/jinlab*) Blessings conferred by one's teachers, realized masters, or through one's own meditation practice and supplications.

ALL-BASIS (Skt. *alaya;* Tib. *kun gzhi/kunshi*) The mindstream. When this is not recognized, it is called all-basis consciousness. When it is recognized, it is called all-basis wisdom.

APPEARANCES (Tib. *snang ba/nangwa*) The objects of the six senses. Also translated as "experiences" or "perceptions."

ARHAT (Tib. *dgra bcom pa/dra-chompa;* foe destroyer) A shravaka or pratyekabuddha who has attained nirvana, or liberation from samsara. *See also* nirvana; liberation.

AVALOKITESHVARA (Tib. *spyan ras gzigs/Chenrezi*) Bodhisattva of compassion.

AWAKENING (Skt. *bodhi;* Tib. *byang chub/changchub*) The state of a buddha. Also translated as "enlightenment."

AYATANAS (Tib. *skye mched/kye-che;* sense-fields)   Twelve sources of perception: the six sense objects and the six sense faculties.

BARDO (Tib. *bar do/bardo;* intermediate state)   Generally refers to the state following death and before the next birth.

BHUMIS (Tib. *sa/sa;* grounds)   The ten stages or levels traversed by bodhisattvas. Attainment of the first bhumi signifies one's first full realization of emptiness. As one progresses through the bhumis, one's realization becomes increasingly profound. There are an additional four paramitas that correspond to and are perfected on the journey of the ten bhumis. To the six paramitas are added: method (Skt. *upaya;* Tib. *thabs*); aspiration (Skt. *pranidhana;* Tib. *smon pa*); power (Skt. *bala;* Tib. *stobs*); wisdom (Skt. *jnana;* Tib. *ye shes*).

BINDU. *See* nadis, pranas, and bindus.

BODHICHITTA (Tib. *byang chub kyi sems/changchub kyi sem;* awakened mind)   Generally, the intention to attain complete buddhahood in order to benefit all beings. Specifically, it is classified as ultimate and relative bodhichitta; the latter being divided into aspiration and application bodhichitta.

BODHISATTVA (Tib. *byang chub sems dpa'/changchub sempa;* awake courageous one)   Awakened Brave One, One Who Has the Courage to Awaken. An aspirant on the path of Mahayana who has vowed to attain complete awakening in order to liberate all beings from samsara. The term may refer to either an ordinary being practicing the trainings of bodhichitta or someone who has attained the realizations of any of the ten bodhisattva bhumis.

BUDDHADHARMA (Tib. *nang pa sangs rgyas pa'i chos/nangpa sangye-pe cho*)   Teachings of the Buddha. Pure Buddhadharma is a genuine science of mind that works with the basic potential of our mind and is a social philosophy of life, a philosophy in action.

BUDDHA NATURE (Skt. *tathagatagarbha;* Tib. *de bzhin gshegs pa'i snying po/deshin shekpe nyingpo*)   The potential to attain complete spiritual awakening that exists in the mindstream of every sentient being.

CAUSAL VEHICLE (Tib. *rgyu'i theg pa/gyu-yi thekpa*) The sutra Mahayana system of the gradual path, which takes the causes for awakening as the path. It includes the Shravakayana, the Pratyekabuddhayana, and the Bodhisattvayana, that is, the Hinayana and Mahayana.

CHAKRAVARTIN (Tib. *'khor lo bsgyur ba'i rgyal po/khorlo gyurwe gyalpo*) An all-powerful universal monarch from traditional Indian cosmology.

CHANDRAKIRTI (Tib. *Zla ba grags pa/Dawa Drakpa*) Indian master, one of the main students of Nagarjuna.

CHITTAMATRA (Tib. *sems tsam/sem-tsam;* mind only) "Mind Only," the Mahayana school that teaches that there are no things that exist as something other than mind and asserts mind—mere clear and aware consciousness—to be truly existent.

COEMERGENT MIND (Tib. *lhan cig skyes pa 'i sems/lhenchik kyepe sem*) The dharmakaya nature of mind; the unborn state of freedom inherent in or inseparable from any expression of mind, such as the arising of a thought or emotion; synonymous with coemergent dharmakaya.

DEFILEMENTS (Tib. *glo bur gyi dri ma/lobur gyi drima*) Impurities that are not indigenous to buddha nature, the nature of mind, but nonetheless obscure our perception of it, like the clouds blocking the rays of the sun. Also called incidental or adventitious stains. *See also* two obscurations.

DEITY YOGA (Tib. *lha'i rnal 'byor/lha-yi naljor*) Meditation practice involving the visualization of a deity to connect with the wisdom embodied by that deity.

DHARMADHATU (Tib. *chos dbyings/choying;* expanse/space of phenomena) The ultimate, primordial expanse of the phenomena of samsara and nirvana, which is nonarising and unceasing, unconditioned and unchanging.

DHARMAKAYA (Tib. *chos kyi sku/chokyi ku;* phenomenal/truth body) "Body of truth," the realization of the essence of vipashyana or the result of perfecting the nature of nonconceptuality. It is the fruition achieved for one's own benefit. In regard to the nature of mind, dharmakaya is mind's empty essence, beyond all speech, thought, and expression. It is also said that it is the nonarising of the mind itself and is free from all conceptual elaborations. From the triad of body, speech, and mind, it is taught as the mind quality of buddhahood.

DHARMATA (Tib. *chos nyid/chonyi;* reality)   The ultimate nature or reality of mind and phenomena. Synonymous with emptiness.

DHATU (*khams/kham;* constituents)   The eighteen aspects of perception: (1–5) the five physical senses; (6–10) the five consciousnesses of the physical senses; (11–15) the five sense objects; (16) the mental faculty; (17) the mental consciousness; and (18) mental objects.

DISPLAY (Tib. *rtsal/tsal*)   The manifesting quality of mind. Also translated as "manifestation" or "expressive power."

DOHA   A type of spontaneous song of spiritual realization, historically sung by masters such as Milarepa.

Düsum Khyenpa (Tib. *Dus gsum mkhyen pa*) (1110–1193)   First Gyalwa Karmapa, one of the foremost students of Gampopa, and founder of the Karma Kagyu.

Dzogchen (Tib. *rdzogs chen*)   "The Great Perfection," the tradition of meditation emphasizing the mind's primordial purity and the methods for realizing it. It is taught to be the most advanced form of meditation practice.

EGO-CLINGING (Skt. *atmagraha;* Tib. *bdag 'dzin/dakdzin*)   The confused tendency of the mind to apprehend a truly existent "me" or "I" within the continuum of body and mind.

EGOLESSNESS (Skt. *nairatmya;* Tib. *bdag med/dak-me*)   Similar in meaning to shunyata. Also translated as "selflessness," it is the absence of something singular, permanent, or independent that could be called an ego, self, soul, identity, or "I." There are two main types of egolessness, that of persons (Skt. *pudgala-nairatmya;* Tib. *gang zag gi bdag med*) and that of phenomena (Skt. *dharma-nairatmya;* Tib. *chos kyi bdag med*).

ELABORATIONS, CONCEPTUAL (Tib. *sprod pa/tropa*)   The conceptual constructs that are falsely imputed to phenomena. Generally, there are four elaborations, which are the four extremes: existence, nonexistence, both, and neither.

EMPTINESS (Tib. *stong pa nyid/tongpa-nyi*)   A term that refers to the lack of true existence of a self of persons or outer phenomena on the absolute level, while not refuting such relative appearances of self. In effect, the natural state of emptiness means that all phenomena are beyond the extremes of existence or nonexistence in any permanent or solid sense.

FIVE PATHS (Skt. *pancha-marga;* Tib. *lam lnga/lam nga*)   The five stages or paths through which one implements the six paramitas and travels in the Mahayana on the journey from being an ordinary samsaric being to becoming a perfect buddha: (1) the path of accumulation; (2) the path of junction; (3) the path of seeing; (4) the path of meditation; and (5) the path of no more learning.

FIVE SENSE PLEASURES (Tib. *'dod yon lnga/doyon nga*)   Beautiful forms, pleasant sounds, fragrant scents, delicious tastes, and soft tangible objects.

FIVE SKANDHAS (Tib. *phung po lnga/phungpo nga;* five aggregates)   The term *skandha* literally means "group," "heap," or "aggregate." The five skandhas are: forms (Tib. *gzugs*), feelings (Tib. *tshor ba*), discriminations (Tib. *'du shes*), formations (Tib. *'du byed*), and consciousnesses (Tib. *rnam shes*). These five comprise all possible aspects of our experience and are said to be the basis of our clinging to a self as well as the basis for the examination of the nonexistence of a self.

FOUR NOBLE TRUTHS (Skt. *caturaryasatya;* Tib. *'phags pa'i bden pa bzhi/phakpe denpa shi*)   The Buddha's first teaching. The first two truths—the Truth of Suffering and the Truth of the Origin of Suffering—present the cause and result of samsara; the second two truths—the Truth of the Cessation of Suffering and the Truth of the Path That Leads to Cessation—present the cause and result of nirvana.

GAMPOPA (Tib. *sGam po pa*) (1079–1153)   Also known as Dakpo Rinpoche (Tib. *Dvags po rin po che*). Foremost student of Milarepa, he also studied with Kadampa teachers. His main disciples include Düsum Khyenpa and Pakmo Drupa.

GREAT EMPTINESS (Tib. *stong pa chen po/tongpa chenpo*)   The inseparability of appearances and emptiness, or the inseparability of clarity and emptiness.

GURU MANDALA   The environment of wisdom invoked through the presence and blessing of the spiritual master, as well as through the devotion and receptivity of his or her students.

GURU RINPOCHE   The Indian master of tantric Buddhism who, through various styles of conventional and unconventional conduct, was primarily responsible for transplanting the teachings of Vajrayana Buddhism to Tibet. Also known as Padmasambhava.

HABITUAL TENDENCIES (Tib. *bag chags/bakchak*)   The propensities created by the mind's habituations, which are stored in a latent form in the all-basis consciousness.

HINAYANA (Tib. *theg pa dman pa/thekpa menpa*)   "Lesser Vehicle." It includes the first two yanas, the Shravakayana and Pratyekabuddhayana, whose fruition is individual liberation.

IMPERMANENCE (Tib. *mi rtag pa/mitakpa*)   An impermanent phenomenon is that which arises, abides, and ceases. Gross impermanence refers to the changes that can be directly observed with the passage of time by undeveloped minds. Subtle impermanence refers to momentary changes, which generally cannot be directly observed.

INTERDEPENDENT ORIGINATION (Tib. *rten cing 'brel bar 'byung ba/tenching drelwar jungwa*)   The interconnectedness of all things; the fact that they arise in dependence on causes and conditions.

KADAMPA (Tib. *bka' gdams pa*)   The tradition brought to Tibet by Atisha, which emphasizes the vinaya and gradual path (Tib. *lam rim*). Gampopa studied with Kadampa teachers prior to becoming a student of Milarepa.

KLESHAS (Tib. *nyon mongs/nyonmong;* mental afflictions)   The negative, deluded states of mind that afflict sentient beings. Also known as afflictive emotions. The six root afflictions are ignorance (Tib. *ma rig pa*), desire (Tib. *'dod chags*), anger (Tib. *khong 'khro*), pride (Tib. *nga rgyal*), doubt (Tib. *the tshom*), and wrong views (Tib. *lta ba*).

LIBERATION (Tib. *thar pa/tarpa* or Tib. *grol ba/drolwa*)   Two different Tibetan terms are translated as the English word *liberation*. *Tarpa* refers primarily to the state of freedom from suffering attained in the Shravaka and Pratyekabuddha yanas, as opposed to the full awakening of a buddha attained through the Mahayana. *Drolwa* has a vaster connotation, and often refers to the spontaneously available, innate liberation that one connects with through the practices of Mahamudra and Dzogchen, such as in the term "self-liberation" (Tib. *rang grol/rangdrol*).

LINEAGE OF THE PROFOUND VIEW (Tib. *zab mo lta ba'i rgyud/'zabmo tawe gyu*)   Lineage of teachings and practices coming from Nagarjuna and Chandrakirti that emphasizes knowledge.

LINEAGE OF VAST CONDUCT (Tib. *rgya chen spyod pa'i rgyud/gyachen chope gyu*)   Lineage of teachings and practices coming from Maitreya and Asanga that emphasizes method.

LUMINOSITY (Skt. *abhasvara;* Tib. *'od gsal/osel*)   The natural quality of clarity and radiance that is inseparable from the shunyata nature of phenomena.

MADHYAMAKA (Tib. *dbu ma pa/umapa;* proponents of the Middle Way) "[Proponents] of the Middle." The Mahayana school of Buddhism founded by the master Nagarjuna that propounds the absence of true existence of all phenomena. Since the Madhyamakas teach the union of the relative and ultimate truths in a way that is beyond the two extremes of permanence and nihilism, they are called "[Proponents] of the Middle." The etymology of the Tibetan *uma* lends insight into Madhyamaka philosophy: *u* means "center" or "middle," whereas *ma* can be understood both as a nominal suffix and a negating particle. Thus, the latter would make the term literally mean "not the middle." This illustrates that this school does not even propound a "middle" that would truly or ultimately exist as a remainder, after the two extremes have been transcended.

MAHAMUDRA (Tib. *phyag rgya chen po/chakgya chenpo;* the Great Seal) A tradition of profound methods of meditation based on direct realization of the mind's true nature.

MAHASIDDHA (Tib. *grub chen/drubchen;* one of great accomplishment) A practitioner of Vajrayana Buddhism who has attained extremely sophisticated states of awareness and spiritual capability.

MAHAYANA (Tib. *theg pa chen po/thekpa chenpo*) "Great Vehicle." Also called the Bodhisattvayana, it is characterized by its dual emphasis on compassion that desires the liberation from suffering of all beings, and wisdom that perceives the true nature of phenomena. Through entering and riding in this vehicle, one brings all sentient beings to the state of complete enlightenment.

MAITREYA (Tib. *Byams pa/Jampa*) The bodhisattva now residing in Tushita Heaven who will be the fifth buddha of this aeon.

MAITRIPA (1012–1097) Indian mahasiddha; one of the principal Mahamudra masters of Marpa Lotsawa.

MANDALA (Tib. *dkyil 'khor/kyilkhor*) The Tibetan term for mandala literally means "the center and its surroundings." In Vajrayana Buddhism, a mandala is the abode of the yidam or meditation deity, the environment composed of pure appearances of buddhafields that communicate the essence of the wisdom of enlightenment.

MANIFESTATIONS (Tib. *'char sgo/chargo*) The manifestations or experiences of mind: thoughts and appearances.

MANTRAYANA   See Vajrayana.

MILAREPA (Tib. *Mi la ras pa*) (1040–1123) One of the foremost students of Marpa Lotsawa and teacher of Gampopa.

NADIS, PRANAS, AND BINDUS (Tib. *rtsa rlung thig le/tsa lung thigle*) The channels, energies or winds, and essences of the physical body. Nadis are channels through which the pranas, or winds, move. The pranas carry the bindus. The channels are the 72,000 nadis and the 40 million minor nadis abiding in the body. The winds are the 21,600 pranas circulating within the nadis. Connected with them, the essences, which are the white and red bindus, permeate.

NAGARJUNA (Tib. *kLu sgrub/Ludrub*)   Indian master of Madhyamaka philosophy.

NATURE OF MIND (Tib. *sems kyi gnas lugs/sem kyi ne-luk*)   A term for the intrinsic state (Tib. *gnyug ma*) or true nature of mind; the uncontrived, natural state, also known as "ordinary mind" or the wisdom of self-arisen awareness. Synonymous with "the way things are" (Tib. *gnas tshul*). Also translated as "natural state," "abiding nature" (Tib. *gnas lugs*), or "abiding mode."

NIRMANAKAYA (Tib. *sprul pa'i sku/trulpe ku*)   "Body of manifestations." The form kaya of a buddha that can appear to both impure and pure beings. It is the fruition that is achieved for the benefit of other sentient beings. Therefore, this kaya is closely associated with compassion. It is also said that the mind, though free from arising and ceasing, manifests in various ways, or that it is the unceasing appearances of the expressive power of mind. From the triad of body, speech, and mind, it is taught as the body quality of buddhahood. According to history that is held in common, the most recent nirmanakaya buddha was Shakyamuni Buddha. However, in the Tibetan tradition, Guru Padmasambhava is also considered a nirmanakaya buddha.

NIRVANA (Tib. *mya ngan las 'das pa/nya-ngen le depa;* pass beyond suffering)   Can either mean the liberation (Tib. *thar pa*) from suffering achieved through the Shravakayana or Pratyekabuddhayana, or the state of omniscience (Tib. *thams cad mkhyen pa*), complete awakening, achieved through the Mahayana.

OBSCURATIONS   *See* two obscurations.

ORDINARY MIND (Tib. *tha mal gyi shes pa/thamal gyi shepa*)   A Mahamudra term that signifies the basic, unfabricated, awake nature of mind. The term "ordinary" is used to indicate that all beings possess this, whether they recognize it or not. In the Mahamudra tradition, it is taught that this aspect of mind must be pointed out by a realized master to a qualified student in order for its realization to occur.

PADMASAMBHAVA Also known as Guru Rinpoche and Padmakara. The lotus-born tantric master who established Vajrayana Buddhism in Tibet in the ninth century at the invitation of King Trisong Detsen. He manifested the attainment of the four vidyadhara levels. He hid innumerable Dharma treasures throughout Tibet, Nepal, and Bhutan to be revealed by destined disciples in the centuries to come. Padmasambhava resides on the summit of the Copper Colored Mountain on the southeastern continent.

PARAMITAS (Tib. *pha rol tu phyin pa drug / pharol tu chinpa druk*) The six perfections that are practiced as areas of training in application bodhichitta: (1) generosity (Skt. *dana;* Tib. *sbyin pa*); (2) discipline (Skt. *shila;* Tib. *tsul khrims*); (3) patience (Skt. *kshanti;* Tib. *bzod pa*); (4) exertion (Skt. *virya;* Tib. *brtson 'grus*); (5) meditation (Skt. *dhyana;* Tib. *bsam gtan*); and (6) transcendental knowledge (Skt. *prajna;* Tib. *shes rab*).

PRAJNA (Tib. *shes rab / sherab*) Wisdom or transcendental knowledge relating to insight into emptiness; also, the naturally sharp discriminating quality of awareness. While prajna functions in our mundane activities, on the highest level it is the awareness that sees impermanence, selflessness, egolessness, and shunyata.

PRAJNAPARAMITA (Tib. *shes rab kyi pha rol tu phyin pa / sherab kyi pharol tu chinpa*) The name given to both the teachings on and the reality of prajnaparamita, or the perfection of supreme knowledge, the realization of emptiness.

PRANA. *See* nadis, pranas, and bindus.

PRATIMOKSHA (Tib. *so sor tharpa / so sor tharpa*) Individual liberation; vows or teachings concerning personal liberation from cyclic existence.

PRATYEKABUDDHA (Tib. *rang sang rgyas/rang sangye;* solitary realizer) Hinayana practitioner who attains nirvana without relying on a teacher and who does not teach.

PRECIOUS HUMAN BIRTH (Tib. *mi lus rin po che/milu rinpoche*) A human birth that is endowed with the favorable conditions required to practice the Dharma. It is taught that in order for a human birth to become precious, one must be endowed with the three qualities of confidence or faith, diligence, and wisdom or supreme knowledge—prajna.

PRIMORDIAL PURITY (Tib. *ka dag/kadak*) One of the two main aspects of Dzogchen teaching, the other being "spontaneous presence." Dzogchen has two main sections: *Trekcho,* or "Cutting Through," and *Togal,* or "Direct Leaping." The former emphasizes primordial purity and the latter spontaneous presence (Tib. *lhun grub*).

RENUNCIATION (Skt. *nihsarana;* Tib. *nges 'byung/nge-jung*) A mind that, motivated by a feeling of disgust with ego-clinging, wishes to be completely free from the prison of samsara.

SAMADHI (Tib. *ting nge 'dzin/ting-nge dzin*) A state of undistracted meditative absorption or meditative concentration. The definition of samadhi is "a one-pointed mind concerning objects to be examined."

SAMAYA (Tib. *dam tshig/damtsik*) Commitments of the Vajrayana path. Samayas essentially consist of outwardly maintaining harmonious relationship with the vajra master and one's Dharma friends and inwardly not straying from the continuity of the practice.

SAMBHOGAKAYA (Tib. *longs spyod rdzogs pa'i sku/longcho dzokpe ku*) "Body of Perfect Enjoyment." In an outer sense, this kaya refers to the manifestations of buddhas as they appear in celestial pure realms, giving teachings only to the assembly of noble bodhisattvas by way of light-bodies, rather than physical ones. The buddhas of the five buddha families taught in Vajrayana Buddhism are sambhogakaya buddhas. However, sambhogakaya in a special sense also refers to the luminous nature of mind, mind's unimpeded, radiant, and blissful energy. From the triad of body, speech, and mind, it is taught as the speech quality of buddhahood.

SAMSARA (Tib. *'khor ba / khorwa;* cyclic existence)   The state of existence, experienced by sentient beings due to their ignorance, in which suffering is the predominant experience.

SHAMATHA (Tib. *zhi gnas / shi-ne*)   Tranquillity meditation. Its aspects are mindfulness (recollection of the object of meditation) and alertness (continuity of mindfulness). *Shama* means "calm" and *tha* means "abiding," so *shamatha* means "calm abiding." In shamatha, distraction toward objects such as form has been calmed and the mind abides one-pointedly in whichever samadhi one is practicing.

SHASTRA (Tib. *bstan bcos / ten-cho*)   A philosophical treatise. Shastras are commentaries on the words of the Buddha by *pandita*s, or learned masters of India and Tibet.

SHRAVAKA (Tib. *nyan thos / nyentho;* hearers)   Hinayana practitioner who attains nirvana through practicing the first cycle of the Buddha's teachings, on the Four Noble Truths.

SHUNYATA (Tib. *stong pa nyid / tongpa nyi;* emptiness)   Emptiness, the true nature or suchness of all phenomena that is devoid of true, inherent, independent existence and is beyond all levels of conceptual elaboration.

SPIRITUAL FRIEND (Skt. *Kalyana-mitra;* Tib. *dge ba'i bshes gnyen / gewe shenyen*)   The name for the teacher in the Mahayana who shows the path of virtue.

SUBTLE VAJRA BODY   The vital life energy of consciousness within the physical body, permeated with an elaborate network of nadis, pranas, and bindus.

SUCHNESS (San. *tathata;* Tib. *de kho na nyid / dekhona-nyi*)   Synonym for emptiness or dharmata, the ultimate nature.

SUGATA (Tib. *bde bar gshegs pa / dewar shekpa;* those gone to bliss)   An epithet for the Buddha or buddhas.

SUTRAS (Tib. *mdo / do;* discourses)   Refers to either (1) the Hinayana and Mahayana teachings given by the Buddha, as opposed to the tantras of the Vajrayana, or (2) the scriptures of the Sutra Pitaka within the Tripitaka, which are concerned with the training in samadhi (Tib. *ting nge 'dzin gyi bslab pa*).

TANTRA (Tib. *rgyud/gyu*)   The Vajrayana teachings given by the Buddha in his sambhogakaya form. The real sense of tantra is "continuity," the innate buddha nature, which is known as the "tantra of the expressed meaning." The general sense of tantra is the extraordinary tantric scriptures also known as the "tantra of the expressing words." *Tantra* can also refer to all the resultant teachings of Vajrayana as a whole.

TATHATA. *See* suchness.

TATHAGATAGARBHA (Tib. *de bzhin gshegs pa'i snying po/deshin shekpe nyingpo*)   The seed or essence of tathagatas that is usually translated as "buddha nature" or "buddha essence." It is the seed or essence of enlightenment possessed by all sentient beings, and which allows them to have the potential to attain buddhahood. Also known as sugatagarbha.

THREE ASPECTS OF SUFFERING (Tib. *sdug bsngal gsum/duk-ngel sum*)   (1) The suffering of conditioning (Tib. *'du byed kyi sdug bsngal/'duje kyi duk-ngel*); (2) the suffering of change (Tib. *'gyur ba'i sdug bsngal/gyurwe duk-ngel*); and (3) the suffering of suffering (Tib. *sdug bsngal gyi sdug bsngal/duk-ngel gyi duk-ngel*).

THREE JEWELS (Tib. *dkon mchog gsum/konchok sum*)   The Buddha (Tib. *sang rgyas*), Dharma (Tib. *chos*), and Sangha (Tib. *dge 'dun*).

THREE KAYAS (Skt. *trikaya;* Tib. *sku gsum/kusum;* the three bodies)   "The Three Bodies," three inseparable aspects of the enlightened nature of mind, three levels of enlightened manifestation: dharmakaya, sambhogakaya, and nirmanakaya. *See* individual entries.

THREE YANAS (Tib. *theg pa gsum/thekpa sum;* three vehicles)   According to the three-yana system, the three yanas are the Hinayana, Mahayana, and Vajrayana. *See also* individual entries.

THREEFOLD PURITY (Tib. *'khor gsum rnam par dag pa/khorsum nampar dakpa*)   The term that refers to the criterion that must be present in order for paramita practice to become genuine. This is the insight into the emptiness of, and the absence of attachment to, the three spheres or aspects of an action: (1) the object of the action; (2) the action itself; and (3) the agent or performer of the action. For example, in the context of generosity, this would mean (1) the person or group toward which the generosity is directed; (2) the generosity itself, which includes the gift given; and (3) the person engaged in giving.

TRIKAYA. *See* three kayas.

TWO ACCUMULATIONS (Skt. *sambhara-dvaya*; Tib. *tshogs gnyis/tsok nyi*) The accumulation of merit and the accumulation of wisdom. The two basic classes of that which is to be gathered or accumulated on the path to enlightenment; the perfection of both of these is synonymous with enlightenment itself.

TWO OBSCURATIONS (Tib. *sgrib gnyis/drib nyis*)   The two classifications of everything that prevents or blocks one from realizing enlightenment: (1) the knowledge obscurations and (2) the klesha obscurations. Knowledge obscurations mainly consist of the ignorance of the true nature of phenomena. This is said to be the more subtle of the two obscurations. The klesha obscurations, or afflictive obscurations, are of the nature of the five root kleshas of anger, pride, passion, ignorance, and jealousy, and their related mental states. Only perfect buddhas are completely free of both obscurations. Also called the two defilements or veils.

TWO TRUTHS (Skt. *dvisatya;* Tib. *bden pa gnyis/denpa nyi*)   Two levels of truth or two ways of perceiving reality: relative truth is what appears to the confused mind of ordinary beings; ultimate truth is what appears to the nondual wisdom mind of realized beings. The realative truth correlates to the way things appear, whereas ultimate truth correlates to the way things are.

TWO WISDOMS OF THE BUDDHA   Also known as twofold knowledge (Tib. *mkhyen pa gnyis/khyenpa nyi*); knowledge of the varieties of phenomena (Tib. *ji snyed mkhyen pa/ji-nye khyenpa*); and knowledge of the mode of phenomena (*ji lta ba mkhyen pa/ji-tawa khyenpa*).

UNBORN (Tib. *skye ba med pa/kyewa mepa*)   A synonym for emptiness. It means that, ultimately, nothing has any true arising or birth, although on a relative level there appears to be arising or birth. Also translated as "nonarising."

UNDERCURRENTS OF THOUGHTS (Tib. *rtog pa 'og 'gyu/tokpa ok-gyu*) Thoughts that operate on a subconscious level and usually go unnoticed.

VAJRA (Tib. *rdo rje/dorje*)   Diamond, or "king of stones." As an adjective it means "indestructible, invincible, firm, adamantine, diamondlike." The ultimate vajra is emptiness; the conventional vajra is the ritual implement of material substance.

VAJRADHARA (Tib. *rdo rje 'chang/dorje chang*)   "Vajra holder." The name of the dharmakaya buddha. Many of the teachings of the Kagyu lineage come from Vajradhara. Often appended to the name of the root guru.

VAJRAYANA (Tib. *rdo rje theg pa/dorje thekpa*)   The tantric teachings of the Mahayana. It is the short path (Tib. *nye lam*) that utilizes a variety of methods that take the results of awakening as the path. Also called Secret Mantra, Mantrayana, or the Resultant Vehicle (Tib. *'bras bu'i theg pa*).

VIPASHYANA (Tib. *lhag mthong/lhaktong*)   Meditation that develops insight into the nature of reality. Vipashyana is practiced on the basis of shamatha meditation. In the word *vi(shesha)pashyana, vishesha* means "special" or "superior," and *pashyana* means "seeing" or "observing." *Vi(shesha)pashyana* thus means "superior seeing," since one sees "the superior"—that is, the nature of phenomena—with the eye of wisdom.

YANA (Tib. *theg pa/thekpa*)   "That which carries," or "vehicle." A set of teachings that enable one to journey toward rebirth in the higher realms, liberation from samsara, or complete buddhahood. There are different classifications of yanas, such as the triple division of Hinayana, Mahayana, and Vajrayana; the triple division of

Shravakayana, Pratyekabuddhayana, and Bodhisattvayana; and the nine gradual vehicles of Shravaka, Pratyekabuddha, Bodhisattva, Kriya, Upa, Yoga, Maha yoga, Anu yoga, and Ati yoga.

YIDAM (Skt. *devata;* Tib. *yi dam/yidam*)   Meditational deities. Also called "the root of siddhis" (Tib. *dngos grub kyi rtsa ba*).

Nalandabodhi Centers

NALANDABODHI U.S.
www.nalandabodhi.org

Nalandabodhi
P.O. Box 95675
Seattle, WA 98145-2657 USA
Phone: 206-985-8887
Fax: 206-985-8878
info@nalandabodhi.org

Nalandabodhi Boulder
Attn: Karen Quirk and Michael Miller
1200 Aurora
Boulder, CO 80302 USA
Phone: 303-443-1401
boulder@nalandabodhi.org
www.nbboulder.org

Nalandabodhi Seattle
Attn: James Meadows
5501 17th Ave. NE
Seattle, WA 98105 USA

Phone: 206-525-6925
Fax: 206-529-0558
seattle@nalandabodhi.org

Nalandabodhi SF Bay Area
Attn: Stephanie Johnston
105 Palm Ave. #12
San Francisco, CA 94118 USA
Phone: 415-422-0002
sfbayarea@nalandabodhi.org

NALANDABODHI CANADA

www.nalandabodhi.org

Nalandabodhi Foundation, Canada
P.O. Box 2355
Vancouver, BC v6B 3w5
Canada
Phone: 604-675-9282
Fax: 604-323-0978
canada@nalandabodhi.org

Nalandabodhi Vancouver
Attn: Stella Young and Rajiv Sankranti
4865 Henry St.
Vancouver, BC v5v 4z2
Canada
Phone: 604-675-9282
vancouver@nalandabodhi.org
www.nbvancouver.org

NALANDABODHI VIENNA

Attn: Heidi Caltik
Herklotzgasse 20

A-1150 Vienna
Austria
vienna@nalandabodhi.org

STUDY GROUPS

Northeast NB Study Group
Attn: Deborah Calloway
11 Davey St.
Simsbury, CT 06070 USA
Phone: 860-651-3863
dcalloway@nalandabodhi.org

Texas NB Study Group
Attn: Jan Puckett and Jean Peters-Do
6121 Coral Ridge
Corpus Christi, TX 78413 USA
Phone: 361-854-0777
jpuckett@nalandabodhi.org
jpeters-do@nalandabodhi.org

Halifax NB Study Group
Attn: Michael Monro
6156 Quinpool Rd., Suite 202
Halifax, NS B3L 1A3
Canada
halifax@nalandabodhi.org

Montreal NB Study Group
Attn: Laurie Milner
4427 Rue de Mentana
Montreal, QC H2J 3B4
Canada
Phone: 514-598-8592
montreal@nalandabodhi.org

Montreal NB French Study Group
Att: Helene Leboeuf
1041, rue Brodeur
Laval, QC H7G 4K6
Canada
Phone: 450-662-2668
montreal.french@nalandabodhi.org

Toronto NB Study Group
Attn: Mary Chung
18 Taylor Wood Ave.
Bolton, ON L7E 1J2
Canada
Phone: 905-857-3788
toronto@nalandabodhi.org

Hamburg NB Study Group
Attn: Acharya Lama Tenpa Gyaltsen and Karl Brunnholzl
Harkortstieg 4
D-22765 Hamburg
Germany
Phone: 49-40-383-238
Fax: 49-40-3861-2435
germany@nalandabodhi.org

Mexico NB Study Group
Attn: Gabriela Monjaraz
gmonjaraz@cuer.laneta.apc.org

CENTERS UNDER THE DIRECTION OF THE DZOGCHEN PONLOP RINPOCHE

Kamalashila Institute
Attn: Lama Sonam Rabgye
Kloster Langenfeld, Kirchstrasse 22a

D-56729 Langenfeld
Germany
Phone: 49-2655-939040
Fax: 49-2655-939041
kamalashila@t-online.de
www.kamalashila.de

Karma Kagyu Tendar Ling
Attn: Claude Diolosa
La Borya Del Cheyrou
24580 Plazac
Dordogne
France
Phone: 0033-553503363
diolosa@hotmail.com
www.karmapa-europe.net

Theksum Tashi Choling
Attn: Acharya Lama Tenpa Gyaltsen
Harkortstieg 4
D-22765 Hamburg
Germany
Phone: 49-40-383-238
Fax: 49-40-3861-2435
germany@nalandabodhi.org
www.ttc-hamburg.de

For more information, please check:
www.nalandabodhi.org
www.nitartha.org
www.dzogchenmonastery.org

NITARTHA INTERNATIONAL

www.nitartha.org

Nitartha International
Att: Lynne Conrad Marvet and Marty Marvet
P.O. Box 85414
Seattle, WA 98145-2414 USA
Phone: 206-985-8887
Fax: 206-985-8878
lcmarvet@nitartha.org
mmarvet@nitartha.org

Nitartha International Document Input Center (NIDIC)
GPO-8974, CPC-150
Kathmandu, Nepal
Phone: 977 (1) 480-511
nidic@ntc.net.np

Archives of Nitartha International
Kathy Penny
156 Palmer Avenue
Mt. View, CA 94043 USA
Phone: 650-967-1399
kpenny@nitartha.org

Editors' Acknowledgments

THE SOURCE OF THESE TEACHINGS is the unbroken lineage of enlightened masters who fully hold the wisdom of their traditions and who transmit the essence of this wisdom to appropriate students. Such masters continually protect and benefit this world and worlds beyond. In this light, we pay homage to all the great masters, especially the supreme emanations of our age, His Holiness the Fourteenth Dalai Lama and His Holiness the Seventeenth Gyalwa Karmapa, Ogyen Trinley Dorje. We are extremely grateful for the presence of their kind remarks here, which creates an auspicious connection between the living lineage of enlightened masters and students in the West. We also offer our respects and gratitude to the peerless Khenpo Tsültrim Gyamtso Rinpoche, who has taught extensively and provided key guidance on the view and practices of Mahamudra and Dzogchen for many years. It has been the honor and pleasure of the editors to undertake the task of compiling and editing these teachings by The Dzogchen Ponlop Rinpoche, which are indistinguishable in intention and significance from the pure wisdom of the lineage.

The Dzogchen Ponlop Rinpoche began teaching Mahamudra and Dzogchen to Western audiences in 1991. At the invitation of the Venerable Sogyal Rinpoche, founder of Rigpa International, Rinpoche traveled to London, where he initiated a major cycle of teachings oriented toward Western students. In 1995, Rinpoche presented teachings on the nine-yana journey of Dzogchen in Vancouver, Canada. From 1997 to 1999, Rinpoche presented another major cycle of teachings on Mahamudra and Dzogchen at the annual Treasury of Knowledge Retreat in San Antonio, Texas, sponsored by the Rigpa Dorje Center of His Eminence Jamgon Kongtrul Rinpoche. These three cycles of teachings constitute the primary sources for the material contained in this text. Additional references were taken from teachings given at a Nalandabodhi San Francisco Bay Area program in 2002.

Rinpoche's teacher and close friend, the most Venerable Alak Zenkar Rinpoche, encouraged Rinpoche to publish these talks, and it is for that reason this project has come to fruition. Therefore, we would like to thank Venerable Zenkar Rinpoche for his support and guidance.

In addition, we are grateful for the assistance of Acharya Sherab Gyaltsen Negi, a wonderful teacher, who reviewed the manuscript and advised us on content and translations of Tibetan terms. Elizabeth Callahan and Tyler Dewar offered valuable assistance with translation and with the adaptation of the glossary, originally compiled by Elizabeth for the publication of the first English translation of the *Ngedon Gyamtso,* by the Ninth Gyalwa Karmapa, Wangchuk Dorje. We also thank Jirka Hladis for assistance with the glossary and Gerry Wiener for his support and advice on translation. We offer special thanks to R. D. Salga and Amita Gupta, artists from the Karma Gardi tradition of Tibet, for the contribution of their meticulously rendered and elegant artwork. Mr. Salga painted the thangka of Padmasambhava; Ms. Gupta painted the thangka of Maitripa.

The editors are indebted to all sponsors of these teaching events, as well as all persons involved in the recording, transcribing, and editing of this material in its earlier forms. We thank Jan Puckett of Rigpa Dorje Center for her enduring generosity and dedication to the spreading of these teachings; Bruce Roe for transcribing and editing the *Treasury of Knowledge* commentaries; Pat Lee for the audio and video recording of these events; and Carole Fleming and Oona Emands for the transcribing and editing of many transcripts. We also acknowledge and thank Martin Marvet for his advice and editorial comments during the development of the manuscript. We thank the Nalandabodhi Executive Council and members of the Nalandabodhi sangha for their support and encouragement of this project. Finally, we especially wish to thank Emily Bower of Shambhala Publications for her perceptive and skillful guidance in the preparation of this manuscript. Whatever oversights or errors remain in this text are due entirely to the limitations and faults of the editors.

Ultimately, we offer our deepest respect and sincere gratitude to The Dzogchen Ponlop Rinpoche for his boundless kindness and pure, compassionate intention to benefit all beings, expressed here through the brilliant transmission of the teachings of profound and perfect liberation.

Illustration Credits

THANGKA PAINTING OF MAITRIPA on page 18 © 2003 by Amita Gupta. Used with permission.

THANGKA PAINTING DEPICTING THE NINE STAGES OF RESTING THE MIND on page 99 from *The Encyclopedia of Tibetan Symbols and Motifs* (Boston: Shambhala, 1999) © 1999 by Robert Beer. Used with permission.

PHOTOGRAPH OF KHENPO TSULTRIM GYAMTSO RINPOCHE on page 110 © 2002 by Ryszard Frackiewicz. Used with permission.

THANGKA PAINTING OF PADMASAMBHAVA on page 174 by R. D. Salga © 1999 by Nalandabodhi and The Dzogchen Ponlop Rinpoche. Used with permission.

CHART OF THE NINE-YANA JOURNEY on page 184 compiled by the Nalandabodhi Editorial Committee. Used with permission.

Index

About the Author

DZOGCHEN PONLOP is acknowledged as one of the foremost scholars and educators of his generation in the Nyingma and Kagyu schools of Tibetan Buddhism. His Holiness the Sixteenth Karmapa and His Holiness the Fourteenth Dalai Lama recognized him as seventh in the line of the Dzogchen Ponlop Rinpoches, and he received the Kagyu and Nyingma lineages of teachings and empowerments from His Holiness Karmapa, His Holiness Dilgo Khyentse Rinpoche, and other great teachers. An accomplished meditation master, calligrapher, visual artist, and poet, The Dzogchen Ponlop is also well versed in Western culture and technology. He is the primary architect of the many websites under the Nalandabodhi umbrella and the publisher of *Bodhi* magazine, an internationally distributed periodical. The Dzogchen Ponlop founded and continues to direct the activities of Nitartha International, Nalandabodhi, and Nitartha Institute, which focus, respectively, on the preservation of endangered ancient texts, study and meditation training, and traditional Buddhist education.

Samadhiraja Sutra
the Torch of Certainty
Torch

words of my perfect teacher

Heart Sutra (as subject)